Thank you
for making our
Riesling rule.

Nicolas Quillé

Riesling
Renaissance

FREDDY PRICE # Riesling
Renaissance

Photographs by Janet Price   FOREWORD BY HUGH JOHNSON

MITCHELL BEAZLEY

To my wife Janet for putting up with me

Riesling Renaissance

by Freddy Price

First published in Great Britain in 2004 by Mitchell Beazley, an imprint of Octopus Publishing Group Limited, 2–4 Heron Quays, London E14 4JP.

A CIP catalogue record for this book is available from the British Library.

ISBN: 1 84000 777 X

Commissioning Editor Hilary Lumsden
Executive Art Editor Yasia Williams
Design Colin Goody
Editor Margaret Rand
Index Ann Parry
Production Gary Hayes

Typeset in Versailles and Helvetica Condensed

Printed and bound by Toppan Printing Company in China

Previous page: Christophe Ehrhart of Domaine Josmeyer explains the principles of biodynamics to Freddy in the Hengst Grand Cru vineyard

Contents

Foreword by Hugh Johnson

There is an international freemasonry of Riesling-drinkers. We know each other by signs non-initiates might miss, of which a slim green bottle (sometimes brown) is the most frequent. We claim unique properties, magic powers almost, for this singular white grape. Not that there is so much competition. Only Chardonnay comes close in quality – and without the crutch of oak would Chardonnay be so interesting? Riesling alone makes pure wine, innocent of oak, that precisely reflects its origin, in a range from flowery and feather-light, through tense, dry, and mineral-laden, to unctuous and creamy, to a piercing liquor like celestial marmalade. Only Riesling can make wine of inconsiderable strength, a mere 7.5 alcoholic degrees, which drinks joyfully from birth and can put on flesh and flavours for twenty years. This is its Moselle manifestation. Only Riesling can ripen on dry Australian hills and emerge lime-fresh with pin-sharp focus. Only Riesling can grow to massive power and density on a rock-ledge above the Danube or on the sunniest slopes of the Vosges, on a gamut of soils from sandstone to marl, and keep its essential form and character: the nervous energy of its fruity acidity.

Nerve, tension, the character of freshness in the mouth is essential for any good white wine – just as a measure of tannic grip is for any red. It is the very essence of Riesling: fruity acidity that can hold the sweetness of honey, as it were, at arm's length, the two elements balancing each other so that your mouth is only aware of a supremely salivating moment.

Forty years ago Riesling was the acknowledged queen of grapes, imitated the world over. Perhaps that was the problem; she was betrayed by imitation and flattery. But the wheel has turned; renaissance is in the air. The freemasonry is feeling buoyant: the range and choice of Riesling – from an increasing number of different regions – is greater than ever and their quality truly exciting.

No one can lead us through the Riesling vineyard with a surer touch, with more experience or more involvement, than Freddy Price, a benign presence in the London wine trade for many years; importer of impeccable examples of the wines he loves and strict critic of peccable ones. Freddy's wife Janet is a photographer whose pictures have illuminated many wine books, my own included. They conceived this book as a joint venture and travelled round the world in its creation. *Riesling Renaissance* could not be more timely. It is the first book, I believe ever, to describe the qualities of the world's finest white wine grape in all its different homes. It will open many eyes to a world of new pleasures.

Riesling vines growing in the steep slate of the Brauneberger Juffer-Sonnenuhr vineyard on the Mosel

Introduction

Why Riesling? The long answer to this question is the whole of this book, because it is the passionate story of my voyage of discovery. The short answer is that Riesling is the most expressive white wine in the world.

I fell in love with Riesling in 1954, when I worked briefly in a cellar in Koblenz. On my days off, I took the train up the Rhine to Rüdesheim or along the Mosel to Bernkastel, tasting the superb 1953s. At this date, the reputation of Riesling was still at its peak; the process by which it was to be undermined, and then blown to bits, by the German wine industry itself, had only just begun.

What was beginning was bad enough. Political motives and technical "advances" in viticulture from 1950 onwards led to the planting of vast areas of Müller-Thurgau and all the other "new" German varieties. Yields increased hugely, as did the labour-saving use of chemical fertilizers, insecticides, and herbicides. Parallel to this were advances in cellar technology and the industrialization of winemaking. The result was mass production of ever-cheaper wines with labels such as *Deutsche Tafelwein*, Liebfraumilch, and Niersteiner Gutes Domtal. Naturally, consumers outside Germany assumed that these were made from Riesling. Naturally, too, wine-drinkers worldwide eventually tired of these *Zuckerwasser* ("sugar-water") wines and turned instead to oak-chip Chardonnay. They turned against Riesling, too – even though they had never tasted it.

The name "Riesling" has been ubiquitous. Until the 1970s, there were no international agreements (except those within the EC) protecting the use of geographical names, let alone the word Riesling on labels, so it was not surprising that everyone used it with equanimity. If Riesling itself was too difficult to grow and to make successfully, producers all over the world tried to copy it with other grape varieties. The major offender was, and still is, known under a number of names: Welschriesling in Austria, Laski Rizling in the former Yugoslavia, Olaszrizling in Hungary, Rizling Vlassky in the Czech Republic, Riesling Italico in Italy, and Riesling de Banat in Romania.

In the New World, other grape varieties were also blatantly sold as Riesling: Crouchen, a forgotten French grape, took the name of Riesling in Australia and South Africa, as did Semillon in Australia, especially in the Hunter Valley. In the USA, Emerald Riesling, Missouri Riesling, and Gray Riesling were and are nothing to do with Riesling.

The view from the top of a mechanical harvester at the Oyster Bay Riesling vineyards in Marlborough, New Zealand

True Riesling reflects its terroir probably more accurately than any other grape. It is a wine that, more than any other white grape, is made in the vineyard – the opposite of, say, Chardonnay, that, much of the time, is made in the winery and reflects in its taste how it has been manipulated.

The Riesling renaissance started in the vineyard – appropriately enough, since it was new plantings in the vineyard that began its fall from grace – and the grape benefits hugely from biodynamic methods: the very opposite of the industrial methods that destroyed the reputation of German wine and Riesling.

Rudolf Steiner set out the principles of biodynamic agriculture in 1924 with the theme "becoming aware of one's humanity". What it means, in practical terms, is applying natural products, such as flower tisanes and specially produced compost, in homeopathic quantities according to the phases of the moon and the planets. Wines grown by biodynamic methods exhibit less of the character of the grape but more of the character of the terroir; it is thus tailor-made for Riesling. In terms of location, the Riesling renaissance started in Germany. The *Verband Deutscher Prädikatsweingüter* (The Association of German Quality Wine Estates, or VDP) was and is the main engine for the renaissance in quality and style. It established, at the end of the 1990s, very strict quality rules for the new classifications.

In Austria, after the 1986 diethylene-glycol scandal, the only direction that the growers could take was upwards to higher quality. In Australia, Chardonnay had lost some of its glamour and Riesling developed a new impetus, especially with the younger generation of wine-drinkers. This renaissance was boosted by interest in matching Riesling with oriental food and an infinite variety of seafood. In New Zealand, once it was proved that Müller-Thurgau was useless there, the growth

Restored Roman Press House discovered in Theo Haart's vineyard in Piesport on the Mosel during the *Flurbereinigung*

of Riesling started in the 1980s. In the USA, half-dry Riesling had been popular, but a change of fashion to Chardonnay almost wiped it out. It survived in Washington State because the producers could make cheap, half-dry Rieslings for the "older consumer". The renaissance started when, realizing that this was not the future, the Washington State wineries began to make dry and premium Rieslings. In Canada, Riesling was the first *Vitis vinifera* vine to be successfully planted in Ontario and one of the first in Okanagan. It is also the finest grape for the very important Ice Wine market.

Australian producers were tired of their wines being ruined by poor corks; Australian wines in general and Riesling in particular were more prone to this. From 1976 to 1983, small quantities of each vintage of Pewsey Vale Riesling were sealed with Stelvin, the brand name of a make of screwcap. However, although the Australian wine industry was convinced of the technical merit of Stelvin, wine consumers were less enthusiastic. Meanwhile, many producers had been making trials, and, for Pewsey Vale Riesling Museum Release, Stelvin was used commercially from 1995. The climax came when all the top Riesling growers in Australia's Clare Valley adopted Stelvin for the 2000 vintage.

By 2003, commercial use had spread to all the New World regions and to Austria, with trials in Germany and Alsace. I have absolutely no doubt that New World Rieslings keep their youthful freshness for longer, while slowly losing primary fruit and gaining finesse. Some European Rieslings have a completely different structure and probably justify the continuing use of real corks. In 2002, a new glass stopper, called Vinolok was launched, and it will be used for most bottlings of the Rieslings of Schloss Vollrads' 2004 vintage. Time will tell whether this will be successful.

A few additional points. New oak is anathema to Riesling, destroying its purity of flavour and character. The malolactic fermentation is also to be avoided; all it can do is to make a simple Riesling less acidic for immediate drinking. Riesling is also best unblended with any other grape variety, although sometimes an addition of Gewürztraminer can make a pretty wine, but never one with the distinction of a pure Riesling.

It is Riesling's purity that is fuelling its renaissance: the realization by growers and consumers alike that a wine that tastes of its terroir is infinitely more profound and satisfying than one that tastes of winery techniques. It can be the most fretful and unforgiving of vines, but its wine can be delicate or concentrated, flirtatious or enchanting. It is a love affair that never fades.

Abbreviations used in this book

Where details of analysis are given for wines in the text, the abbreviations used are:

g.s.: grams per litre residual sugar

g.a.: grams per litre acidity

alc.: degrees of alcohol

ha; hl/ha: hectares; hectolitres/hectare

BA; TBA: Beerenauslese; Trockenbeerenauslese

A note on minerals and Riesling

The flavour of most dryish Rieslings can be described using terms that fall into three basic categories. Fruit is the most common – citrus or lime fruit, apples, and all sorts of other fruit. Some Rieslings are evocative of flowers, and others of minerals.

What does it mean to say a wine tastes of minerals? I mean the character of minerals in a wine where there is little or no fruit or flower character, but where my first impression is of a pristine quality and a dry, fresh flavour I associate with natural mineral waters (with or without minerals from deep below ground). I associate such wines with vineyards, particularly in Alsace, Austria's Wachau, Germany's Mosel-Saar-Ruwer, and the USA's Finger Lakes, in all of which terroir is so important.

Professor Alex Maltman of the Institute of Geography and Earth Sciences, University of Wales at Aberystwyth, published a fascinating paper entitled *Wine, Beer and Whisky: the role of Geology* in January 2003. It includes his interpretations of Chablis, the hill of Corton, and Sonoma County, California. He indicates that minerals have no taste and that they cannot be dissolved by the vine's roots. He also explains different sorts and usages of the term "minerals". When I consulted him, he pointed out that, "Geologists use the term to mean the chemical compounds that make the earth and its soils. Quartz (silicon dioxide), calcite (the mineral of which limestone is largely composed), and mica are all examples of minerals." However, he added that, "In the context of horticulture and foodstuffs, 'mineral', normally means inorganic elements. Thus fertilizers may contain potassium, phosphorus or other 'minerals' as plants need them to grow; food may contain things like calcium. So when wine writers talk about the mineral content of vine leaves, sap, must, wine, and so on, then they are presumably using the term in this sense." He stresses that almost all minerals (meaning rocks) lack any taste. "When we taste 'minerals' in, say, bottled waters it's the soluble ions that we sense... If the water has come from the ground, the connection with the host rocks is clear – the ions have been dissolved out of the host rock." But, getting them into the vine and through to the wine is a different matter. If there is a mechanism for this, we don't know about it. "In any case," Maltman concludes, "the chemical compositions of granite and slate are virtually identical."

What we do know for certain is that Riesling grown on slate tastes different from Riesling grown on granite. Throughout this book I have indicated the style and flavour imparted to Riesling by different types of soil and certain types of rock in the soil. There may be physical reasons (such as drainage) for this, but there is no doubt that the rocks play an integral part in the character of a wine. Certainly the wine-growers in Alsace, Germany, and Austria are completely convinced that this is so.

Germany

Rheingau vineyards from a ferry across the Rhine at Bingen

The Story of German Riesling

Centuries before the Romans arrived, Celtic tribes in Germany were cultivating wild grapes. The history of organized wine production in Germany, however, really begins with the Romans, when the Rhine became the border between Roman civilization and the many tribes that subsequently came from the east.

In AD286, Trier, on the Mosel, became the capital of the western Roman Empire – the massive city gate (Porta Nigra) still stands today, as do the Imperial Palace and huge amphitheatre. Not surprisingly, both the Roman legions and the citizens of this prosperous city demanded quantities of wine. Fortunately, the nearby Mosel Valley was famous for its vineyards. The poet Ausonius (AD309–390) wrote glowingly about Mosel wines, especially those from Piesport – where recent excavations at the base of the Goldtröpchen vineyard have revealed a large Roman press house.

The Geilweilerhof Institute of Ampelography announced in 2002 that in vineyards just south of Heidelberg, where the vines were between 100 and 200 years old, they had discovered the parent of Riesling, as well as seventy-five other German varietals. The vine is the Weisser Heunisch – the legendary grape of the Middle Ages – which had been thought to be extinct. The first likely written reference to Riesling is in Kintzheim, Alsace, in a 1348 map of showing *zu dem Russelinge*. However, an invoice for twenty-two *soliden,* a contemporary currency, for *umb seczreben Riesslingen in die wingarten* (six Riesling grape vines in the vineyard), dated March 13, 1435, from the cellar of the castle of the counts of Katzenelbogen in Rüsselsheim, near Hochheim in the Rheingau, is the first proof positive in Germany, because this spelling is repeated in other documents. One document shows that Sanctus Jacobus (now part of Weingut Vereinigten Hospitien in Trier) bought 1,200 *Risselingen reben* (Riesling vines) in 1464. In 1490, in Worms there was a reference to *Risslinge hinder Kirssgarten* Riesling behind the cherry orchard). And in 1511 *ein Rissling weingart* (a Riesling vineyard) in Pfeddersheim, on the outskirts of Worms was recorded.

The herbalist Hieronymus Bock wrote in his Latin *Herbal* of 1552: "Rissling grows in the Mosel, Rhein and in the Worms region". From the sixteenth century, Riesling became recognized as the finest white wine grape in Germany, which then included Alsace, but this did not mean that it was widely planted. The Thirty Years' War devastated the wine regions of Germany as it did Alsace. But even there, Riesling, because of its low yield, was a luxury grape that was only

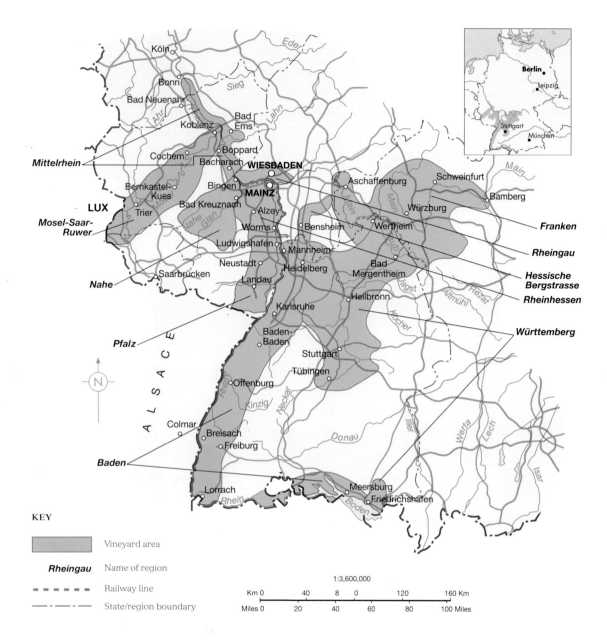

KEY

▨	Vineyard area
Rheingau	Name of region
– – – – –	Railway line
–––––·–––·–	State/region boundary

1:3,600,000

Km 0	40	8	0	120	160 Km
Miles 0	20	40	60	80	100 Miles

planted on the best sites for the connoisseurs of the time: the church and the aristocracy. In 1669, Johann Hoffmann, the headmaster of the Trarbach Hochschule on the Mosel, wrote a book about wine. He described Trarbacher Ungsberg as one of the most prestigious vineyards, and said that it was planted with Riesling despite its yield being half or one-third of that of the Elbling grape. This meant a great financial sacrifice, because the tax was fifty per cent of the crop. In 1672, the St Clara convent in Mainz instructed its tenants in Geisenheim, in the Rheingau, to replace their red vines with good *Riesling-Holz* (Riesling-wood). In 1763, Johannes

Hau, the Pastor of Piesport, succeeded in persuading his parishioners to plant nothing but Riesling vines and started on a mission to convert growers in other nearby villages. He planted Riesling in his own vineyard, Kreuzwingert, which Weingut Reinhold Haardt now owns. Haardt takes selected cuttings from these ungrafted old vines for planting direct in his vineyards.

It was not until the middle of the eighteenth century that the punitive fifty per cent tax on wines was removed and Riesling became paramount in the best vineyards of the Mosel. Meanwhile, in 1716, the prince-bishop of Fulda bought the monastery at (Schloss) Johannisberg in the Rheingau, and 294,000 vines were planted in 1719 and 1720, including 38,500 Rieslings. This later became the first vineyard to be planted with 100 per cent Riesling. In 1744, the prince-bishop of Speyer, in the Pfalz, ordered that all Elbling vines should be pulled up and replaced with noble vines, among them Riesling. The prince-elector of Trier, Clemens Wenzeslaus, decreed in 1786 that all wine-growers should pull up "poor" vines within seven years and replant with "good" vines – he meant Riesling, as this was the only "good" white grape in the Mosel-Saar-Ruwer at that time. In 1803, Father Otto Staab, the last cellarmaster of Schloss Johannisberg for the Benedictine Abbey of Fulda, wrote that the whole of the Rheingau should be planted with no other vine than Riesling. No other grape variety has had such a continuous aristocratic pedigree, throughout its history.

In the 1960s, there was a plethora of Müller-Thurgau and other early ripening grape crossings planted on flat fields better suited for sugar beet. This presaged a huge increase in the production of cheap wines. The legal addition of *süssreserve* (sweet unfermented grape juice) to fermented dry wine was introduced, and this is when the derogatory term *Zuckerwasser* (sugar-water) was coined. The 1971 German Wine Laws had the opposite effect to that which was intended because it encouraged mass production of poor wines, and labels became more difficult to understand. Ernst Loosen of Bernkastel, Mosel said that, "Germany has massive and precise wine laws goose-stepping through the vineyards – get rid of the whole lot, talk about vineyards, not laws; we should have the right to do everything, within reason". In spite of the great vintages of 1971, 1976, and 1983, the boom of ever-cheaper German wines insidiously dragged down the image of fine German wines until the markets for both fine and cheap wines virtually collapsed.

The VDP (*see* page 10) was founded in 1910. In 2003, there were over 200 members; and tastings, auctions, and other activities are held throughout the year. Riesling is at the heart of the VDP and its strict rules concerning reduced yields and other aspects, leading to better quality, are far higher than the minimum legal requirements. The VDP committee of each region instigated a classification of vineyards that was finally confirmed in 2003. In the middle of the nineteenth century beautiful and incredibly accurate maps of some regions were published for taxation purposes, showing the vineyards classified in three qualities. The new classification is remarkably similar, except that there is just one class with three different titles: *Erstes Gewächs* (First Growth) in the Rheingau (incorporated by law in the State of Hessen in 2001), *Erste Lage* (First-class Site) in the Mosel-Saar-Ruwer, and *Grosses Gewächs* (Great Growth) in all the other regions. *Grosses Gewächs* wines must be labelled with the vineyard name and not the village name and must be dry. Mosel-Saar-Ruwer *Erste Lage* wines can be both dry and sweet *Prädikat* (quality level, *see* page 21) wines. *Erstes Gewächs* laws in the Rheingau are slightly different and are noted in the Rheingau introduction.

I have marked the wines that qualify in each profile of a Weingut as EG (*Erstes Gewächs*), EL (*Erste Lage*), and GG (*Grosses Gewächs*), respectively. At the time of writing, only members of the VDP qualify for EL and GG, but this may be widened to include other producers who can prove that they abide strictly by all the VDP classification rules, which are even stricter than VDP membership rules. I have given more detail, including the qualifying grape varieties, in the introduction to each region.

Eiswein

Eiswein, made from grapes frozen on the vine and pressed before the grapes thaw, thus separating the ultra-sweet juice from the water, is effectively a twentieth century discovery. The first reported Eiswein in Germany was in 1794 in Franken. In 1842, a grower in Traben-Trarbach picked his grapes, in spite of their being frozen, and was surprised to find that the wine he made was wonderful. Minute quantities of eight vintages were reported between then and 1960.

The advent of the pneumatic bladder press made the production of Eiswein practical, and a few were made in 1961 and over the next decade, usually of Spätlese and Auslese quality. Since the 1982 vintage, Eiswein has been legally required to have the must-weight level of a Beerenauslese (BA).

Riesling is the only grape that can make sensational Eiswein in Germany and Austria, because no other grape can have the perfect balance of acidity and sugar; Eiswein made with other grapes tastes of very sweet grapes without the counterbalance of refining acidity. The chart of Max Ferd. Richter vintages shows how risky and tiny the production of Eiswein is. Provided that any botrytized grapes have been pre-picked, it is the elixir of pure Riesling: intensely fresh, with high acidity to balance its concentrated sugar, and all the terroir character of Riesling from wherever it is grown. This is a wine for celebration.

Grapes for Eiswein should be perfect with no damage or botrytis; it follows that the later the date of picking, the lower the quality of the Eiswein. When the temperature is forecast to drop below -10°C (14°F), the serious grower will send his pickers out in advance to pick every botrytized grape (to make a BA) and discard any damaged ones. On the night itself, if the temperature has fallen to 10°C (14°F) by 3am, the grower alerts his team and they pick from about 4.30am until dawn. Selective picking is important not just for Eiswein;

Max Ferd. Richter – Riesling Eiswein From Mülheimer Helenenkloster

Yr.	Vintage	Date	Description	Oechsle	Acidity	Litres
1	1961	23 Nov 23, 1961	feinste Spätlese Eiswein	110	13,5g	550
2	1966	Nov 2, 1966	feinste Spätlese Eiswein	116	11,6g	1 600
3	1970	Dec 23, 1970	feinste Spätlese Eiswein	114	13,0g	900
4	1971	Nov 20, 1971	Auslese Eiswein	150	10,3g	300
5a	1973	Dec 1, 1973	Auslese Eiswein	130	9,3g	700
5b	1973	Dec 2, 1973	Beerenauslese Eiswein	170	11,5g	550
6a	1975	Nov 23, 1975	Auslese Eiswein	115	9,5g	650
6b	1975	Nov 24, 1975	Beerenauslese Eiswein	127	10,2g	1 000
7	1976	Dec 10, 1976	Auslese Eiswein	137	9,2g	330
8	1979	Jan 13, 1980	Spätlese Eiswein	127	8,6g	180
9	1983	Nov 15, 1983	Eiswein	164	13,1g	1 350
10	1985	Dec 31, 1985	Eiswein	128	13,0g	750
11	1986	Dec 25, 1986	Eiswein – Christwein	145	14,6g	300
12	1987	Dec 9, 1987	Eiswein	122	16,4g	550
13	1988	Nov 22, 1988	Eiswein	160	11,3g	780
14	1989	Nov 26, 1989	Eiswein	140	13,2g	680
15	1990	Dec 8, 1990	Eiswein	130	13,7g	300
16	1992	Dec 30, 1992	Eiswein	149	11,5g	400
17	1993	Nov 24, 1993	Eiswein	130	12,9g	500
18	1994	Jan 5, 1995	Eiswein	150	10,0g	120
19	1995	Nov 6,1995	Eiswein	120	12,0g	1 000
20	1996	Dec 26, 1996	Eiswein – Christwein	138	16,5g	150
21	1997	Jan 28, 1998	Eiswein	166	9,0g	100
22	1998	Nov 21, 1998	Eiswein	168	15,0g	510
23	1999	Jan 25, 2000	Eiswein	125	10,0g	300
24	2000	Dec 23, 2000	Eiswein	140	10,0g	300
25a	2001	Dec 24, 2001	Eiswein – Christwein	176	11,0g	200
25b	2001	Dec 24, 2001	Eiswein**-Christwein	223	13,0g	200
26	2002	Jan 8, 2003	Eiswein	190	11,0g	200
27	2003	Jan 3, 2004	Eiswein	200	9,0g	250

it is the rule for Riesling in Germany, and the reason why a single grower can make a range of qualities according to the year. Ideally, the first picking of grapes is of perfectly ripe bunches with no botrytis; then, perhaps towards the end of October, autumn mists begin to get trapped in the valley at night, to be burnt off by the strong sun in the morning. This provides perfect conditions for the spread of botrytis.

In 2003, the area planted with Riesling in Germany was 21,514 hectares, representing 20.8 per cent of the total area of 103,605 hectares. Riesling is a demanding grape variety and terroir is very important, so there is a limited number of sites where Riesling is at home. Riesling is grown in all the wine regions of Germany, but Ahr (forty hectares) is more famous for its Spätburgunder and Sachsen (seventy hectares) and Saale-Unstrut (virtually none) are so far north that the weather and the quality are unpredictable and I have not included them.

German quality definitions

Kabinett, Spätlese, and Auslese labelled *trocken* or *halbtrocken* are dry or half-dry, otherwise they are sweet, of which most Auslesen include botrytized grapes. BA and Trockenbeerenauslese (TBA) are made with selected heavily botrytized grapes. Ideally, Eiswein is made without any botrytized grapes, but must have at least the minimum sugar level of BA. (Please also see the Glossary, page 187).

Mosel-Saar-Ruwer

The best way to see the vineyards of the Mosel-Saar-Ruwer is to paddle downstream in a kayak from Serrig on the Saar, winding through the vineyards to join the Mosel. A couple of miles downstream, take a short detour up the little Ruwer stream to Karthäuserhof and Maximin Grünhaus and then back to the Mosel, Trittenheim and its 360-degree bend of the river, Piesport and its amphitheatre of vines, Brauneberg Juffer and its long, steep vineyard and its sundial, the medieval village of Bernkastel and the Doktor vineyard, Wehlen and its sundial, Ürzig and its Würzgarten, and Erden and its Prälat. Then carry on through countless twists and turns of the Mosel, passing unsung vineyards, villages, and woods until you reach Winningen and Heymann-Loewenstein's extraordinary vineyards perched on the cliffs close to Koblenz where the Mosel joins the Rhine.

Terroir, meaning the combination of soil, climate, and topography that makes each vineyard unique, explains why Riesling can flourish so far north. The deep, twisting valley protects the vines from the worst of the weather in spring and the steep south-facing vineyards bask in the sun in the summer. The slate rock stores the heat and reflects it onto the grapes, whose sugar levels rise sharply in the lead-up to the vintage. Ideally, the first picking of grapes is of perfectly ripe bunches with no botrytis, then perhaps towards the end of October the autumn mists may be trapped in the valley at night, to be burnt off by the strong sun in the morning. This provides perfect conditions for the spread of botrytis.

The slate has different colours, for example, brown at Brauneberg, black at Bernkastel, blue at Wehlen, and pink at Erden, and there are recognizable differences of taste in the wines. Ürzig is the exception, with volcanic rocks containing red sandstone which recurs in a tiny part of Winningen. There is, as yet, no published scientific research on these different slates.

For some estates, the ideal Riesling vine is not a clone and is ungrafted, over fifty years old, grown up a single pole with the canes trained in a heart shape, and planted at up to 10,000 vines per hectare. It must be remembered that a hectare is measured horizontally, and on steep slopes the area of vines is actually perhaps twenty-five per cent greater; this increases both the number of vines and the hectolitres-per-hectare calculation, making them seem much higher than in top vineyards in France. There has been no phylloxera in some slate vineyards, and it is perfectly legal to take cuttings from your best vines rather than buying

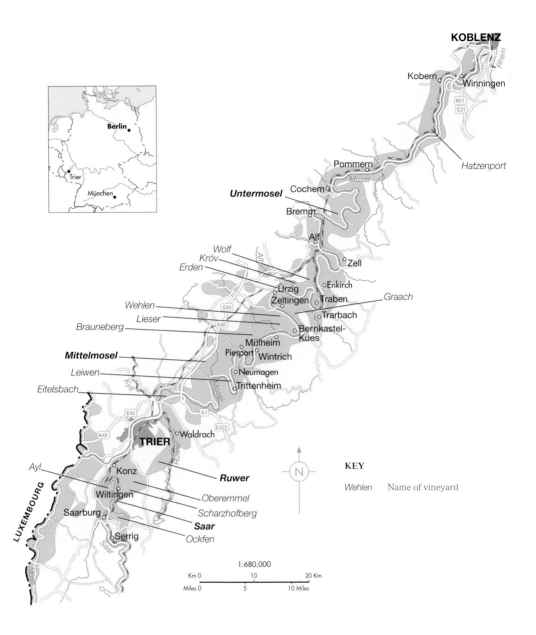

prepared cloned vines grafted onto American rootstocks. If the vineyards have been restructured by *Flurbereinigung* (the important re-structuring and then re-planting of steep vineyards and building roads to give proper access to the vines), each grower must sign up to planting grafted vines. Thus, for example, Brauneberger Juffer has had phylloxera, has been restructured, and is planted with grafted vines, whereas Wehlener Sonnenuhr has not had phylloxera and there was considerable objection to *Flurbereinigung* until recently; it was being planned at the time of writing.

In 2003, out of 9,300 hectares of vines, fifty-six per cent was Riesling and seventeen per cent Müller-Thurgau, which is a slow but sure change, as in 1994 the proportion was fifty-four per cent and twenty-one per cent, respectively. Müller-Thurgau has partly been replaced by Weisser Burgunder and red grapes, especially Spätburgunder (Pinot Noir) and Dornfelder, on the flat vineyards. Nevertheless, this is a far cry from the statistics in 1960, when there were 8,052 hectares, of which eighty-five per cent was Riesling, ten per cent Elbling, and four per cent Müller-Thurgau.

The area under vine has decreased, however, whether in the inaccessible, cold, and windy vineyards with little soil at the top of the slopes or flat vineyards where the soil is too heavy for Riesling. A smallholder who has, say, two parcels of a quarter of a hectare each, might find them too small to be of use. A successful estate has between seven and twenty hectares, and has carefully organized its finances and its team; more vineyards mean employing more people, and social costs to an employer are extremely high in Germany. Most larger estates have been quietly reducing their holdings for the last twenty years to improve control and quality as well as to reduce the payroll.

Even some excellent vineyards on steep slopes are sold at very low prices when the older generation retires or dies. Their neighbours buy some because, if they are left to run wild, all sorts of diseases may affect the adjacent ones. Apart from vintage-time, the average number of hours per annum for working a flat vineyard is about 300 per hectare, compared with 1,200 hours for Riesling on a steep site. The prices fetched and the yields are impossible to calculate accurately because they vary so much, but as a generalization Riesling sells at twice the price of Müller-Thurgau and the yield is half as much. So, as the costs of working a Riesling vineyard are treble those of a flat vineyard, the Riesling grower makes much less profit, even though his major asset is his steep vineyard which, in principle, is more valuable. I am not an accountant, but this does not add up unless you ignore the value of your vineyard or you are able to sell very fine Rieslings for much higher prices.

The best sites in the Mosel are usually in the lower two-thirds of the slope; those near the top of the slope have cooler temperatures, high winds and little soil, and the work is more difficult.

Riesling expresses terroir more directly than any other grape variety. The steep slate soil gives Mosel Riesling its unique character. Where else in the world could you find perfection with 46.5 g.s., 8.3 g.a., 7.5 alc. (as in a traditional Spätlese);

A venerable tractor plays a leading part in the vintage on Mülheimer Sonnenlay in the Mosel Valley

213 g.s., 15 g.a., 8.5 alc. (as in a TBA); and 5.7 g.s., 6.9 g.a., 13 alc. (as in an Auslese Trocken) from the same grower, vineyard, and vintage? I am doubtful about Mosel Auslese Trocken, however; until now I have found it too heavy. Filigree elegance is the theme. You can love both a Kabinett Trocken and a sweet Kabinett, provided that the balance of sugar, acidity, and alcohol is right, though sweet Rieslings mature better and last longer.

The VDP classification is *Erste Lage*; there are thirty-nine classified vineyards. Only Riesling qualifies and this is the only region where wines may be sweet or dry from Kabinett upwards. Vineyards that qualify are marked "EL" under "best vineyards". Only members of the VDP can qualify.

Weingut Fritz Haag

Dusemonder Strasse 44, D-54472 Brauneberg
(Middle Mosel)
tel 49 (0)6534 4410, fax 49 (0)6534 1347
email weingut-fritz-haag@t-online.de
internet www.weingut-fritz-haag.de
estate 7.5 ha, 100% Riesling
best vineyards Brauneberger Juffer-Sonnenuhr EL
and Juffer EL
average annual production 65,000 bottles
Member VDP

Wilhelm Haag took over the Weingut in 1961 and
he slowly increased his holding of Brauneberger
Juffer-Sonnenuhr, of which he owns 3 ha: a larger
slice than any other grower.

A Roman press-house, discovered recently
at the base of the great, steep, brown, slate slope,
shows that they, too, knew the best site. Juffer-
Sonnenuhr (*Sonnenuhr* means "sundial") is the
best part of the slope, close to the river; the rest
is Brauneberger Juffer. Everything in the vineyards
and cellars of this Weingut is traditional and all the
fine wines are matured in *Fuder*.

Wilhelm gave me a tasting of Brauneberger
Juffer-Sonnenuhr Rieslings. The Spätlese 1999 was
already smooth and gently civilized, with hints of
apple and the structure to develop with time in
a different way from the Spätlese 1988; it was still
fresh and strong, perfectly mature with a gentle,
creamy finish so typical of this underrated vintage.
In each vintage he makes several Auslesen from
different parts of the vineyard.

We tasted two 1999s, a 1993 and three 1994s,
but much to my regret, I do not have space here
to do them justice individually. This tasting was
a revelation, showing how the final wine was
influenced by the specific differences between
the vintages, the timing of the picking, the depth
of soil, the precise angle of exposure to the sun.
I think that Wilhelm knows every vine in the vineyard
by its first name.

Weingut Reinhold Haart

Ausoniusufer 18, D-54498 Piesport (Middle Mosel)
tel 49 (0)6507 2015, fax 49 (0)6507 5909
email info@haart.de
internet www.haart.de
estate 6.5 ha, 100% Riesling
best vineyards Piesporter Goldtröpfchen EL, Domherr EL
and Kreuzwingert, Wintricher Ohligsberg EL
average annual production 50,000 bottles
Member VDP

The Haart family is the oldest wine-growing family
in Piesport, with records going back to 1337.
Theo Haart practises sustainable viticulture, using
no chemicals herbicides or fungicides, and this
protects the indigenous yeasts, which he uses
for fermentation. The rest is orthodox modern
winemaking: cold fermentation, in stainless steel
for dry wines and old-oak *Fuder* for sweet ones.

Concentrating on Haart's Piesporter Rieslings
in the tasting, the Goldtröpchen Spätlese 1999 from
the best slate slope had fine acidity, showing supreme
delicacy and minerally flavour. Domherr Spätlese
1999 had a much deeper, richer quality, with a
lingering Riesling flavour and a touch of botrytis
on the finish. This vineyard is completely different
to Goldtröpchen, and has deep, heavy soil – but still
with some slate – and always greater botrytis from
the mists that rise from the river. Goldtröpchen
Auslese Goldkapsel 1999 was still an infant but
already showed a multitude of flavours, concentration,
and elegance. The greatest Rieslings of Piesport.

Weingut Heymann-Löwenstein

Bahnhofstrasse 10, D-56333 Winningen, (Lower Mosel)
tel 49 (0)2606 1919, fax 49 (0)2606 1909
email weingut@heymann-loewenstein.com
internet www.heymann-loewenstein.com
estate 12 ha, 95% Riesling
best vineyards Winninger Uhlen EL and Röttgen EL,
Hartzenporter Kirchberg and Stolzenberg
average annual production 80,000 bottles
Member VDP

Reinhard Löwenstein spent some years in Cuba, but he forswore communism and came back in 1980 to run the estate, then just 4 ha. It was an inauspicious start because 15 centimetres (6 inches) of snow fell in the vineyards during that vintage; it was the worst in living memory. The village of Winningen is between two spectacular terraced vineyards: Uhlen and Röttgen. Both are so steep that trolleys on rails are needed for people to get up to the vines.

The vineyards are practically biodynamic, and terroir is Reinhard's passion. Uhlen lies in an amphitheatre facing due south, and there are three completely different soil types. He uses the old vineyard names for these plots. At the top is blue-grey slate (this plot he calls Blaufüsser-Lay), similar to that at Wehlen; below that is slate with fossils (this plot he calls Laubachschichten), with the highest lime content in the whole region; at the bottom is red slate (this one he calls Rot-Lay) with iron and quartzite. He makes a dry Winninger Uhlen and Röttgen QbA, but does not make any Kabinetts or Spätleses. If he can make an Auslese from each soil type, he labels them Uhlen "B", "L", and "R" to denote the three soil types. The Uhlen Auslese 1998 (made before the codes) was intensely concentrated, with exotic fruit, while Röttgen Auslese 1998 was softer and had more botrytis but tasted less sweet – both great wines. All the wines are fermented in stainless steel and are kept for a long time on the fine lees.

Weingut von Hövel

Agritiusstrasse 5–6, D-54329 Konz-Oberemmel (Saar)
tel 49 (0)6501 5384, fax 49 (0)6501 8498
email weingutvonhoevel@t-online.de
estate 10 ha, 100% Riesling
best vineyards Oberemmeler Hütte EL, Scharzhofberg EL
average annual production 50,000 bottles
Member VDP

Eberhard von Kunow is always smiling and joking and he only makes wines that he likes to drink himself. Oberemmeler Hütte is his steep monopoly vineyard on a round slate hill close to his mansion and vaulted cellars; he also owns almost 3 ha on Scharzhofberg, and a great collection of funny and serious corkscrews. The monastery of St Maxim was set up here in the eleventh century, and Eberhard's ancestor, Balduin von Hövel, bought the estate in 1802 at auction after the secularization of church properties.

In the early 1980s, the estate converted to organic methods in vineyards and cellars – no chemical sprays, fungicides or even copper sulphate. Eberhard does not really like dry wines, so only five per cent are dry for the local market. He says, "Trocken is almost a religion in Germany." Oberemmeler Hütte Kabinett 1998 was very precise and a typical Saar Riesling with mineral extract, character and longevity (only 7.5 alc.). The Auslese 1999 had a wonderful scent of autumn flowers leading into flavours of ripe fruit and honey – a wine that will develop creaminess in time – while the Auslese Goldkapsel for the Grosser Ring auction had the same genes, with even greater potential and twice as much of everything. The Auslese 1997 was totally different: very closed with superb acidity and demanding at least seven years from the vintage. Scharzhofberger Spatlese 1999 had a delightful rich style; the 1997 freshness, purity, and elegance; and the 1994 power and maturity.

Weingut Karthäuserhof

Am Kartäuserhof 9, D-54292 Trier-Eitelsbach (Ruwer)
tel 49 (0)6515 121, fax 49 (0)6515 3557
email mail@karthaeuserhof.com
internet www.karthaeuserhof.com
estate 19 ha, 93% Riesling
best vineyard Eitelsbacher Karthäuserhofberg EL
average annual production 150,000 bottles
Member VDP

Given to the Carthusian monks in 1335 by Prince Balduin of Luxemburg, this estate was secularized and sold at auction in 1811 to an ancestor of Christoph Tyrell. He took it over in a very bad state in 1986 and transformed it.

Biological methods were immediately put into practice in the vineyard, partly to reduce erosion, and the vineyard was totally reorganized. This, with the latest stainless-steel technology, gave the wines their hallmark mineral purity of flavour. *Eitelsbach* means "iron brook", and the soil is full of minerals, including iron, phosphorus, zinc, and calcite.

We tasted the splendid 2001 vintage. Christoph is very proud of his dry Rieslings, and the Spätlese Trocken was slim and racy, with a mineral and wild flower scent, and fresh green-apple flavours, balanced by powerful but ripe acidity. Auslese "S" Trocken, his top dry wine, had terrific power in the fruit, with elegance. The traditional Spätlese had an unmistakable fragrant and delicate quality, with higher residual sugar and lower alcohol. To differentiate the finest selective pickings of the sweet Auslesen, each has a number. Auslese No. 38 had fantastic extract of minerals and honeyed fruit (88 g.s., 8.35 g.a., 9 alc.). Auslese No. 33 had a cornucopia of wild fruit on the nose and intricately sublime mineral flavours that stayed on and on. (117 g.s., 7.23 g.a., 9.3 alc.). The Eiswein I tasted was picked in the middle of November with no botrytis; the mineral flavours were pronounced and in perfect balance with the sugar, acidity, and alcohol (163 g.s., 9.7 g.a., 7.5 alc.).

Weingut Reichsgraf von Kesselstatt

Schlossgut Marienlay, D-54317 Morscheid (Ruwer)
tel 49 (0)6500 91690, fax 49 (0)6500 916969
email weingut@kesselstatt.com
internet www.kesselstatt.com
estate 40 ha, 100% Riesling
best vineyards Josephshofer, Wehlener Sonnenuhr EL, Bernkasteler Doktor EL, Piesporter Goldtröpchen EL and Domherr EL, Scharzhofberger EL, Kaseler Nies'chen
average annual production 280,000 bottles
Member VDP

In 1377, Friedrich von Kesselstatt was put in charge of the elector's wine cellars in Trier. The Günther Reh family bought the Kesselstatt family estate 601 years

later. Since 1983, Annegret Reh-Gartner has managed it and the superb modern winery at Schloss Marienlay, high up in the Ruwer.

The grapes are collected in 700-litre stainless-steel containers, which are closed to prevent oxidation, and fermentation and maturation are entirely in stainless steel to keep the wines as reductive as possible. Cellarmaster Bernward Keiper says, "A wine cellar that smells strongly of fruit aromas is a bad sign, because the aromas that you smell in the air have left the soul of the wine." He uses indigenous yeast and extended lees contact, both of which improve the aroma and structure of the wines.

We tasted the 1999 Rieslings and these particularly struck me. Scharzhofberger: the straight Kabinett had the classic balance of acidity with the fruit of the Saar. Piesporter Goldtröpchen: the Spätlese was an exciting wine with freshness and great complexity, while for the Auslese, with its soft background of botrytis, my note was a bit over the top – "diamonds on velvet". The Auslese from the monopoly vineyard in Graach, Josephshofer, was sheer delight, like a Dégas *danseuse*: perfectly poised.

Weingut Schloss Lieser

Am Markt 1, D-54470 Lieser (Middle Mosel)
tel 49 (0)6531 6431, fax 49 (0)6531 1068
email info@weingut-schloss-lieser.de
internet www.weingut-schloss-lieser.de
estate 7 ha, 100% Riesling
best vineyards Lieser Niederberg Helden EL
average annual production 50,000 bottles
Member VDP

This horror-film *Schloss* was once a great *Weingut*. In 1992, its remaining run-down vineyards in Lieser and the cool, damp cellars tunnelled under the vineyard were acquired by Thomas Haag, the elder son of Wilhelm Haag of Weingut Fritz Haag. In the vineyards, Thomas applied the philosophy "as little as possible, as much as necessary" – to encourage

Vines clinging
to the slate slope
at Ürziger
Würzgarten
"Erste Lage",
with a drop
of 150 metres
(492 feet) to
the Mosel

nature by natural methods, in other words. In the cellars, he installed state-of-the-art stainless-steel fermentation equipment and vats, alongside well-maintained old-oak *Fuders*.

The vintage is made by selection after selection until the last grapes are picked. The fermentation is with indigenous yeast, because Thomas is convinced that the essential character of each individual vineyard is only fully expressed in this way. Lieser Niederberg Helden is the only vineyard name on his labels, and all the grapes from his other vineyards are blended and labelled as Weingut Schloss Lieser.

Every vintage has been good for Thomas. His wines have brilliance and are perfectly structured, with a similar reductive style to that of his father, which guarantees that, though delicious when young, they will develop with time. In 1993, a great botrytis year, he made a superb range of Spätleses, Auslesen, a BA and a TBA. 1997 was a great year for him and one of the most remarkable wines of his that I have tasted was Lieser Niederberg Helden Auslese *** 1997 which had no botrytis and 115 Oechsle, leaving 150 g.s.

Weingut Dr. Loosen

St Johannisof, D-54470 Bernkastel (Middle Mosel)
tel 49 (0)6531 3426, fax 49 (0)6531 4248
email dr.loosen@t-online.de
internet www.dr.loosen.de
estate 18.8 ha, 100% Riesling
best vineyards Bernkasteler Lay EL, Wehlener Sonnenuhr EL, Ürziger Würzgarten EL, Erdener Treppchen EL and Prälat EL
average annual production 100,000 bottles
Member VDP

Ernst Loosen is like Papageno, with his hair in little curls, his magic flute, and his magic bells. He appears anywhere and everywhere and plays his inspired tunes about Mosel and about Riesling worldwide – talking, like Papageno, all the time. He says outrageous things but plays his magic bells

and no one could ever be cross with him. Having qualified at Geisenheim Wine Institute, he had decided to study archaeology at Mainz University, but his father's health was deteriorating and he asked him to supervise the vintage. He never looked back.

He calls himself a "terroirist" and he wants each of his wines – from Bernkastel, Graach, Wehlen, Ürzig, and Erden – to express its own site. Ernst is inordinately proud of his old, ungrafted vines, with their deep roots, very small yields, and high extract, while younger vines in the same parcels give freshness. He is ferociously opposed to laboratory-selected clones, because they mean dull uniformity.

He is passionately against bureaucracy (*see* page 18). In addition to his *Weingut*, he has a brand – Dr. L Riesling – that is a blend of Mosel wines from other producers. He has taken over Weingut J.L.Wolf in the Pfalz, and he is consultant to the huge Château Ste-Michele Winery in Washington State and helped it to create Eroica Riesling.

One unforgettable wine sums up his vision: Erdener Prälat Riesling Auslese Long Goldkapsel 2001. This is from a minute 1.44-ha vineyard close to the river in an amphitheatre of red volcanic rocks. The wine has unbelievable botrytis concentration and is perfectly clean, balanced by high acidity, and wrapped up in fruit with layers of different flavours.

Weingut Markus Molitor

Post 54492 Zeltingen, Klosterberg, D-54470 Bernkastel-Wehlen (Middle Mosel)
tel 49 (0)6532 3939, fax 49 (0)6532 4225
email weingut.markus.molitor@t-online.de
internet www.wein-markus-molitor.de
estate 37 ha, 92% Riesling
best vineyards Zeltinger Sonnenuhr and Schlossberg, Wehlener Sonnenuhr, Graacher Domprobst, Bernkasteler Graben, Ürziger Würzgarten
average annual production 260,000 bottles

Markus Molitor has risen like an interplanetary rocket. In 1984, at the age of twenty, he took over the then 7-ha estate from his father. By 1994, he had 14 ha; in 2000, 20 ha; and in 2002, 37 ha. On his 2001 wine list he was able to offer over 150 different Rieslings, including 60 Auslesen (dry and sweet), 13 Eisweins, 17 BA, and 15 TBA.

Markus' greatest passion is Riesling Auslese, for which he selects and picks the grapes as late as December, long after the normal vintage. His approach to vineyard and cellar work is very traditional, and the musts are fermented in *Fuder* with indigenous yeasts. His prime holding is 4.5 ha of Zeltinger Sonnenuhr, and my notes on these wines follow:

Spätlese Trocken 2001 had a pristine freshness backed by beautiful, intense, mineral extract; Spätlese 1999 was round, exquisitely delicate yet full-flavoured. The different Riesling Auslesen are classified by stars: Auslese 2001 ** was a superb, rich wine of this great long-term vintage, and 1994 * had a barley-sugar richness that showed the wonderful botrytis of the year balanced with the creamy flavour of maturity. Trockenbeerenauslese 1993 – a wine to put before a queen, gold that glisters in tears on the inside of the glass, classic botrytized Riesling in the core of the wine, surrounded by flavours of honey and dried apricots, balanced by the highest acidity.

Weingut Mönchhof – Robert Eymael
Weingut J.J. Christoffel

Mönchof, D-54539 Ürzig (Middle Mosel)
tel 49 (0)6532 93164, fax 49 (0)6532 93166
email moenchhof.eymael@t-online.de
internet www.moenchhof.de
estate Mönchhof 10 ha, J.J. Christoffel 2.2 ha,
both 100% Riesling
best vineyards Erdener Treppchen EL and Prälat EL,
Ürziger Würzgarten EL
average annual production Mönchhof 60,000 bottles,
J.J. Christoffel 20,000 bottles
Member VDP

Robert Eymael is a proud man because he has completely restored his historic manor and taken over the small but very distinguished Christoffel estate.

The Christoffel Rieslings have perceptible differences in style from those of Mönchhof, because Hans Leo Christoffel continues to oversee his vines, and decides when and how to pick the grapes. Also, he watches the fermentation of each wine as he has always done in tank or *Fuder*, in a completely separate cellar in Mönchhof. Christoffel has a special reputation for its dry Spätlesen in Germany but also makes exotic, spicy, sweeter wines such as a superb Ürziger Würzgarten Auslese ** 2001, the stars denoting one of five different bottlings of 2001 Würzgarten Auslese.

Erdener Treppchen is on pink slate soil and has an elegant style, that can reach perfection from the tiny Prälat vineyard at its heart. Ürziger Würzgarten is from the deep, ochre-red, volcanic, weathered sandstone soil, which gives the wines their unique spicy (*Würz*) flavour.

Robert can be equally proud of his Mönchhof wines, which are mostly made in the traditional style with some residual sugar, reflecting the fact that exports represent eighty per cent of the total production. All the *Prädikat* wines at this estate are fermented with indigenous yeast in oak *Fuder* in the cool, damp, underground cellars originally dug out by the monks of the Abbey of Himmelrod, who built their first house in Ürzig in 1177.

Among many of Robert's young wines that I have tasted, his Erdener Treppchen Riesling 2002 showed admirably its distinctive, elegant, baroque style. After our tasting, Robert brought up from the cellar an unlabelled bottle of Ürziger Würzgarten Riesling Auslese 1975 from his father's time. It was pure poetry, with less richness but greater acidity than 1971 or 1976, and still with great freshness.

Weingut Egon Müller-Scharzhof

Scharzhof, D-54459 Wiltingen (Saar)
tel 49 (0)6501 17232, fax 49 (0)6501 150263
email egon@scharzhof.de
internet www.scharzhof.de
estate 8 ha Scharzhof, 4 ha Le Gallais, 98% Riesling
best vineyards Scharzhofberger EL,
Wiltinger Braune Kupp EL
average annual production 70,000 bottles
Member VDP

The Scharzhofberg vineyard was originally planted by the monks of the monastery of St Maria and Martyres. In 1735, French troops plundered the monastery buildings and the vineyard fell into disuse. In 1794, France annexed the west of Germany right up to the Rhine, and in 1797, Johann Jacob Koch bought the estate at auction after the secularization of church properties.

His son-in-law, Felix Müller, started to build the new manor in 1829, but by 1851 the ownership of the estate was shared by seven members of the family, and Clara Koch, who had inherited the monastic buildings, wine cellar, and some vines, sold these to the Hohe Domkirche in Trier. This caused friction (and still does). Egon Müller I took over his family's part of the estate in 1880, followed by Egon II.

Egon III totally revived the estate in 1945, purchased the Le Gallais family vineyard Wiltinger Braune Kupp, and eventually handed everything over in fine fettle to his son Egon IV, who had graduated from the Geisenheim Wine Institute. Egon V was born close to the millennium, so the future is bright.

The Egon Müller estate owns the best part of Scharzhofberg, the lower section directly behind the estate buildings. There is a good proportion of old vines from which cuttings are taken for the new vines, thus obviating the need to buy laboratory-selected clones and retaining diversity of plant material. I tasted the 2002 Rieslings in London, and Scharzhofberger Spätlese was charismatic, polished steel in its youth and intensity, with the promise to develop over fifteen years into a multifaceted wine, while the Auslese Goldkapsel had concentration and wild-honey botrytis complexity – for Egon V's twenty-first birthday.

Egon Müller IV greeted us with an unlabelled bottle. The wine was immensely rich, with a sense of equal amounts of sun-dried and botrytized grapes in its flavours, plus a dry touch on the finish – wonderful. He revealed that it was 1971 Scharzhofberger Auslese. A second unlabelled bottle appeared. The wine was a beautiful pale yellow with a touch of green: fresh yet fully mature with fine acidity and a supreme elegance that lingered on the palate long after we left. The 1976 – sheer bliss.

Weingut Dr. Pauly-Bergweiler und Peter Nicolay

Gestade 15, D-54470 Bernkasteler-Kues
(Middle Mosel)
tel 49 (0)6531 3002, fax 49 (0)6531 7201
email info@pauly-bergweiler.com
internet www.pauly-bergweiler.com
estate 13 ha, 90% Riesling
best vineyards Bernkastler Alte, Badstube am Doktorberg, Wehlener Sonnenuhr, Graacher Himmelreich, Brauneberger Juffer-Sonnenuhr, Erdener Treppchen and Prälat
average annual production 110,000 bottles

Peter Pauly qualified at Geisenheim Wine Institute and then took his doctorate in business studies. He returned to sort out the vineyards of his own family on the Bergweiler and Prüm side, mainly from Wehlen to Brauneberg, now labelled Dr. Pauly Bergweiler. Then, having married Helga Beeres, whose family owned Weingut Nicolay, he set about sorting out those of the Beeres family (mainly Ürzig and Erden, labelled Nicolay) as well.

The result was one operation, with a new winery outside Bernkastel and a home and office in the beautifully restored baroque Weingut of the elector of Trier in Bernkastel. This has a pretty little chapel, vaulted cellars, a wine shop, and rooms for events and tastings. The company owns vines in almost every great vineyard between Brauneberg and Erden, including Peter's pride and joy, Bernkasteler alte Badstube am Doktorberg (Peter spent seventeen years fighting the administrators of the 1971 wine laws to get this 0.5-ha monopoly vineyard on the map).

The 1994 Auslese from this vineyard was gloriously rich and beginning to acquire the creamy feel of a mature Mosel. Other high points included Ürziger Goldwingert Spätlese 1999, from a monopoly vineyard, which was mouth-filling, extremely spicy, exotic and herbal in flavour and deeply satisfying. Ürziger Goldwingert Trockenbeerenauslese 1990 was fantastic, as rich as Croesus: sheer beauty in harmony with botrytis in a great year when there was little of the latter.

Although it was so young, Erdener Prälat Auslese 1999 was my favourite wine of the tasting. It showed the most wonderfully civilized, ethereal, stylish complexity imaginable.

Weingut J.J. Prüm

Uferallee 19, D-54470 Bernkastel-Wehlen (Middle Mosel)
tel 49 (0)6531 3091, fax 49 (0)6531 6071
estate 14 ha, 100% Riesling
best vineyards Wehlener Sonnenuhr EL, Graacher Himmelreich EL
average annual production 120,000 bottles
Member VDP

Prüm has been a great name in the Mosel since the sixteenth century, when a Prüm managed the vineyards in Graach owned by the archbishop of Trier. Johann Joseph Prüm was the eldest of seven children, and the vineyards were split up after his death in 1911. J.J.'s grandson, Dr. Manfred Prüm, is carrying the flag today and his wines are legendary. Today, absolutely no one is allowed in the cellars, but in 1975 they were described by Hans Ambrosi as "extensive vaulted cellars, parts of which are centuries old, with long rows of barrels and a rare wine library".

I asked Manfred Prüm for his secret of success. "Quite simply, perfect grapes. We have some of the best sites close to the river, where the mist encourages botrytis; a dedicated and experienced team in the vineyards, which are all close to the cellars; some original ungrafted vines over

Dr. Manfred Prüm, scion of the great J.J. Prüm estate in Wehlen, Mosel

three months in cask to make them less reductive. Sadly, today the general demand is for last year's Rieslings but it is criminal to drink J.J. Prüm wines too soon.

Graacher Himmelreich Riesling Spätlese 1995 *was* quite dry, though not *trocken,* with pronounced minerality and secondary aromas beginning to develop but still far too immature at 8 years old. Then, Wehlener Sonnenuhr Riesling Spätlese 1993 – the secondary aromas in this wine were in full ascendancy and the wine was nearing its prime, though it would last another eight years; purity and filigree elegance were the keynotes. The wines here have always captivated me, and by general accord, the Wehlener Sonnenuhr Lange Goldkapsel Auslesen of every vintage are to die for.

Weingut Max Ferd. Richter

Hauptstrasse 37/85, D-54486 Mülheim (Mosel)
tel 49 (0)6534 933003, fax 49 (0)6534 1211
email weingut@maxferdrichter.com
internet www.maxferdrichter.com
estate 15.5 ha, 93% Riesling
best vineyards Brauneberger Juffer-Sonnenuhr, Graacher Dompropst, Wehlener Sonnenuhr, Mülheimer Helenenkloster, Veldenzer Elisenberg
average annual production 120,000 bottles

Dr. Dirk Richter is "The King of Eiswein". He represents traditional ideas in a very determined and modern way. The family business in Mülheim goes back to 1680, and the family lives in its historic baroque mansion built in 1774.

The offices are above deep, cool cellars built in 1881; the temperature is permanently around 10°C (50°F) and the humidity is eighty-five per cent, allowing it to keep its "museum" bottles of most vintages back to the nineteenth century. After taking his doctorate in economics and then graduating

100 years old that are trained in the traditional heart shape on single stakes, with just two branches, to reduce the yield; a team which knows exactly when, where, and how to pick the right grapes." The fermentation is in stainless-steel vats, almost always with indigenous yeast, and the wines are disturbed as little as possible to allow the natural CO_2 to retain their freshness. Just a few wines spend

at the Geisenheim Wine Institute, Dirk joined his father Horst in 1975, and they decided to focus entirely on Riesling and to buy more parcels of vines in the best sites. Dirk is a great ambassador for fine German Rieslings and I wish I knew why he has not yet been invited to join the VDP.

Traditionally, after pressing, the free-run juice and the pressed juice are kept separate in temperature-controlled oak *Fuder*, where the natural fermentation takes place spontaneously at 12–15°C (54–59°F), with indigenous yeast if possible. Thus, each *Fuder* develops at a different rate and in a different way. Dirk produces some dry wines, mostly for German enthusiasts, but for him, the unique quality of Mosel Riesling is expressed in mature, sweeter styles with about 8 alc., with the advantage that "You can drink a bottle with lunch and work in the afternoon."

Brauneberger Juffer-Sonnenuhr is his best vineyard, but in vintages with extreme heat and drought, Veldenzer Elisenberg produces finer Rieslings. Wehlener Sonnenuhr is more elegant, and Graacher Dompropst, with its heavier clay and slate soil, is deeper and richer. Himmelreich is always very attractive.

Dirk orchestrated a memorable dinner in London to celebrate my sixtieth birthday, with the six other *Weingüter* I represented in the UK. Among the wines served, representing the first half of my life, were three Richter Riesling Auslesen: Braunberger Juffer 1959, perfectly balanced like a string quartet playing Mozart, creamy tone with a clear finish, elegance, depth, and length of expression; Mülheimer Johannisberg 1949 had fabulous golden botrytis gradually reaching noble old age; Graacher Himmelreich 1937 had a touch of crème brûlée on the nose, and long, seamless Riesling flavour leading into a dry, elegant finish.

Weingut Schloss Saarstein

D-54455 Serrig (Saar)
tel 49 (0)6581 2324, fax 49 (0)6581 6523
email info@saarstein.de
internet www.saarstein.de
estate 11 ha, 95% Riesling
best vineyard Serriger Schloss Saarstein (monopoly) EL
average annual production 60,000 bottles
Member VDP

The *Schloss*, with its wine cellar tunnelled into the summit of the vineyard, was completed in 1900. From below it looks like a Prussian battleship breasting a huge wave, and from the *Schloss* the view down is of a regiment of vines marching down the steep slate slope to the meadow of the Saar River.

Dieter Ebert bought this very rundown estate in 1956 and transformed it. His son Christian took it on in 1986, and later married Andrea, the daughter of Dr. Heinrich Wirsching of Weingut Wirsching in Franken

It used to be said that the wines of the Saar were magnificent in great vintages but not so good as those of the Mosel in difficult ones. The vineyards are at a higher altitude, more exposed, and the climate is more extreme, but the wines are much more consistent than they used to be. Biological methods are strictly adhered to in the vineyard at Schloss Saarstein.

The Kabinetts and Spätlesen have the archetypal delicate mineral character unique to the Saar, while the Auslesen, BAs, and Eiswein have the high natural acidity and concentration to give sublime and elegant balance with their massive sugar levels.

I have tasted most of the wines made in the last twenty years, and the best all-round vintages here have been 1996 and 1997. The Auslese Lange Goldkapsel 2002 is one of the greatest Rieslings of this century.

Weingut Sankt Urbans-Hof

Urbansstrasse 16, D-54340 Leiwen (Middle Mosel)
tel 49 (0)6507 93770, fax 49 (0)6507 937730
email St.Urbans-Hof@t-online.de
internet www.weingut-st-urbans-hof.de
estate 38 ha, 90% Riesling
best vineyards Leiwener Laurentiuslay EL,
Ockfener Bockstein EL, Wiltinger Schangengraben,
Piesporter Goldtröpfchen EL
average annual production 250,000 bottles
Member VDP

Hermann Weiss increased the size of his estate
to 35 ha during 1989 and 1990. In 1996, he purchased
a small parcel in Piesporter Goldtröpchen.
Meanwhile, he had developed a multi-clone vine
nursery specializing in Riesling and spent a great
deal of time in Ontario, founding the successful
Vineland Winery in 1988, which he sold in 1992. He
also assisted other wine-growers in Canada, supplying
them with vines, including Cave Springs Winery.

Hermann's charming and urbane son, Nik,
completed his studies at the Geisenheim Wine
Institute in 1997, and Hermann immediately
appointed Nik general manager of the estate.
His first vintage was 1998, and he started to use
indigenous yeast for the fermentation. He found
that each part of each vineyard had different yeasts
and that one type of yeast ended up dominating
the others. This, and fermenting in *Fuder*, have
an important influence on the terroir character
of each wine. So that Hermann could concentrate
on his vine nursery, he handed total responsibility
for the *Weingut* to Nik.

Of the 2001 Rieslings that we tasted, Ockfener
Bockstein Spätlese had the typical Saar mineral-rich
complexity and fresh, lemony acidity. Piesporter
Goldtröpchen Spätlese, from a heavier soil with
layers of slate, had exotic fruit and natural charm.
In the first week of November after the first frost,

The gateway to the steep Maximin Grünhaus Abtsberg vineyard
in the Ruwer Valley

they picked the Leiwener Laurentiuslay Auslese, the "home" vineyard, which gave perfectly ripe grapes with good botrytis. The wine had real nobility, great concentration, power, and elegance and needed several years fully to harmonize into a great wine. This *Weingut* showed a dynamic development from 1989, and with someone so young and positive at the helm, there is an even greater future ahead.

Gutsverwaltung von Schubert-Maximin Grünhaus

Maximin Grünhaus, D-54318 Mertesdorf (Ruwer)
tel 49 (0)6515 111, fax 49 (0)6552 122
email info@vonschubert.com
internet www.vonschubert.com
estate 34 ha, 97% Riesling
best vineyards Maximin Grünhäuser Abtsberg, Herrenberg, and Bruderberg
average annual production 200,000 bottles

On October 6, 966, Emperor Otto I gave the buildings, vineyards, and land here to the Benedictine monastery of St Maxim in Trier. In 1781, the average production of wine was 400 *Fuder*: say over 500,000 bottles – rather more than today. Napoleon secularized church properties, and in 1810 the estate was sold at auction to a private owner. It was acquired in 1882 by the great-grandfather of Dr. Carl-Ferdinand von Schubert, who has run it since 1981.

This estate is on the opposite side of the Ruwer to the former Carthusian monastery, Karthäuserhof, which has been its rival since 1335. The real difference is the soils. Here there are three different parts of the vineyard: Bruderberg, which is the lower part of the hill with weathered slate soil, giving powerful wines; Herrenberg, which has a mixture of blue and light-red slate, giving flowery, strong-flavoured wines; and Abtsberg – in the steepest part in the centre of the vineyard – which has blue slate, giving the finest wines.

This estate has a special reputation for its dry wines, and Bruderberg Auslese Trocken 1997 had a certain richness with a touch of botrytis to balance the very small amount of residual sugar. Herrenberg Kabinett 1998 was very open, with wonderful style, and Herrenberg Kabinett 1983 had perfect balance and freshness without a hint of petrol, showing just how these wines develop after twenty years in bottle. The last five wines were from the Abtsberg vineyard: Kabinett 1998 still had some spritz and very high acidity (10 g.a.), and Dr. von Schubert guaranteed it for at least another twenty years. Auslese 1999 Fuder No. 165 had a very high Oechsle level and tremendous concentration, with subtle background flavours and long-term potential. Beerenauslese 1999 was of course even more concentrated, with greater botrytis and beautifully integrated. Finally, 1993 Eiswein had the special "green" nose that typifies Mosel Eiswein, and the fresh fruit balanced by high acidity which will allow it to keep forever. At the time of writing, the estate was not a member of the VDP, and so the three vineyards are not registered as *Erste Lagen*, but Herrenberg and Abtsberg are among the finest vineyards in the Mosel-Saar-Ruwer.

Weingut Selbach-Oster

Uferallee 23, D-54492 Zeltingen (Middle Mosel)
tel 49 (0)6532 2081, fax 49 (0)6532 4014
email info@selbach-oster.de
internet www.selbach-oster.de
estate 14 ha, 97% Riesling
best vineyards Zeltingen Sonnenuhr, Schlossberg, Wehlener Sonnenuhr, Graacher Domprobst
average annual production 105,000 bottles

The Selbach family can trace its ownership of vineyards in Zeltingen back to 1661, but in recent years it has increased this considerably. In 1992, it owned 9 ha, and by quietly buying small parcels in top-quality sites close to its cellars it has increased this to 14 ha. Johannes Selbach joined his father

Hans in the business in 1988 and took over running the *Weingut* in 1993. He is a very personable and positive man and travels indefatigably all over the world, yet still keeps everything on the boil at home.

Hans and his sister continue to run the other side of the business separately. This is J.&H. Selbach, with different labels from those of the *Weingut*, in a much larger cellar at Ürziger Mühle. This wholesale business buys grapes, musts, and wines under long-term contracts, and also buys individual casks for a range of single-vineyard wines; these wines are treated in the same way as the wines of the *Weingut*. There is also brokerage service for almost every type of wine in bottle, shipping from all regions to customers in Germany and internationally, including buying at the famous regional auctions.

The Selbach Weingut motto is hands-on in the vineyards and hands-off in the cellar. In the vineyards, it is immensely proud of its old, ungrafted vines and the diversity this brings. It uses no chemical fertilizers, and everything is worked in as "green" a fashion as possible. It aims for low yields and has a very skilled team selecting and picking the grapes. In the cellar, hands-off means natural and traditional: slow pressing, slow fermentation, using indigenous yeasts, mostly in *Fuder*, though cultured yeasts are used for the dry wines which require much shorter, controlled fermentations.

Zeltinger Sonnenuhr is the largest holding and it may make up to twelve different wines here, from Kabinett to Eiswein. There may be four different Ausleses, the standard one without a star and the finest with three stars on the label.

My notes on three 2001 Rieslings from Zeltinger Sonnenuhr were as follows: the Spätlese Trocken was dry but not sour, making it very food-friendly, while the sweet Spätlese * tasted so minerally as to be almost ethereal, and as balanced as a ballerina on her points. The Auslese ** was hinting at how it will evolve into a gentle,

sophisticated Mosel to sip slowly on a summer evening. The magic Rieslings of Selbach are not the result of brilliant winemaking but of encouraging nature to take its course.

Weingut Wwe. Dr. H. Thanisch-Erben Thanisch

Saarallee 31, D-54470 Bernkastel-Kues (Mosel)
tel 49 (0)6531 2282, fax 49 (0)6531 2226
estate **6 ha, 100% Riesling**
best vineyards **Bernkaster Doktor, Lay, and Badstube, Braunberger Juffer-Sonnenuhr**
average annual production **50,000 bottles**

Bernkasteler Doktor is the unique vineyard of just 3.4 ha. This vineyard was once the most valuable agricultural land in Germany. If you do not suffer from vertigo, from the vineyard you can look straight down onto the old village and the river Mosel as it snakes through the valley.

Dr. Thanisch died in 1895 and his widow (Witwe) continued to produce wines from his two ha. In 1988, the two lines of the Thanisch family divided their holding to have 1 ha each. The Wegeler family own the other 1.3 ha.

In addition to the vineyard being so precipitous, the soil is completely covered with black slate, and faces due south. This means that the snow melts first here and as a result Eiswein is very rare. Its terroir gives Riesling a heavier style than that of the other famous Mosel vineyards.

Among the wines that we tasted: a Doktor Spätlese 1999 had elegant fruit, with both finesse and body. A legendary Doktor Auslese 1990 was still young at 11 years old, and, yet, had developed great length and breadth of flavours that will remain in my memory (and as long as the 1953 that we drank on the first evening of our honeymoon).

Mittelrhein

This is the epitome of the romantic Rhine landscape: all castles and cliffs, straggling medieval villages, and precipitous vineyards. It extends for about 110 kilometres (seventy miles) from Bingen to Bonn. In 2003, there were only 505 hectares of vines, of which seventy per cent were Riesling. Most vineyards are around Bacharach and on the great curve of riverbank from Boppard to Spay. Their steepness and inaccessibity explains why the area of vines is only a third of what it was fifty years ago. The soil is Devonian slate with veins of quartzite, which gives the Rieslings their wonderful mineral character. In winter it can be very cold; here, the turbulent Rhine was completely frozen over in 1928. The VDP classification is *Grosses Gewächs* and, at the time of writing, there were six classified vineyards, which are marked GG under "best vineyards"; only dry Rieslings qualify.

Weingut Toni Jost-Hahnenhof

Oberstrasse 14, D-55422 Bacharach am Rhein
tel 49 (0)6743 1216, fax 49 (0)6743 1076
email tonijost@debitel.net
estate 8.5 ha, 85% Riesling
best vineyards Bacharacher Hahn GG and Wolfshöhle GG
average annual production 70,000 bottles
Member VDP

Peter Jost is the best-known grower, and Bacheracher Hahn the best-known vineyard in the whole region. The Jost family has owned 4.2 of the 5 ha of Hahn for five generations. It lies just downstream from the village on a steep, curving, slate slope, half of which faces the river; the reflection of the sun from the water warms the vines and helps to ripen the grapes.

I have tasted and loved the Jost wines in every vintage from 1989, and was particularly impressed with Bacharacher Hahn Riesling Spätlese Halbtrocken 2000 for its lovely, definitive Mittelrhein character: tight structure and faintly salty, mineral taste. His Beerenauslese 2000 was a magnificent wine, loaded with apricot and honey and all things bright and beautiful.

Weingut Matthias Müller

Mainzer Strasse 45, D-56322 Spay
tel 49 (0)2628 8741, fax 49 (0)2628 3363
email weingut.matthias.mueller@t-online.de
estate 7.2 ha, 84% Riesling
best vineyards Bopparder Hamm Feuerberg, Mandelstein, Engelstein, and Ohlenberg
average annual production 74,000 bottles

Matthias Müller is a young grower whose Rieslings have great precision and character. The terroir of each vineyard shows most clearly in his dry wines, and he attributes this to his use of indigenous yeasts. All the wines we tasted were from the wonderful 2001 vintage. Bopparder Hamm Engelstein Kabinett was clear and dry, with ripeness and fine balance. Engelstein Spätlese MM had more power and finesse, tasting slightly less dry.

Among the sweet Rieslings, Mandelstein Spätlese (69 g.s.) had lovely delicacy, freshness, and primary fruit; the Engelstein Auslese MM, (82 g.s.) was a meticulous, crystalline, "modern" wine, with hardly any botrytis – expressing the steep-slate terroir.

Weingut Ratzenberger

Blücherstrasse 132, D-55422 Bacharach
tel 49 (0)6743 1585, fax 49 (0)6743 3260
email weingut-ratzenberger@t-online.de
internet www.weingut-ratzenberger.de
estate 9 ha, 75% Riesling
best vineyards Steeger St Jost GG, Bacharacher Posten,
and Wolfshöhle GG
average annual production 65,000 bottles
Member VDP

Jochem Ratzenberger and his son Jochen work alongside each other to produce a range of pure Rieslings with Saar-like precision. Some of their vineyards are on eighty per cent slopes, which rise from 80 to 250 metres (262 to 860 feet) in altitude and are extremely hard to cultivate.

The Ratzenbergers uprooted one row of vines in three in order to plant grass and to allow the weeds to grow. This enabled them to reduce the erosion problem and to plough the weeds back in, to give humus to the poor slate soil. When working in the vines, they park a tractor at the top of the slope, which pulls up a tiny wheeled machine on which the driver sits and controls by radio the rate of pull by the tractor.

Spacious cellars are tunnelled into the rock, maintaining the temperature and moisture level. This is perfect for the stainless-steel tanks and the large, old-oak barrels in which all their Spätlesen and Auslesen are fermented with indigenous yeast and then matured before bottling.

Among the Rieslings I tasted, Bacharacher Wolfshöhle Spätlese 1999 had wonderful depth and harmony (52 g.s., 9 g.a., 8.5 alc.). They have made Eiswein in every recent vintage; the bunches of grapes destined for this are wrapped in clear plastic on the vine to protect them from birds. Bacharacher Kloster Fürstental Eiswein 2001 was a masterpiece, with 220 Oechsle and 17.2 g.a. Their perfectionism and hard work is completely justified by the quality and authenticity of their wines.

Weingut Weingart

Mainzer Strasse 32, D-56322 Spay
tel 49 (0)2628 8735, fax 49 (0)2628 2835
email mail@weingut-weingart.de
internet www.weingut-weingart.de
estate 9.5 ha, 93% Riesling
best vineyards Bopparder Hamm Feuerberg,
Mandelstein, Engelstein, and Ohlenberg
average annual production 80,000 bottles

Florian Weingarten studied at the Geisenheim Wine Institute and took on the *Weingut* from his father in 1996. He has state-of-the-art, stainless-steel winemaking equipment, with a press which allows good skin contact with the must but no contact with air, and a subtle system whereby the temperature of the fermentation is controlled by the amount of CO_2 emitted by the must – if the yeast is weak the temperature is increased, and vice versa.

I was most impressed with their 2001s. The dry Kabinetts and Spätlesen all showed the wonderful, clear, mineral flavour and freshness that typifies the Rieslings of the Mittelrhein. The Feuerlay had a lovely elegance due to its thin soil; and Ohligsberg, with its deeper soil, had more power and concentration. The potential is there for *Grosses Gewächs* style and quality.

Among the sweet wines the Ohlenberg came out trumps in both the Spätlese and the Auslese categories, the former was ripe and luscious, and the latter was young and rich, lingering on the palate long after our departure.

Rheingau and Hessische Bergstrasse

From the end of the seventeenth century, the Rheingau led the development of Riesling in Germany. By the early nineteenth century, the growers in the Rheingau were the aristocracy of German wine in general and of Riesling in particular. This was partly because the wines were magnificent and partly because the aristocratic estates were large and well-managed.

The golden age of Rheingau Riesling was from 1870 to 1930. In the 1950s, scientists advised the planting of new high-yielding clones and the use of new labour-saving cellar technology. Yields mushroomed, and sterile filtration made it possible to manipulate wines with residual sugar in order to mimic the rare botrytized wines.

For the last two decades of the millennium, every large Rheingau estate was under pressure because its buildings and cellar equipment were so costly to modernize. And also because the cost of employing workers in Germany was so much greater than that of a smaller family estate where everyone works when there is a job to be done.

Gradually, with large investments, the scene changed again and those estates that had fallen back began to make great wines again: they still owned some of the most esteemed vineyards in Germany. In the meantime, a number of focused smaller estates had taken the initiative and developed modern Rheingau Rieslings.

In 1984, a group of producers founded the "Charta" Association, guided by two remarkable personalities: the late Graf Erwein Matuschka-Greiffenclau, twenty-seventh generation owner of Schloss Vollrads, and Bernhard Breuer of Weingut Georg Breuer. The purpose of Charta was the rediscovery of dry Rheingau Rieslings. Back in the 1970s, Bernhard Breuer had been something of an *enfant terrible* because he insisted that many Rheingau Rieslings used to be dry, having been matured in cask for long periods to clarify them and to reduce their acidity; only those wines made from botrytized grapes were sweet. The rest of the world had got hold of the idea that all Rheingau Rieslings should be sweet. At that time, seventy per cent of Rheingau wines were sweet; by the middle 1990s, the percentages had reversed, with seventy per cent being dry Riesling.

Charta also carried out the original research into the best vineyard sites, which in time led to the system of *Erstes Gewächs*, or First Growths, being enshrined in law. In order to select the pieces of vineyard that should be

The Monks'
Dormitory at Kloster
Eberbach though
very beautiful must
have been bitterly
cold in winter

accorded this title, the terroir of the Rheingau was studied by the Geisenheim Wine Institute; the soils were analyzed and mini-weather-stations were placed in the vineyards at twenty-five-metre (eighty-two-foot) intervals. The studies were completed in 1998 and 1999 and meanwhile Charta was taken over by the VDP.

One-third of the whole area – 1,132 hectares of the 3,216 hectares – was then classified *Erstes Gewächs*. This is a far larger area than that recommended by the VDP, and Bernhard resigned from the VDP because he believed that the new laws were too weak and the scientific tests on the terroir were based on the wrong criteria. Nevertheless, the fact remains that he and Erwein set in motion the renaissance of German Riesling.

Producers do, of course, still make and label many wines in accordance with the 1971 Wine Law. Modern dry Rieslings with 12.5 to 13 degrees of alcohol are not everyone's choice, and traditional, delicate Rieslings of all sorts, with residual sugar and lower alcohol levels, will continue to be made.

The Rheingau is in effect one great slope facing due south. It was created by the once-enormous Rhine hitting the solid rock of the Taunus Mountains, turning due west and depositing earth and stones until it found a softer section of slate and schistose deposits at Rüdesheim that it cut through to force its way north again, forming the steep Lorelei Gorge. The Taunus Mountains and forests protect the slope from the worst weather from the north, and there is an occasional little valley (*Tal* or *-thal*, as in Rauenthal). Lorch and the great *Berg* ("hill") of Rüdesheim

are very steep and have a thin layer of soil with slate and quartzite, giving a fresh and subtle quality to the wines. From the east of Rüdesheim to Walluf, there is a varying mixture of quite deep loam with stones and, in some places, wind-blown loess. Following the slight undulations of the slope, some sites face southwest and benefit from the evening sun. Just north of Eltville there are several superb sites in Kiedrich and Rauenthal with phillite stones added to the loess and loam. The soil in Hochheim further to the east is slightly heavier loam and sand deposited by the river Main. Wines from certain monopoly vineyards were always labelled with just the name of the estate without the village name, in particular Schloss Johannisberg, Schloss Vollrads, Steinberg, and little Schloss Reichartshausen. All of these are classified *Erstes Gewächs*.

The Rheingau is in many ways a more cohesive region than many, not least because it is small: the heart of the region from Eltville to Rüdesheim is less than twenty-one kilometres (thirteen miles) long and a maximum of 4.8 kilometres (three miles) deep, extending from the Rhine to the foothills of the Taunus mountains. In 2003, Riesling covered seventy-nine per cent of the vineyard.

The 450 hectares of vines of the tiny Hessische Bergstrasse region is clustered along the hills just north of Heidelberg. Fifty-three per cent is planted with Riesling. The VDP classification is *Grosses Gewächs* and currently there are three classified vineyards (marked GG under "best vineyards") and only dry wines made with Riesling, Spätburgunder, and Grauburgunder qualify.

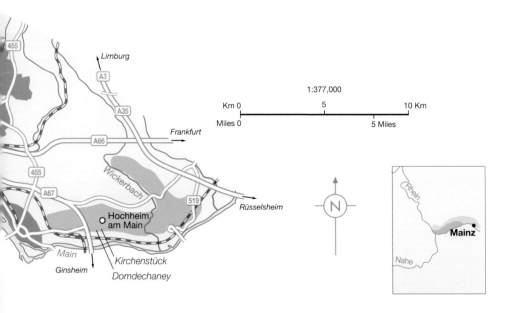

The elegant marker
indicating fifty degrees
latitude is planted
among the vines of
Schloss Johannisberg
in the Rheingau

Weingut Georg Breuer

Grabenstrasse 8, D-65385 Rüdesheim
tel 49 (0)6722 1027, fax 49 (0)6722 4531
email georg-breuer@t-online.de
internet www.georg-breuer.com
estate 24 ha, 88% Riesling
best vineyards Rüdesheimer Bischofsberg EG,
Berg Schlossberg EG, Berg Rottland EG,
Rauenthaler Nonnenberg
average annual production 100,000 bottles

Bernhard Breuer and his brother Heinrich run
four successful businesses. Firstly, they buy
grapes under contract to supply restaurants and
merchants with dry Rheingau Rieslings labelled
Abfüllung ("bottling") Georg Breuer; secondly,
they own the prominent Georg Breuer Hotel
and Restaurant in Rüdesheim; thirdly, Bernhard
is a consultant in vineyard management and
wine production in Germany and worldwide
in partnership with Bernd Philipp of Pfalz ; fourthly,
their splendid *Weingut*.

Their philosophy is to protect the environment
by natural viticulture: reduced yields, a diversity
of clones, cover crops. The effects of cover crops
are water retention, stress to the vines at the right
times, improved insect life, reduced erosion,
and humus for the roots of the vines when
ploughed in.

The Breuers never use Kabinett or Spätlese
descriptions on labels and, at these levels, they
make only *trocken* and *halbtrocken* wines. They
make superb sweet Auslesen and higher qualities,
but their main focus is their dry wines. Bernhard
demonstrated how pure, dry Rheingau Rieslings
develop with three vintages of Rüdesheimer Berg
Schlossberg Riesling: 1997, incredibly refined
and elegant, with vibrant acidity for long
development; 1990, slim and aristocratic with
typical Rheingau length and still developing:
1983, wonderful creamy character of mature
Riesling – but dry.

Domdechant Werner'sches Weingut

Rathausstrasse 30, D-65234 Hochheim
tel 49 (0)6146 835037, fax 49 (0)6146 835038
email weingut@domdechantwerner.com
internet www.domdechantwerner.com
estate 12.3 ha, 98% Riesling
best vineyards Hochhheimer Domdechaney EG,
Kirchenstück EG, Stein EG, Hölle EG, Stielweg EG
average annual production 90,000 bottles
Member VDP

Dr. Franz-Werner Michel's ancestor, Dr. Franz
Werner, the father of the dean (*Domdechant*)
of Mainz Cathedral, bought the estate in 1780,
and Dr. Michel was the most affable director
of the German Wine Institute in Mainz when I first
met him. All his wines are from the best vineyards in
Hochheim, and the sweet ones benefit from keeping.
This was perfectly illustrated by the following two
wines: 2002 Domdechaney Auslese, though so young,
had the Hochheim terroir flavour and had begun to
spread its wings, thanks to its cask ageing. The 1983
was gloriously enhanced by time in bottle, which
brought out the terroir character and the botrytis
raisin and apricot flavours.

Schloss Johannisberg

Schloss, D-65366 Geisenheim-Johannisberg.de
tel 49 (0)6722 70090, fax 49 (0)6722 700933
email info@schloss-johannisberg.de
internet www.schloss-johannisberg.de
estate 35 ha, 100% Riesling
best vineyard Schloss Johannisberg EG
average annual production 250,000 bottles
Member VDP

The influence of Schloss Johannisberg has been
so important in the story of Riesling and of German
wine. It was the first 100 per cent Riesling estate; the
first to bottle all its best wines and also (by mistake)
to make wines from a completely botrytized vintage
in 1775; and the first to introduce selective picking
of botrytized grapes in 1787.

It was eventually passed to Prince von Metternich-Winneburg whose descendant currently lives in the palace. Wolfgang Schleicher was director until he retired in 2004 and he did everything conceivable to restore the wines to their former glory. He was aware that the competition had caught up and that no longer could it be said of Johannisberg that, in the words of Goethe, *"Der Johannisberg thront doch uber alles"* ("Johannisberg dominates everything").

I have tasted the wines countless times, focusing on Auslesen, and those of 2002, 1990, 1989, 1983, 1976, and 1945 have all been glorious, as have the Beerenauslese 2002 and 1999 and the Eiswein 2001. The 1945 was the finest Riesling Auslese that I have ever tasted – despite the fact the *Schloss* had been destroyed by bombs, the men were still away after the end of the war, and Germany was bankrupt.

Weingut Johannishof

Grund 63, D-65366 Johannisberg
tel 49 (0)6722 8216, fax 49 (0)6722 6387
email info@weingut-johannishof.de
internet www.weingut-johannishof.de
estate 17.7 ha, 99% Riesling
best vineyards Johannisberger Klaus EG and Hölle EG, Rüdesheimer Berg Rottland EG and Berg Roseneck EG, Winkeler Jesuitengarten EG
average annual production 120,000 bottles
Member VDP

A stream runs past the Johannishof cellar, cooling it to a constant 8°C (46°F) with 100 per cent humidity; Johannes Eser says that these two factors are fundamental both to fermenting Riesling in cask with indigenous yeast and to maturing it in bottle.

Hans Hermann Eser, Johannes' father, was an innovator and had shocked his father by planting cover crops between the rows when he took over the *Weingut* in 1968; they have continued to work each vineyard in as ecological a manner as possible. In 1996, just before handing over the *Weingut* to

Johannes, Hans Hermann bought 4 (precious) ha of Rüdesheimer Berg Rottland, Berg Roseneck, and Kirchenpfad from the liquidators of the once-celebrated Schloss Groenesteyn.

This purchase meant that Johannes now had vineyards in both the principal terroirs of the Rheingau – slate and quartz at Rüdesheim, giving an elegant mineral concentration to the wines; and loam and loess with stones at Johannisberg and Winkel, giving broader, more fruit-driven wines.

Johannes Eser does not make wines to win medals and trophies, but creates reserved styles, both dry and sweet, with classic virtues, that deserve four or five years before they are ready to drink.

Johannes gave me a thought-provoking tasting of 1999 vintage Rieslings. If I had to choose just one wine, it would be Rüdesheimer Berg Rottland Spätlese 1999, which had the wonderfully fresh, elegant character that typifies this great vineyard.

Weingut August Kesseler

Lorcher Strasse 16, D-65385 Assmannshausen
tel 49 (0)6722 2513, fax 49 (0)6722 47477
email info@august-kesseler.de
internet www.august-kesseler.de
estate 18 ha, 50% Riesling
best vineyards Rüdesheimer Berg Schlossberg EG, Berg Roseneck EG, Bischofsberg EG
average annual production 105,000 bottles
Member VDP

August Kesseler is a perfectionist. Both his parents died in 1977 when he was still at school. In 1983, he took full charge of the *Weingut* and set his mind to making the finest Pinot Noirs and Rieslings in the Rheingau. But, he needed extra regular income, and in 1992 he became co-director at Weingut Schloss Reinhartshausen. There he made major improvements but experienced the problems that have dogged almost every large wine estate in Germany, until another change of ownership in 1999 gave him good cause to resign.

He made his name with his Spätburgunders (or Pinot Noirs); his Rieslings only came to the fore in the mid-1990s. They are the essence of modern dry Riesling. Now their reputation, but not their price, is as high as that of his Spätburgunders.

His approach to Riesling is very modern and reductive. In both the 1999 and 2001 vintages, his Rüdesheimer Berg Roseneck Spätlese Trocken had a bouquet of summer flowers, and complexity of minerals on the palate with no sense of dryness or sweetness. The Berg Schlossberg Spätlese 1999 and the 2002 with residual sugar both had miraculous balance of fruit and acidity with Auslese depth but little botrytis. Towards the end of our five-hour marathon we tasted a cavalcade of unforgettable botrytized Riesling Ausleses, BAs, and TBAs. An incredible experience.

Weingut Peter Jacob Kühn

Mühlstrasse 70, D-65375 Oestrich
tel 49 (0)6723 2299, fax 49 (0)6723 87788
email info@weingutpjkuehn.de
internet www. weingutpjkuehn.de
estate 13 ha, 85% Riesling
best vineyards Oestricher Lenchen EG and Doosberg EG
average annual production 72,000 bottles

Jacobus Kühn owned vines in Oestrich in 1786, but his descendent, Peter Jacob Kühn, nevertheless appeared like a comet in the night sky in 1992, when the tasting panel of Germany's best wine and food magazine, *Feinschmecker* ("Connoisseur"), chose his range of 1991 dry Rieslings as the finest in Germany. Peter Jacob uses fully organic methods in the vineyards, including cover crops planted between the rows of vines in late summer.

Peter Jacob likes to keep things simple in the vineyards and cellar, but his wines are actually very sophisticated. All his Rieslings are fermented slowly with indigenous yeasts in temperature-controlled stainless-steel tanks. In his inflexible resolve to keep freshness in all his Rieslings,

Peter Jacob was, for the 2001 vintage, one of the first German producers to bottle his Rieslings with Stelvin screwcaps, following the initiative of the Australian Riesling producers.

All the Rieslings are from Oestrich, and he uses just two vineyard names: Doosberg is always *trocken*, and Lenchen always has residual sugar; both are *Erstes Gewächs*. Auslese and higher qualities are given no vineyard name. All his wines have great intensity of flavour. His Doosberg Spätlese Trocken expresses the minerality of this terroir, while the gravel and loam terroir of Lenchen makes the wines quite opulent in a ripe vintage; his Auslesen are impeccable, with striking acidity to match their great fruit and concentration. His BAs are like nectar to a bee: you want to put your nose right into the glass to take in the wild flower, fruit, and honey flavours. His Eiswein are the essence of Riesling.

Weingut Franz Künstler

Freiherr-vom-Stein-Ring/Kirchstrasse 38,
D-65239 Hochheim
tel 49 (0)6146 82570, fax 49 (0)6146 5767
email info@weingut-kuenstler.de
internet www.weingut-kuenstler.de
estate 26 ha, 85% Riesling
best vineyards Hochheimer Hölle EG, Kirchenstück EG, and Domdechaney EG
average annual production 150,000 bottles
Member VDP

From 1988, Gunter Künstler made a succession of great dry Rieslings from the Hölle vineyard. In 1996, he and a financial partner bought Weingut Aschrott, which came with 12 ha of the finest vineyards in Hochheim. The cellars were refurbished, and stainless-steel tanks were installed.

The vineyards are farmed organically, and in August a severe green harvest is carried out to reduce the crop. The soil is relatively light near

The enchanting Hansel
and Gretel manor house
built by Sir John Sutton,
now the headquarters of
Weingut Robert Weil

the village, and Kirchenstück, Domdechaney, and Steilberg give the wines finesse. I have tasted their wines frequently, and for elegance Kirchenstück is wonderfully consistent, both dry and sweet. There is more clay and loam near the Main River, where the Hölle vineyard lies, giving fruit and richness. Hölle Spätlese Trocken 1999 was beautifully balanced, ultra-clean in taste and clear, dry and very spicy on the palate. The sweet Auslese 1998 was a superb wine with a long life ahead.

Weingut Balthasar Ress

Rheinallee 7, D-65347 Hattenheim
tel 49 (0)6723 91950, fax 49 (0)6723 919591
email weingut@ress-wine.com
internet www.ress-wine.com
estate 33 ha, 91% Riesling
best vineyards Schloss Reichartshausen EG, Hattenheimer Wisselbrunnen EG and Nussbrunnen, EG Rüdesheimer Berg Schlossberg EG, and Berg Rottland EG, Oestricher Doosberg EG
average annual production 220,000 bottles
Member VDP

Stefan Ress has collected vineyards like postage stamps and has almost a complete set of top vineyards from Eltville to Assmannshausen. In addition, the Hattenheim Cooperative decided to close in the late 1990s, just when Stefan needed a new cellar. He bought it complete, including most of the almost-new equipment and stainless-steel vats at bargain prices. The old cellars are now a splendid location for concerts, wine tastings, weddings, and cultural events. For these they often need Sekt, and Stefan has a first-class Balthasar Ress "Von Unserm" Riesling Vintage Brut *méthode traditionelle* Sekt.

In the 1999 vintage, the monopoly vineyard wine Schloss Reichartshausen Spätlese was particularly restrained and aristocratic, while the opulent Auslese from Hattenheimer Nussbrunnen and the more minerally Rüdesheimer Berg Schlossberg both showed great class.

Domänenweingut Schloss Schönborn

Hauptstrasse 53, D-65347 Hattenheim
tel 49 (0)6723 91810, fax 49 (0)6723 918191
email schloss-schoenborn@ t-online.de
internet www.schoenborn.de
estate 50 ha, 91% Riesling
best vineyards Erbacher Marcobrunnen EG, Nussbrunnen EG, and Pfaffenberg EG, Rüdesheimer Berg Schlossberg EG and Rottland EG, Hochheimer Domdechaney EG
average annual production 300,000 bottles
Member VDP

This is another large traditional estate (established in 1349), making the transition from the twentieth to the twenty-first century, thanks in part to the skills and dedication of director Günter Thies. Its vineyards are ideal: steep slate above Rüdesheim, gentle sloping loam and loess close to the Rhine at Erbach, sandy loam leading down to the river Main at Hochheim.

The dry wines are altogether fresher and of greater appeal than in the past. Erbacher Marcobrunnen Erstes Gewächs 1997 had majesty and power; Hattenheimer Pfaffenberg Spätlese 1997 was chic, deliciously fresh, and full-bodied. Rüdesheimer Berg Schlossberg Auslese 1999 was concentrated and expressive of its slate terroir, with little botrytis. From the great Domdechaney and Kirchenstück vineyards, Hochheimer Trockenbeerenauslese 1990 had an unbelievable 300 g.s. and 12.5 alc. and was a fabulous finale.

Hessische Staatsweingüter Kloster Eberbach

Schwalbacher Strasse 56–62, D-65343 Eltville
tel 49 (0)6123 92300, fax 49 (0)6123 923090
email info@staatsweingüterhessen.de
internet www.staatsweinguterhessen.de
estate 140 ha, 99% Riesling
best vineyards Steinberger EG, Rauenthaler Baiken EG, Erbacher Marcobrunn EG, Rüdesheimer Berg Schlossberg EG, Hochheimer Domdechaney EG
average annual production 800,000 bottles
Member VDP

In 1136, Cistercian monks (whose first vineyard was Clos Vougeot) founded the monastery Kloster Eberbach high above the Rhine in the forest of the Taunus Mountains. A few hundred yards downhill they hacked away trees and dug the stony soil to make the 35-ha Steinberg vineyard.

Incredibly, in the Middle Ages the monastery was said to be the largest wine producer in the world! Today, it is a national monument and the home of the Hessische Staatsweingüter; the offices and main cellars are still in Eltville, but are to be moved here.

Dieter Greiner was appointed Director in 2000, and he has instituted profound changes: modern, organic methods in the vineyards and reducing yields; smaller lots of individual wines to allow each to express the terroir of its site; and a number of passes through the vineyards to pick only the perfect grapes. Formerly, they used only stainless-steel tanks, but now they have the choice of fermenting and maturing in stainless steel or oak casks. Greiner wanted to re-discover character aspects of past Rieslings, so he started researching in the library of old vintages – recording each wine by taste and by scientific analysis. In particular, they were trying to establish the dry Rheingau Riesling style from the golden age – 1870 to 1930.

In 2003, I tasted Steinberg Riesling Erstes Gewächs 2001 with Steinberg Riesling Cabinet 1921 to compare the two. The former was closed, but it expressed the strong terroir of the stony soil. Dry, with relatively high alcohol, it had a sense of sweetness that would diffuse in a couple of years. The latter was full of life, its Riesling nose had faded a little, but it had a powerful character, and the finish was creamy but dry. This was the vintage of the century, proving thatboth great dry and botrytized Rieslings had been made in Rheingau since the eighteenth century. Previously, Dieter had organized a tasting of eleven top wines. The Rauenthaler Gehrn GG Spätlese

Trocken 1999 had finesse and power at the same time, with relatively low acidity and high alcohol. Steinberger QbA 1999 was a surprise, because it was so mineral and concentrated that it almost had a hint of Eiswein; while the Spätlese 1998 again showed its mineral freshness and elegance with harmonious acidity. The Rauenthaler Baiken Auslese 1995 was a brilliant green-gold colour, with the raisin flavour of botrytis giving it great length – this is one of my favourite vineyards. A glimpse of the future of a great *Weingut*!

Staatsweingut Bergstrasse

Grieselstrasse 34–36, D-64625 Bensheim
tel 49 (0)6251 3107, fax 49 (0)6251 65706
email bergstrasse@staatsweinguterhessen.de
estate 38 ha, 65% Riesling
best vineyards Heppenheimer Centgericht GG, Heppenheimer Steinkopf GG and Bensheimer Streichling, Bensheimer Kalkgasse
average annual production 240,000 bottles

This *Weingut* was established in 1904, and is now a subsidiary of the Hessische Staatsweingüter Kloster Eberbach. For almost a century, one family managed it – Johann Hillebrand, Jean (director of the vine nursery), Josef, and Heinrich. The new owners have total respect for their terroir, and viticulture is virtually organic. They use oak barrels and stainless steel for fermentation and maturation. Their wines always have a frank, open style.

Heppenheimer Centgericht Riesling Kabinett 1998 was light and friendly, whereas the Auslese 1994 was wonderfully exotic, with a flavour of dried figs and the strong botrytis of the vintage, balanced by fine acidity. Heppenheimer Steinkopf Spätlese Trocken 1999 was a perfect dry Riesling: exquisitely fresh with ripe acidity. Bensheimer Streichling Spätlese Trocken 1998 expressed its granite and mineral terroir and was quite herbal on the nose, with lime balancing its dry, but ripe, fruit. The Auslese 1989 was even more exotic, with hints of guava and light botrytis.

Weingut Schloss Vollrads

Schloss Vollrads, D-65375 Oestrich-Winkel
tel 49 (0)6723 660, fax 49 (0)6723 6666
email info@schlossvollrads.com
internet www.schlossvollrads.com
estate 56 ha, 100% Riesling
average annual production 400,000 bottles
Member VDP

The tragic death of Erwein Graf Matuschka-Greiffenclau in 1997 ended 667 years of ownership of Schloss Vollrads by his family. The Nassau Bank took it over in 1999 and appointed Dr. Rowald Hepp as director. The vineyards are spread around five villages. Steep slopes are twenty per cent of the total area, sixty per cent is on gentle slopes, and twenty per cent is on flat land. Grapes from the lesser parts, with malolactic fermentation to soften the acidity, make Schloss Vollrads Sommer Riesling – delicious young.

Graf Matushka spent twenty years promoting German wines internationally, yet he did not make the best of his own dry wines. The 1999s showed how quickly Dr. Hepp transformed everything and the Schloss Vollrads Spätlese Goldkapsel was rich and concentrated but not heavy, with great elegance. The 2000 Spätlese Halbtrocken was delicate and the sweet version was classic and complete. The 2000 Auslese Weissgold was a superb wine, finer than any Vollrads Auslese I had tasted for years, but then it had an almost BA level of 123 Oechsle and was picked on 23 December! The 2002s showed the improvements made by the new regime. Dry Erstes Gewächs, sweet Spätlese, and BA were each immaculate.

Weingut Robert Weil

Mühlberg 5, D-65399 Kiedrich
tel 49 (0)6123 2308, fax 49 (0)6123 1546
email info@weingut-robert-weil.com
internet www.weingut-robert-weil.com
estate 65 ha, 98% Riesling
best vineyards Kiedricher Gräfenberg EG and Wasseros EG
average annual production 450,000 bottles
Member VDP

In 1875, Robert Weil bought the vineyards and the house, and by the 1890s it had become one of the most famous estates in the Rheingau. Wilhelm Weil, Robert's great-grandson, is the present director and he has transformed the estate since 1988, when a majority shareholding was sold to the giant Japanese company, Suntory. A huge investment was made in state-of-the-art equipment and in buying fine vineyards, bringing the estate up from 18 ha to its present 65 ha.

Wilhelm devised an ideal *modus operandi*: he sells all the wines except Gräfenberg under the estate name only, without mention of the vineyard. Gräfenberg (9.5 ha) is the jewel in the crown. The steep slope faces southwest, benefiting from long evening sunshine; the slate and phyllite soil is rare in the Rheingau and gives a wonderful mineral character to the wines. The viticulture is exacting: green cover-crops, stringent pruning controls, thinning after flowering, leaf plucking, green harvest. There are about seventy pickers who make up to seventeen selective pickings between mid-October and early December. Each picking is pressed and fermented separately in computer-controlled stainless-steel tanks, some containing as little as 100 litres. The fermentation of the sweet wines is stopped by deep-cooling the must in order to retain the fructose, carbonic acid gas, and freshness. Then the wine rests with the fine lees for as long as possible to achieve maximum flavour extraction before bottling.

The style of the Robert Weil wines is unmistakable. There is absolute purity and mineral, citrus-fruit flavour in the dry wines, with no angular acidity and a crescendo of concentration and white peach fruit in the sweet wines. There are several different Auslesen and relatively large amounts of Eiswein, and sometimes I think I taste a tiny dose of this in the top Auslesen. I have fond memories of the Gräfenberg Auslese 1953 from here that I used to sell nearly fifty years ago.

Nahe

The best Nahe vineyards start at Monzingen. From here, the valley runs for about 160 kilometres (100 miles) in a great semi-circle from the west before joining the Rhine at Bingen. Some five miles downstream from Monzingen, the river starts to make a series of sharp bends as it cuts through porphyry volcanic rock and slate hills. Here, around Niederhausen-Schlossböckelheim, are the most famous vineyards of the region, and it was here that the Prussian state set up a Staatsdomäne in 1902, now privatized (Gutsverwaltung Niderhausen-Schlossböckelheim, *see* page 59). After another bend in the river you are confronted by a massive cliff of rock towering 180 metres (600 feet) above the little wandering Nahe River; the cliff changes to a pink and golden glow and then to a sensational red in the evening light. At the base of the cliff, like a little steep-sloping beach, is all the mineral debris that has fallen over millions of years. This unique vineyard is Traiser Bastai.

Bad Kreuznach is the main city of the region, and fine vineyards are spread out like a fan to the north of the city. The soil is loam and loess, giving Rieslings with extra body and great concentration. Unfortunately, the wines are not as great as they were up to the 1990s, and I dearly hope that they will be restored to their former glory.

From Monzingen to Bad Kreuznach, the vineyards face south. Then the river turns north and the vineyards of the villages of Langenlonsheim, Dorsheim, and Münster-Sarmsheim face south and are in side valleys, where the soils are more mixed, less volcanic, and with good amounts of slate; they give a broader style of Riesling.

Nahe Rieslings have a unique place. They have great elegance and lightness of touch with more body than those of the Mosel-Saar-Ruwer, less earthy richness and weight than some Pfalz Rieslings, and more subtlety than those of the Rheingau. The VDP classification is *Grosses Gewächs* ("Great Growth"), and at the time of writing there were thirty-three classified vineyards; only dry Riesling qualifies. Vineyards that qualify are marked GG under "best vineyards".

The bridge over the river Nahe from Weingut Dönnhoff to the Niederhausen vineyards was built by convicts!

Weingut Dr. Crusius

Hauptstrasse 2, D-55595 Traisen
tel 49 (0)6713 3953, fax 49 (0)672 8219
email weingut-crusius@t-online.de
internet www.weingut-crusius.de
estate 15 ha, 70% Riesling
best vineyards Traiser Bastei GG and Rotenfels GG,
Schlossböckelheimer Felsenberg GG, Niederhäuser
Felsensteyer GG, Norheimer Kirschheck GG
average annual production 80,000 bottles
Member VDP

The Crusius family can trace its wine-growing
ancestors back to 1586 in Traisen. In 1990, Peter
Crusius took over from his father. His philosophy
is sustainable viticulture and he never uses sulphur
either on the vines or in the cellar.

Traiser Bastei, at the base of the great Rotenfels,
is the jewel in the Crusius crown. The Spätlese
Trocken 1999 was cool-fermented in stainless steel,
and with 92 Oechsle and relatively low acidity it
was a scintillating, minerally wine, dry but not acidic.
The classic, sweet Riesling Spätlese 1999 was
attractive and soft. The Auslese 1998 had powerful
botrytis and needed time to gather itself together,
whereas the Auslese 1999 was open and elegant,
though still very young. Traiser Rotenfels Eiswein
1998 was the essence of fragrant Nahe Riesling.

Schlossgut Diel

D-55452 Burg Layen
tel 49 (0)6721 96950, fax 49 (0)6721 45047
email info@schlossgut-diel.com
internet www.schlossgut-diel.com
estate 16 ha, 70% Riesling
best vineyards Dorsheimer Pittermännchen GG,
Goldloch GG, and Burgberg GG
average annual production 90,000 bottles
Member VDP

Peter Diel bought the ruined twelfth century castle,
the mansion and its vineyards in 1802. Armin Diel
is the sixth generation, and took over from his father,
Dr. Ingo Diel, in 1987. Armin became a lawyer

and began writing about gastronomy in 1978.
He and Joel Payne write the influential *Gault Millau
Wein Guide Deutschland*. His father proudly
made countless BAs and TBAs with all the
"new" German grape varieties and Armin promptly
pulled them up, replacing them with Riesling and
the Burgundian vines. Armin initially concentrated
on dry wines but later started to make sweet
Spätlesen and Auslesen. Meanwhile, he had
drastically reduced the yields by sharp pruning.
He uses no chemical fertilizers.

The three *Grosses Gewächs* vineyards are
contiguous along a steep, south-facing hill about
500-metres (1,650-feet) long, but the soil in each
vineyard is entirely different. Pittermännchen has
pebbles and sandstone with slate and quartzite, and
the Spätlese 1999 was beautifully fresh and mineral.
Goldloch has about 0.6 metres (two feet) of clay and
pebbles above primary rock, and the Spätlese 1998
was *spritzig* with voluptuous, juicy fruit, and great
length. Burgberg has slate and loam tinged brown
by iron, and the Spätlese 1998 was quite powerful,
with depth and breeding, deserving time in bottle
to develop.

In the cellar Armin uses indigenous yeasts for
the fermentations whenever this is viable. He has
large, old-oak barrels for fermenting and maturing
most of the Rieslings, barriques for his Burgundian
wines, and stainless-steel vats for others.

Weingut Dönnhoff

Bahnhofstrasse 11, D-55585 Oberhausen
tel 49 (0)6755 263, fax 49 (0)6755 1067
email weingut@doennhof.com
internet www.doennhof.com
estate 14.5 ha, 75% Riesling
best vineyards Niederhäuser Hermannshöhle GG,
Oberhäuser Brücke GG, Schlossböckelheimer
Felsenberg GG and Kupfergruber GG,
Norheimer Kirschheck GG and Dellchen GG
average annual production 100,000 bottles
Member VDP

Weingut Hermann Dönnhoff has the greatest
reputation in the Nahe region. Helmut Donnhöff
can trace his ancestors as wine-growers back
to 1750, but he has done more in twenty-five years
than they did in 250.

The 1-ha Oberhäuser Brücke is between
Schlossböckelheimer Kupfergrube ("copper mine")
and Niederhäuser Hermannshöhle. The volcanic soils
here are extremely complex.

Helmut is traditional and meticulous in his
cellars, using large old barrels and stainless steel.
He led me through a memorable tasting of 1999s.
Three Spätlesen: the Kupfergrube was typical in its
finesse and charm but with an undercurrent of its
terroir – you can see the green of oxidized copper
in the soil – that would express itself fully in a few
years time. The Brückes was very restrained with
greater depth; the Hermannshöhle was quite

full-bodied, with lots of minerals and great length. Two Auslesen: the Hermannshöhle Auslese was without any botrytis, very delicate and long with relatively high acidity for the long term; the Brückes had more structure and depth with a touch of exotic guava in the flavour. The Brückes Eiswein was all ripe Riesling with no botrytis and great acidity (12 g.a.). Finally, two Brückes Beerenauslesen – the 1999, picked on November 17 was all finesse, with botrytis and fine acidity – "with no complications" as Helmut said – and 1998, picked on November 27 with 210 Oechsle (TBA had he so wished) – the richest Riesling imaginable, but balanced with the ripest acidity.

Weingut Emrich-Schönleber

Naheweinstrasse 10a, D-55569 Monzingen
tel 49 (0)6751 2733, fax 49 (0)6751 4864
email Weingut@Emrich-Schoenleber.com
internet www.emrich-schoenleber.com
estate 14.5 ha, 76% Riesling
best vineyards Monzinger Halenberg GG and Frühlingsplätzchen GG
average annual production 110,000 bottles
Member VDP

The first monastic record of vines at Monzingen is dated 778. But because Monzingen is at the extreme west of the region and there was no famous *Weingut*, it was forgotten until Werner Schönleber, at the age of nineteen, won the National Viticultural Competition and took over the *Weingut* from his father in 1993.

Today, his wines are on a par with Dönnhoff. The climate is benign; a warm west wind wafts down the valley and the steep vineyards face directly south, protected from cold north winds by the Hunsrück hills.

The grapes are whole-bunch pressed. The *trocken* wines are usually fermented in stainless steel with cultured yeasts, but the sweeter wines are fermented with indigenous yeasts in large oak casks.

Werner's wines illustrate the difference between the two vineyards. Frühlingsplätzchen has quartzite, basalt, green, blue, and red slate (with volcanic

minerals like those of Ürzig on the Mosel). The Riesling Spätlese Trocken 1998 had a fresh, elegant bouquet that expanded on the palate, with mineral flavours dominant. Halenberg has quartzite, basalt, and blue Devonian slate like that of Wehlen on the Mosel. The Riesling Spätlese Trocken 1998 was equally fresh but had a pervasive scent of wild roses, great delicacy, and length. The Spätlese 1998 with residual sugar was neat, precise, and delicious. Werner's sweet Halenberg Auslese Goldkapsel 1998 was sensational. A perfect modern Riesling: crystal-clear on the nose, essence of fresh apricot and white peach, given a touch more acidity by a smidgen of Eiswein, which are among the finest in Germany.

Weingut Kruger-Rumpf

Rheinstraase 47, D-55424 Münster-Sarmsheim
tel 49 (0)6721 43859, fax 49 (0)6721 41882
email weingut@kruger-rumpf.com
internet www.kruger-rumpf.com
estate 19.5 ha, 65% Riesling
best vineyards Münsterer Dautenpflänzer GG, Pittersberg GG, Rheinberg GG and Kapellenberg GG, Dorsheimer Goldloch GG, and Burgberg GG
average annual production 120,000 bottles
Member VDP

The Kruger family can trace its *Weingut* back to 1790, and in 1860 it was one of the largest estates in the Nahe, with 70 ha of vines. The vineyards were gradually sold and the wines sold in bulk to other producers, until Stefan took over the *Weingut* and just 8.5 ha from his parents in 1984. He doubled the size of the estate by buying land in the best vineyard sites.

There is plenty of slate in the vineyards and the soils are very mixed. We tasted the 1999 Rieslings. The Dautenpflänzer Spätlese Trocken Silberkapsel was "international" in style, 12.5 alc., with low acidity, good concentration and great charm. The Pittersberg Kabinett Halbtrocken Silberkapsel had a nose of fresh flowers, with citrus and minerals – a delightful wine.

Gutsverwaltung Niederhausen-Schlossböckelheim

Ehemalige Weinbaudomäne, D-55585 Niederhausen
tel 49 (0)6758 92500, fax 49 (0)6758 925019
email info@riesling-domaene.de
internet www.riesling-domaene.de
estate 34 ha, 90% Riesling
best vineyards Niederhäuser Hermannsberg GG and
Hermannshöhle GG, Schlossböckelheimer Kupfergrube
GG and Felsenberg GG, Traiser Bastai GG
average annual production 200,000 bottles
Member VDP

The Prussian State created the Staatsdomäne
in 1902 as a model winery. Convict labour cleared
the oak trees, scrub, and massive rocks on the
surrounding hills and the disused copper mine
(*Kupfergrube*), creating a huge amphitheatre of vines
around the winery, which had the latest equipment
and techniques. The estate flourished, producing
many fabulous vintages until the late 1980s, when
the quality dropped, as it did for so many large
estates in Germany. To concentrate the estate back
to its original amphitheatre, the RheinlandPfalz State
put 10 ha of vines in Münster and Dorsheim on the
market, and Diel, Kruger-Rumpf, and others snapped
them up. In 1998, Erich Mauer, an agricultural
products manufacturer, bought the estate.

It takes time and financial investment to restore
vineyards and to modernize an old winery. This one
made Auslesen and above in 1998 and in 1999 a fine,
concentrated traditional Schlossböckelheimer
Kupfergrube Auslese and a superb Niederhäuser
Hermannshöhle Trockenbeerenauslese with
incredible concentration and subtlety. The 2002
vintage seemed to show that the transformation was
completed across the range. Schlossböckelheimer
Kupfergrube Spätlese Trocken shone with mineral
intensity and finesse, and contrasted with the sweet
Spätlese from the same vineyard. The Niederhäuser
Hermannshöhle Auslese was refined and
concentrated, with great potential.

Weingut Prinz zu Salm-Dalberg, Schloss Wallhausen

Schlossstrasse 3, D-55595 Wallhausen
tel 49 (0)6706 944411, fax 49 (0)6706 944424
email salm.dalberg@salm-salm.de
internet www.salm-salm.de
estate 11.7 ha, 60% Riesling
best vineyards Wallhäuser Johannisberg GG
and Felseneck GG, Roxheimer Berg GG
average annual production 70,000 bottles
Member VDP

The Salm-Dalberg family has owned Schloss
Wallhausen since 1200, and the present incumbent
is Michael Prinz zu Salm-Salm. From 1980 to 1988,
he was director of the Castell Domäne in Franken
and then, briefly, chief executive of the Castell Bank.
In 1982, he inherited the Schloss Wallhausen estate
with 3 ha of vines, the splendid mansion, and plenty
of land. Immediately, he set about re-establishing
the vineyards.

In 1990, he was elected president of the VDP. He
steered the negotiations through the intricacies of the
new classifications with charm and determination.

In 1988, the vineyards of Schloss Wallhausen
started to be converted to organic practices and they
were officially tested and confirmed by Naturland
as fully organic in 1995.

We tasted the 1999 vintage at the *Schloss* and
these are my notes. Roxheimer Berg Spätlese was
brisk and fresh, with pristine mineral flavours and
typically Nahe; the soil is loam tinged red with iron,
and this vineyard has long been famous for Riesling.
Wallhäuser Felseneck Spätlese had greater fruit
and depth of character, with racy acidity to retain
its freshness, from the green slate in the soil.
Wallhäuser Johannisberg Auslese had superb
richness, concentration and harmony: the
red-slate soil with volcanic minerals is like that
in Ürzig, and gives a spicy richness. These wines
all express to the full their individual terroirs,
as organic wines should.

Rheinhessen

Until forty years ago the Rieslings of Nierstein were on a par in reputation with those of Piesport, Rüdesheim, and Forst. It was the infamous 1971 Wine Law that encouraged Rheinhessen to become synonymous with Liebfraumilch, Bereich Nierstein, and Niersteiner Gutes Domtal, where mass-produced Müller-Thurgau and the disgusting Morio-Muscat – to name but two of the culprits – were planted instead of sugar beet on flat agricultural land. Even in 2003, though matters have improved, there were 26,333 hectares of vines in Rheinhessen, of which twenty-two per cent were red grapes, twenty per cent Müller-Thurgau, eleven per cent Silvaner, and only ten per cent Riesling, leaving thirty-seven per cent of awful "new", mass-production, early ripening, white grapes.

Nevertheless, there are a few great Rieslings from the red soil of the Rheinfront (or Roten Hang or Rheinterrassen or Rotschiefer, as it is variously called). This strip of steep vineyards faces almost due east, but the grapes achieve phenomenal ripeness because the sun is reflected from the broad expanse of the Rhine here and the soil retains the heat. The Rheinfront starts at Nackenheim and finishes about five kilometres (three miles) upstream with the cluster of famous Nierstein vineyards. The deep, red-brown soil is sandstone and schist. Weingut Gunderloch in Nackenheim and Heyl zu Herrnsheim in Nierstein are the finest estates in this tiny area. About a dozen growers have grouped together to form the "Roter Hang" Association.

Wonnegau ("the happy land") is an area roughly between Alzey and Worms, where Riesling was recorded as existing in 1490. The climate is perfect for vines and the soil is very variable; it changes every 100 metres (305 feet) or so, due in part to this having been the basin of the Rhine before the Alps rose.

In 2003, there were just four estates, with a total of seventy hectares, making fine wines – and I am not only talking about Riesling. Two estates, near Nierstein, are survivors from before the 1971-inspired decline; two in Wonnegau are the starting point for the renaissance of Riesling in Rheinhessen. The example of these four will encourage some other growers to try to make fine wines from good sites, and there are some around Nierstein, Oppenheim, Alsheim, and Wonnegau but, assuming that mass-produced sweet German wines continue to lose customers, sooner or later the farmers – because that is all most of them are – will return to producing other crops.

It is my view that most Rheinhessen Rieslings are best when *trocken* except those affected by botrytis, because the fruit and alcohol in the wine will naturally balance the acidity.

The VDP classification is *Grosses Gewächs* ("Great Growth"), and at the time of writing there were sixteen classified vineyards; only dry Riesling and Spätburgunder qualify. Vineyards that qualify are marked GG under "best vineyards".

Weingut Gunderloch

Carl-Gunderloch-Platz 1, D-55299 Nackenheim
tel 49 (0)6135 2341, fax 49 (0)6135 2431
email weingut@gunderloch.de
internet www.gunderloch.de
estate 12.5 ha, 80% Riesling
best vineyards Nackenheimer Rothenberg GG,
Niersteiner Pettenthal GG, and Hipping GG
average annual production 85,000 bottles
Member VDP

Agnes and Fritz Hasselbach first hit the headlines with their 1989 vintage. They had radically reduced yields, while others were increasing theirs and introduced strict selection during the picking. They had kept the old 600-litre oak barrels for fermenting and maturing their wines on fine lees for between two and ten months, but replaced the old press with a new slow, low-pressure one, and made 101 other improvements. Niersteiner Pettenthal is the most famous Rheinhessen vineyard, and Nackenheimer Rothenberg adjoins it on the same red soil. The Hasselbachers have made a scintillating range of Nackenheimer Rothenberg Rieslings every year from 1989 onwards.

Among recent vintages, the Spätlese 1999 with residual sugar had spritz, giving great freshness on the palate and exquisite purity with subtle hidden fruit; the grapes were picked from the end of November to December 22, without a speck of botrytis. The 1999 Auslese had tremendously concentrated fruit, with white peach, lovely acidity, and fantastic botrytis giving it a touch of crème brûlée on the finish. The 2000 Auslese Goldkapsel

surpassed the 1999 in depth, richness, and complexity and will take a long time to reveal all its secrets. It was from selected single grapes from the steepest terrace of the vineyard and had 135 Oechsle. It qualified as BA, but it was too subtle and refined to be so labelled.

Freiherr Heyl zu Herrnsheim

Langstrasse 3, D-55283 Nierstein
tel 49 (0)6133 57080, fax 49 (0)6733 570880
email info@heyl-zu-herrnsheim.de
internet www.heyl-zu-herrnsheim.de
estate 24 ha, 68% Riesling
best vineyards Niersteiner Brudersberg (monopoly) GG,
Pettenthal GG, Hipping GG, and Oelberg GG,
Nackenheimer Rothenberg GG
average annual production 200,000 bottles
Member VDP

Freifrau Isa von Meding-Heyl inherited this splendid *Weingut* in 1969. Immediately, she and her husband, physicist Peter von Weymarn, started to transform the vineyards to organic viticulture. In the cellars many small improvements were made to allow gentle handling of the grapes and the wines. They made dry Rieslings for the first time and continued to make great sweet Auslesen and above until 1994, when they sold the estate to the Ahr family. Under the aegis of Markus Winfried Ahr, Michael Burgdorf, the young manager of the *Weingut*, follows the philosophy established by the von Weymarns.

The simplest wines are labelled only with the grape variety and the vintage: Riesling Trocken 1999 was fresh and juicy. The second level is labelled

Klaus-Peter Keller of Weingut Keller, at Dalsheimer Hubacher,
a *Grosses Gewächs* and their finest Riesling vineyard

Rotschiefer ("red schist") Riesling Spätlese Trocken
and the 1999 had real red-soil terroir character. The
third level is *Grosses Gewächs*, dry Rieslings from
four vineyards; Brudersberg 1999 showed the great
power and concentration of an Auslese fermented
to dryness and 13 alc., somewhat in the style of an
Alsace Grand Cru. The richer, sweeter qualities are
fermented in old-oak barrels and remain on the light
lees for anything from eight to twenty months. The
fourth level consists of sweet Auslesen and above.
Just to choose one, the Oelberg Goldkapsel Auslese
1998 had a glorious medley of fruit, richness, and
power plus sophistication, and remained on my
palate for ages. This was from a parcel of 45-year-old
vines, that only produced 18 hl/ha – but the Oechsle
level was 125! Alas this meant that the quantity was
only 600 litres.

Weingut Keller

Bahnhofstrasse 1, D-67592 Flörsheim-Dalsheim
tel 49 (0)6243 456, fax 49 (0)6243 6686
email info@weingut-keller.de
Internet www.weingut-keller.de
estate 12.5 ha, 50% Riesling
best vineyards Dalsheimer Hubacher GG and Bürgel GG
average annual production 100,000 bottles
Member VDP

The Keller family has been making wine in Dalsheim
in Wonnegau since 1789, yet suddenly its wines are
being recognized as among the finest in Germany.
Klaus Keller, with the help of his son Klaus-Peter,
fresh from the Geisenheim Wine Institute, has
performed this miracle.

The microclimate here is ideal and the soil is
mixed, there is red loam, clay, and limestone with
minerals. Each vine is treated as special, and
whatever they do – pruning, leaf-plucking, green
harvest, picking – is timed to perfection. The cellar
is as clean as a whistle.

When I visited, Klaus-Peter had just finished his studies at Geisenheim Wine Institute. He was busy experimenting with special metal sheets that were laid down to reflect the sun upwards to the bunches of grapes. The technique was also used to retain moisture and keep the soil cool at night – allowing a temperature variation of as much as 15°C (59°F). He had already done a green harvest to reduce the crop and was debating when to carry out leaf plucking. There is an element of *Vorsprung durch Technik* (leading through technique), because father and son do everything to a plan and they never fail with Riesling.

The estate's best Riesling vineyard is Dalsheimer Hubacher, and we tasted its fine 1999s. The Spätlese Trocken was golden-green, with spritz, fine acidity, and exotic fruit flavours (8.5 g.a., 12.5 alc.). The Spätlese "No. 26" was exquisite, with minerals and acidity framing the concentrated (but in no way cloying) fruit; it was very late-picked, with a yield of 25 hl/ha from a parcel of old vines. The Auslese itself was the essence of Riesling, with a flavour of ripe William's pear – perfect.

Perhaps their Rieslings will not improve greatly in bottle and be as great as Wilhelm Haag's, Egon Müller's or Helmut Dönnhoff's, but Keller Rieslings have pure varietal perfection.

Weingut Wittmann

Mainzer Weinstrasse 19, D-67593 Westhofen
tel 49 (0)6244 905036, fax 49 (0)6244 5578
email info@wittmannweingut.com
internet www.wittmannweingut.com
estate 20 ha, 47% Riesling
average annual production 150,000 bottles
best vineyards Westhofener Morstein GG, Kirchspiel GG, and Aulede GG
Member VDP

When Günter Wittmann took over the *Weingut*, he commenced acquiring or exchanging vineyards to get more on limestone soil. He joined the organic organization Naturland and his vineyards were recognized as being fully organic in 1989. The effects were visible to all, because his garden is full of Mediterranean flowers, birds, butterflies, and insects. His son Philipp, having completed his wine studies and worked with Bassermann-Jordan in the Pfalz and in Tuscany, Burgundy, and California, took on responsibility for the *Weingut* in 1999; Günter continues with the viticulture. They have a tall, deep cellar that was built in 1829, which they use for their large, old-oak barrels and stainless-steel tanks. It is linked to an adorable little fifteenth century vaulted cellar that they acquired in 2002.

The successful export company von Valkenberg owns the historic 20-ha Liebfrauenstifts Kirchenstück. The original vineyard was planted with Riesling in the ninteenth century. Die berühmte Lieben Frauen Milch zu Worms (the famous Liebfraumilch at Worms), as it was described in 1744, was from the vineyards surrounding the Liebfrauenkirche.

In 2001, with the encouragement of the von Valkenberg estate manager, Wittman bought the grapes from 1 ha, "to see what they could make with Riesling from there". The sandy soil of the vineyard gives the wine lots of fruit, which is completely different in style from the estate's other Rieslings.

We tasted the brilliant 2001 Westhofener Rieslings. Aulede Spätlese Trocken was from 50-year-old vines on heavy clay, broken limestone, and sand, giving a full, balanced, and concentrated wine with 13 alc. Kirchspiel Spätlese Trocken, from a warmer vineyard with deep limestone and red slate, had finesse and elegance and just 10 alc.

Among the 2001 Rieslings with residual sugar, Morstein Spätlese had a bouquet of wild meadow flowers and gentle rounded flavours on the palate, and Morstein Auslese "S" was immensely rich, with a cornucopia of autumn fruit flavours that lasted forever – not a normal Auslese but almost a TBA without the treacle. (160 g.s., 9.8 g.a., 8 alc.). Organic viticulture in a perfect micro-climate and hard work is their recipe for success.

Pfalz

Die Pfalz ist ein Garten von Eden ("the Pfalz is a garden of Eden"), as they say here. The climate is benign: almonds, apricots, lemons, and figs ripen in the autumn sunshine. In spring, the pink blossom of the almond trees illuminates the still-dormant vines. Vineyards flank the foothills of the Haardt Mountains right up to the French frontier. Riesling is the most important grape variety and covers twenty-one per cent of the vineyard, and the growers are planting more Riesling and Burgundian varieties, at the expense of the ghastly Müller-Thurgau and other "new" crossings.

The classic wines come from the villages along the sixteen-kilometre (ten-mile) stretch of the *Weinstrasse* ("wine route") below the hills of the Mittelhaardt – villages like Kallstadt, Bad Dürkheim, Wachenheim, Forst, Deidesheim, and Ruppertsberg, but also less well-known ones, such as Königsbach, Gimmeldingen, Haardt, and Müssbach. The soil on the slopes has a fine mineral content, with limestone in some places, especially in Wachenheim, and volcanic porphyry and basalt elsewhere, especially in Forst (one of the *Grosses Gewächs* is called *Pechstein* which means "basalt"). Sometimes these are overlaid with weathered, red sandstone and wind-blown loess. The soil of the vast plain, with its soft hills across to the Black Forest – this was the original Rhine Valley – is loess and alluvial sand and gravel, which means that the wines lack the complexity of those from the slopes.

In the middle of the nineteenth century, the Pfalz suddenly joined the Rheingau and the Mosel as a great wine region largely because of three famous estates "The Three Bs": Bassermann-Jordan, Bürklin-Wolf, and von Buhl. Today, these three still own some of the best sites in the Mittelhaardt.

From Neustadt to the French border, the *Südliche Weinstrasse* ("southern wine route") continues along the Haardt Mountains, but everything here is on a broader scale. The mountains are higher, the forests are thicker, the views are longer, the vineyards are larger, and the prices of the wines are lower. The terroirs are not yet as clearly defined as in the Mittelhaardt, and much of the flat land continues to produce large volumes of simple wines.

However, Weingut Bergdolt in Duttweiler, just south of Neustadt, makes excellent Rieslings. Further south, stretching about three miles along the *Weinstrasse*, the estates of Rebholz in Siebeldingen, Wehrheim in Birkweiler, and Siegrist in Leinsweiler have already proved that they can produce great wines, including Rieslings, on their very special terroirs. There is considerable potential for high-quality Rieslings to be produced in this sub-region.

There are two contrasting styles of Riesling in the Pfalz. There is the restrained elegance of, for example, Bassermann-Jordan and Mosbacher, and the florid, aromatic style of Dr. Bürklin-Wolf and Müller-Catoir; between the two poles is Christmann – for me, the great discovery of my last visit. It is my view that most Pfalz Rieslings are best when *trocken*, except those that have botrytis, because the fruit and alcohol in the wine will naturally balance the acidity.

The VDP classification is *Grosses Gewächs* ("Great Growth") and at the time of writing there were thirty-four classified vineyards; only dry wines made with Riesling, Spätburgunder, and Weissburgunder qualify. Vineyards that qualify are marked GG under "best" vineyards.

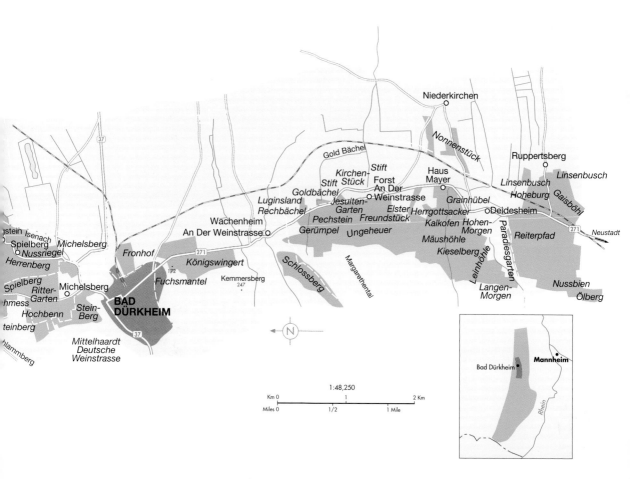

The village of
Grosskarlbach in
the Pfalz with Rainer
Lingenfelder's Weingut in
the foreground
and an approaching
summer storm

Prädikats Weine

Lingenfelder
Weingut

PROBE+
VERKAUF

Weingut Geheimrat Dr. von Bassermann-Jordan

Kirchgasse 10, D-67142 Deidesheim
tel 49 (0)6326 6006, fax 49 (0)6326 5008
email hauck@bassermann-jordan.de
internet www.bassermann-jordan.de
estate 42 ha, 90% Riesling
best vineyards Deidesheimer Grainhübel GG,
Hohenmorgen GG and Kalkofen GG, Forster Kirchenstück
GG, Ungeheuer GG, Pechstein GG, and Jesuitengarten GG
average annual production 300,000 bottles
Member VDP

Like other large wineries, for about fifteen years this estate's wines were disappointing. Ulrich Mell became cellarmaster in 1997, and gave the dry Rieslings a fresh, modern style: his sweet wines have been sensational. Gunther Hauck, the director, told us that the first priority was the vineyards. In the cellars, there is slow pressing and slow, cold fermentation with indigenous yeasts in old-oak barrels.

We tasted the 2001 Rieslings. Forster Jesuitengarten Spätlese Trocken had great finesse, fine, ripe acidity, and a subtle, volcanic background flavour; it was dry, but rich, with fruit and depth. It contrasted perfectly with the Jesuitengarten Spätlese 2001, with residual sugar – wonderful dried-apricot fruit and a touch of botrytis, with acidity to develop over ten years (65 g.s., 9.5 alc.). Ruppertsberger Reiterpfad TBA was a dream Riesling – caramel, glycerol, crème brulée, and butterscotch (185 Oechsle).

Weingut Bergdolt

Klostergut Sankt Lamprecht, D-67435 Duttweiler
tel 49 (0)6327 5027, fax 49 (0)6327 1784
email info@weingut-bergdolt.de
internet www.weingut-bergdolt.de
estate 23 ha, 32% Riesling
best vineyards Kirrweiler Mandelberg GG, Duttweiler
Kalkberg GG, Ruppertsberger Reiterpfad GG
average annual production 155,000 bottles

The *Weingut* is southeast of Neustadt, with varying mixtures of loess and sandstone soils. The brothers Rainer and Günther run the estate now, and towards the end of the 1990s they bought vineyards in Ruppertsberg, which gave them an extra string to their bow, the soil having extra mineral and volcanic elements from the Haardt Mountains.

We tasted a range of 2001 Rieslings. Duttweiler Kalkberg Spätlese Trocken (6.6 g.s., 8 g.a., 12 alc.) was subtle and drier from the limestone in the soil. Kirrweiler Mandelberg Spätlese Trocken was richer and more aromatic, but Ruppertsberger Reiterpfad GG was altogether more powerful, with less sugar, more acidity, and higher alcohol. What struck me most was the unmolested purity of these Rieslings.

Weingut Dr. Bürklin-Wolf

Weinstrasse 65, D-67157 Wachenheim
tel 49 (0)6322 95330, fax 49 (0)6322 953330
email bb@buerklin-wolf.de
internet www.buerklin-wolf.de
estate 85.5 ha, 72% Riesling
best vineyards Forster Kirchenstück GG,
Jesuitengarten GG, Ungeheuer GG and Pechstein GG,
Ruppertsberger Reiterpfad GG and Gaisböhl (monopoly)
GG, Deidesheimer Hohenmorgen GG, Lagenmorgen GG,
and Kalkofen GG
average annual production 600,000 bottles
Member VDP

In the 1980s, this estate was in the doldrums. But in the 1990s, Bettina Bürklin-von Guradze and her husband Christian von Guradze reorganized the vineyards, reduced the yields, and modernized the cellars, with temperature-controlled, traditional *Doppelstück* (2,500 litre barrels).

Wachenheim Gerümpel Spätlese 2000 had a fragrant bouquet and sang of its terroir. Gaisböhl Grosses Gewächs 2000 was a fantastically complex wine – a concentrated cornucopia of ripe fruit. Wachenheimer Gerümpel Auslese 1990 was a perfect example of a powerful, rich, late-picked Riesling, with minimum botrytis and peach and apricot flavours.

Ruppertsberger Gaisböhl Trockenbeerenauslese 1989 (189 g.s., 10 alc.) was the great botrytis vintage – hedonistic essence of honey and dried apricots.

Weingut Reichsrat von Buhl

Weinstrasse 16, D-67146 Deidesheim
tel 49 (0)6326 96500, fax 49 (0)6326 965024
email info@reichsrat-von-buhl.de
internet www. reichsrat-von-buhl.de
estate 50 ha, 88% Riesling
best vineyards Forster Freundstück GG,
Jesuitengarten GG, Pechstein GG, Kirchenstück GG,
Ungeheuer GG, Deidesheimer Kieselberg GG,
Ruppertsberger Reiterpfad GG
average annual production 350,000 bottles
Member VDP

Like many other large estates, von Buhl had problems in the poor vintages of the 1970s and 1980s, though it made great wines in 1971 and 1976. In 1989, the estate and cellars were leased to sixty Japanese wine merchants, who invested heavily to improve quality. From 1994 to 2000, it made excellent dry wines and superb sweet wine in every vintage, but 2000 was a disaster, rain having caused uncontrollable grey rot.

We tasted the 2001 vintage. Deidesheimer Herrgottsacker Kabinett Trocken had a flowery bouquet with fine acidity and balanced richness. Ruppertsberger Reiterpfad Spätlese Trocken Grosses Gewächs had great power and concentration. Forster Ungeheuer Spätlese Trocken had depth and a rich, oily flavour from the black volcanic basalt in the soil.

Weingut A. Christmann

Peter-Koch-Strasse 43, D-67435 Gimmeldingen
tel 49 (0)6321 66039, fax 49 (0)6321 68762
email weingut.christmann@t-online.de
internet www.weingut.christmann.de
estate 14 ha, 67% Riesling
best vineyards Ruppertsberger Reiterpfad GG,
Königsbacher Idig GG, Gimmeldinger Mandelgarten GG,
Deidesheimer Hohenmorgen GG
average annual production 110,000 bottles
Member VDP

This *Weingut* can challenge its neighbour Müller-Catoir for the title of greatest Pfalz Riesling estate. Ruppertsberger Linsenbusch Kabinett Trocken 2001 had a fresh, lemony nose and a delicious flavour of pink grapefruit; the 2002 had a bouquet of wild flowers and powerful Pfalz concentration on the palate. Königsbacher Idig Spätlese Trocken 2000 (4.9 g.s., 7.1 g.a., 13.2 alc.) was even more concentrated and characteristic and, although it is very dry, it tasted almost sweet; on the palate it opened like a flower in ultra-slow-motion. Gimmeldinger Mandelgarten Grosses Gewächs 2002 (6.2 g.s., 8.0 g.a., 13.1 alc.) was still closed, but the high acidity and alcohol will allow it to develop the glorious flavours of ripe peaches, apricots, and mandarins already so evident in the marvellous 1997 from the same vineyard. Gimmeldinger Biengarten Spätlese Trocken 2001 was the epitome of Pfalz Riesling, and Ruppertsberger Reiterpfad Auslese 2000 (134 g.s., 12.1 g.a., 9.2 alc.) was all luscious fruit, balanced by very high acidity.

Weingut Koehler-Ruprecht

Weinstrasse 84, D-67169 Kallstadt
tel 49 (0)6322 1829, fax 49 (0)6322 8640
email berndphilippi@t-online.de
estate 12.5 ha, 56% Riesling
best vineyards Kallstadter Saumagen, Steinacker,
and Kronenberg
average annual production 100,000 bottles
Member VDP

Bernd Philippi uses indigenous yeasts for fermenting his Rieslings in barrels, never cools them during fermentation and then leaves them with the light lees for bottling the following September. His Rieslings are "old-fashioned" because they spend so long in cask that the primary fruit aromas are hardly perceptible and some tartaric acid has precipitated inside the barrel, making the wines softer. His finest

Villa Wolf, the unique Italianate *Weingut* in Forst, where Ernst Loosen has restored the vineyards and the wines

vineyard is Kallstadter Saumagen. Its limestone sub-soil gives his Rieslings a special mineral quality and also retains water, so the vines are never stressed. He does not practise green harvests because his vines are in balance and never produce more than 55 to 60 hl/ha; he does, however, practise green viticulture, using humus and no chemicals. The Auslese Trocken 1999 was very dry, tremendously concentrated, and powerful, with peachy overtones.

He labels his best wines "R" and releases them six years after the vintage. The Auslese "R" 1997 showed just how a wine with such tremendous concentration improves with time.

Weingut Lingenfelder

Hauptstrasse 27, D-67229 Grosskarlbach
tel 49 (0)6238 754, fax 49 (0)6238 1096
email wine@lingenfelder.com
internet www.lingenfelder.com
estate 15 ha, 40% Riesling
best vineyards Freinsheimer Goldberg and Musikanenbuckel, Grosskarlbacher Osterberg
average annual production 150,000 bottles

Rainer-Karl Lingenfelder is a man with passion bordering on obsession for wine. He is scientific, with a rebellious attitude to status quo and bureaucracy. He is passionate about his "Green *Zeitgeist"* (organic viticulture). He uses stainless steel and indigenous yeasts for his Rieslings, with no fining or stabilization.

First, we tasted Rainer's 2001 dry Spätlese Rieslings: Musikantenbuckel ("musicians' hill") has sandy gravel soil; the Riesling was pretty and fresh as a daisy. Osterberg is loess on a sandy sub-soil, and had a positive, modern, clear, Pfalz, ripe-fruit charm, with fine acidity; Goldberg has light sandy soil – the wine had a bouquet of wild flowers and greater depth from a high proportion of old vines. Goldberg Auslese 1994 had luscious roses on the nose and a peacock's tail of fruit flavours, with obvious quince. Goldberg Trockenbeerenauslese 1989 burst with exotic, dried fruit, sultanas, and golden syrup.

Weingut Georg Mosbacher

Weinstrasse 27, D-67147 Forst
tel 49 (0)6326 329, fax 49 (0)6326 6774
email Mosbacher@t-online.de
internet www.georg-mosbacher.de
estate 13.8 ha, 90% Riesling
best vineyards Forster Ungeheuer GG, Freundstück GG and Pechstein GG, Deidesheimer Mäushöhl, and Kieselberg GG
average annual production 120,000 bottles
Member VDP

I have long admired the purity of the Rieslings from this unpretentious estate. A very high proportion of its wines are fermented dry, and rightly so, but its does produce the occasional great sweet Auslese and BA. It does all the right things in the vineyards, from ploughing-in natural manure to hard pruning, and green harvesting in August to reduce the yield. What appeals to me most is the subtle mineral character of the Rieslings, which is such a contrast with the heavier style of some estates. Its Rieslings have been more consistent over the past decade than those of any other Pfalz estate.

The focus is on Spätlese Trocken: Forster Pechstein 2002 had great freshness combined with mineral backbone and length; Forster Ungeheuer 1997 Trocken had combined power and finesse, while the Grosses Gewächs 2001 had rich sophistication.

Weingut Müller-Catoir

Mandelring 25, D-67433 Haardt
tel 49 (0)6321 2815, fax 49 (0)6321 480014
email weingut@mueller-catoir.de
internet www.mueller-catoir.de
estate 20 ha, 58% Riesling
best vineyards Haardter Herrenletten, Burgergarten, and Herzog, Gimmeldinger Mandelgarten GG, Mussbacher Eselhaut
average annual production: 135,000 bottles

Müller-Catoir makes the most extrovert white wines in Germany: great, concentrated, spicy, barley-sugar

Riesling; gloriously hedonistic Scheurebes, uniquely perfumed Muskatellers; powerful, expressive Weiss- and Grauburgunders; and the finest Rieslaners in the world.

I fell in love with Haardter Bürgengarten Riesling Spätlese Trocken 2001 for its exuberance, and the 2000 for its purity, so difficult to achieve in this vintage with so much rain in the Pfalz.

Weingut Pfeffingen-Fuhrmann-Eymael

Pfeffingen an der Weinstrasse, D-67098 Bad Dürkheim
tel 49 (0)6322 8607, fax 49 (0)6322 8603
email info@pfeffingen.de
internet www.pfeffingen.de
estate 10.2 ha, 59% Riesling
best vineyards Ungsteiner Weilberg GG,
Herrenberg GG
average annual production 90,000 bottles

The soil here is a mixture of loam and loess, with some limestone and volcanic soil. A precursor of *Grosses Gewächs*, Ungsteiner Herrenberg Riesling Spätlese Trocken 1993 (which I drank in 2003) showed me precisely how a dry Riesling can develop with time – magic wine, with focus, in perfect harmony. It had hardly any residual sugar, 13 alc. but no heaviness, and loads of ripe Pfalz fruit, soft acidity, and great length. Herrenberg Spätlese Trocken 2001 and Weilberg Grosses Gewächs 2001 were great wines and had potential to mature over ten or twenty years.

Weingut Ökonomierat Rebholz

Weinstrasse 54, D-76833 Siebeldingen
tel 49 (0)6345 3439, fax 49 (0)6345 795
email wein@oekonomierat-rebholz.de
internet www.oekonomierat-rebholz.de
estate 13.5 ha, 35% Riesling
best vineyards Birkweiler Kastanienbusch GG,
Siebeldingen im Sonnenschein GG
average annual production 70,000 bottles
Member of VDP

I have not visited this estate, so will only mention the wines that I have tasted. Birkweiler Kastanienbusch GG is high in the mountain, facing southeast, and the soil is red slate, which seemed to give the 2001 Riesling a rich complexity that deserved several years to develop into a rare wine. Siebeldingen Im Sonnenschein GG 2001 on stony, sandy soil was more open, with a softer, rounder intensity.

Weingut J.L. Wolf

Weinstrasse 1, D-67157 Wachenheim
tel 49 (0)6322 989795, fax 49 (0)6322 981564
email J.L.Wolf@drloosen.de
internet www.drloosen.com
estate 10.5 ha, 80% Riesling
best vineyards Forster Jesuitengarten GG,
Ungeheuer GG and Pechstein GG,
Wachenheimer Gerümpel GG and Goldbächel
average annual production 70,000 bottles
Member VDP

Ernst Loosen (*see also* page 30, 163) of the Mosel took over running this sleeping beauty of a wine estate in 1996. Because Ernst is convinced that Mosel Rieslings need to be sweet to show their true character, he decided to come to the Pfalz to make dry wines – all his Kabinetts, Spätlesen, and *Grosses Gewächs* here are *trocken*. Ernst has launched the brand name "Villa Wolf" to market inexpensive wines from other producers – these are labelled "bottled for Villa Wolf".

The vineyards are top sites in the Pfalz, four of them *Grosses Gewächs*, but they were in a poor state and the cellars had no proper equipment, so it was a challenge. 1998 was Ernst's first great vintage, with four outstanding dry Spätlesen, a brilliant Auslese, and an Eiswein. In 1999, Forster Jesuitengarten Spätlese Trocken was the star. Ernst's dry Spätleses show his Mosel instincts, which makes them lighter, more elegant, and less smoky than some Pfalz Rieslings.

Baden

Baden has eight wine regions, which stretch some 320 kilometres (200 miles) from just southwest of Würzburg via Heidelberg, Baden-Baden, Offenburg, and Freiburg to Basle, and 160 kilometres (100 miles) east to Lake Constance. In 2003, Riesling was planted in only around six per cent of the total 15,856 hectares of vineyards. In most places, the terroirs and micro-climates are not right for Riesling, and there are only a few villages where there is any Riesling tradition. Also, some seventy-five per cent of the wines are produced by cooperatives whose members are more interested in quantity than quality. The average holding of vines in Baden is significantly less than one hectare. It is only in the Ortenau and Kaiserstuhl regions that a few estates have the terroir and the ability to make fine Rieslings. Even here, however, I have found little character in Rieslings from the co-ops.

Ortenau – where Riesling is also known as *Klingenberger* – is in the foothills of the Black Forest. The biggest concentration of Riesling is around Durbach, tucked into a beautiful steep valley, but even here only twenty-five per cent of the vines are Riesling. The climate is rainier and cooler than that of Alsace, and the slopes are of weathered granite with some red sandstone and slate – similar soil to that of Alsace's Grand Cru Brand vineyard – which gives Riesling good fruit and acidity.

The Kaiserstuhl is a volcanic complex forced up through the basin of the wide valley of the Rhine, and covered with up to thirty metres (ninety-eight feet) of loess: finely ground rock blown from glaciers over aeons. This is particularly light and malleable soil, containing minerals, and it retains heat well; it also retains water in summer. Traces of volcanic rock add exotic flavours and complexity to Rieslings here, and there is limestone at the southern edge of the Kaiserstuhl that favours Riesling. However, this region's main claim to fame is its Weiss-, Grau-, and Spätburgunders.

In the 1950s, the wine-growers agreed that most of the steep, terraced vineyards in the Kaiserstuhl should be levelled to flat benches – each roughly the size of a football pitch – to make them easy to cultivate with tractors and spraying machines. They did not realised that they would lose some fifteen per cent of the actual area of vines in the process. This was the extreme form

Extreme *Flurbereinigung* in the Kaiserstuhl, where steep vineyards were bulldozed into broad flat terraces

of *Flurbereinigung* and would not have been possible without the depth and lightness of the loess. All Baden Rieslings, up to Spätlese quality, are best dry. Sweeter wines are occasionally produced in Kaiserstuhl near the Rhine and Durbach, but botrytis is rare here and autumn rains start earlier in Baden than in Alsace.

The VDP classification is *Grosses Gewächs* ("Great Growth"); there are thirty-four classified vineyards. Dry Riesling, Spät-, Weiss-, and Grauburgunder qualify.

Weingut Bercher

Mittelstadt 13, D-79235 Vogtsburg-Burkheim
(Kaiserstuhl)
tel 49 (0)7662 90760, fax 49 (0)7662 8279
email info@weingutbercher.de
internet www.weingutbercher.de
estate 22 ha, 12% Riesling
best vineyards Burkheimer Schlossgarten GG and Feuerberg GG, Sasbacher Limburg GG
average annual production 150,000 bottles
Member VDP

The Bercher family live and work in this lovely eighteenth century house with its huge, deep cellar below. In 1966, they owned just 5 ha of vines and bought grapes from other growers. As the cooperatives were increasing their influence, the Berchers decided to buy the best sites as and when the growers were prepared to sell.

The family believe that Riesling should be grown on white loess, not black volcanic soil, which they say reduces acidity, though it seems to me that this is not always the case. The estate uses mostly large, oak barrels for fermentation and maturation.

Sasbacher Limburg Kabinett Trocken 1998, from loess soil, was all flowers with remarkable concentration and length for a Kabinett, and the Spätlese Trocken 2001 was very fresh and exotic, needing time to blossom. In complete contrast, Burkheimer Feuerberg Spätlese 1998, from volcanic soil, was rich (22.5 g.s.), gentle, peachy, and stylish.

Burkheimer Schlossberg Auslese 1999 is quite close to the Rhine (it was once a port) and early

morning autumn mists creep up into the vineyard, encouraging the spread of botrytis that gave this wine its barley-sugar, ripe apricot richness.

Weingut Dr. Heger

Bachenstrasse 19, D-79241 Irhringen (Kaiserstuhl)
tel 49 (0)7668 205, fax 49 (0)7668 9300
email info@heger-weine.de
internet www.heger-weine.de
estate 16.5 ha, 24% Riesling
best vineyards Ihringer Winklerberg GG, Ackarrer Schlossberg GG, Freiberger Schlossberg GG
average annual production 100,000 bottles
Member VDP

This estate has the reputation of being the best estate in Baden. Joachim Heger's two finest limestone-and-loess terraced vineyards, Achkarrer Schlossberg and Ihringer Winklerberg, are in the southeast corner of the Kaiserstuhl slopes. Ihringen claims to be the hottest and driest village in Baden, and therefore in Germany.

Ihringer Winklerberg Riesling Spätlese Trocken 2001 was a fresh wine for enjoying young. Achkarrer Schlossberg Riesling Auslese 1998 was exquisite and honeyed (ninty per cent botrytis), with the subtlety of a Nahe Auslese. Joachim runs two other businesses. There is Weingut Fischer, a 15-ha estate with great potential, situated on a small volcanic hill half a kilometre (one-third of a mile) east of the Kaiserstuhl, which he runs on behalf of its owners, and Weinhaus Joachim Heger, the wines for which are made from grapes from sixteen other growers.

Weingut Andreas Laible

Am Bühl 6, D-77770 Durbach (Ortenau)
tel 49 (0)7814 1238, fax 49 (0)7813 8339
email info@weingut-laible.de
internet www.weingut-laible.de
estate 6 ha, 58% Riesling
best vineyard Durbacher Plauelrain GG
average annual production 34,000 bottles
Member VDP

Plauelrain is the best, and to the eye the steepest, vineyard in Durbach. The soil is weathered granite and the microclimate is cool and damp. Andreas Laible (an eccentric genius, if ever there was one) makes five different Spätlese Trocken each year, plus various others, yet his total production of Riesling is less than 2,000 cases. He also has nine other grape varieties, making a total of ninety different bottlings – plus a range of *eaux de vie*.

The three finest Durbacher Plauelrein Riesling Spätlese Trocken 2001s summarize his talents. *Alte Reben* ("old vines") is from a parcel of vines planted in 1960 on an eighty-five per cent slope. It had a bright, clear nose, wonderfully concentrated with faint lemon and grapefruit hints, and a soft, elegant finish. "SL" (it stands for *Selection Laible*) was also from old vines, and had a green-gold colour and even more concentration, great finesse, and acidity in balance. "Achat" was from even older vines, and had little tears of concentration and glycerol on the glass. On the palate it had such harmony that, with 13 alc.: it tasted neither dry nor sweet.

Weingut Salwey

Hauptstrasse 2, 79235 Oberrotweil, (Kaiserstuhl)
tel 49 (0)7662 384, fax 49 (0)7662 6340
email weingut@ salwey.de
internet www.salwey.de
estate 20 ha, 8% Riesling
best vineyards Oberrotweiler Kirchberg GG and Eichberg GG, Glottertaler Eichberg GG
average annual production 150,000 bottles
Member VDP

Oberrotweiler Kirchberg is in the heart of the Kaiserstuhl, where the climate is warm and where there is loess and volcanic soil. The Riesling Spätlese Trocken 1998 from here had a rich intensity with a clear, dry finish. Glottertaler Eichberg is about 24 kilometres (14 miles) away in the foothills of the Black Forest. It has a cooler, damper climate and granite soil similar to that of Durbach. The Riesling Kabinett Trocken 1999 (0.3 g.s., 6.4 g.a. 12.7 alc.) was elegant, subtle, bone-dry but with relatively low acidity and quite high alcohol – so tasted less dry than the analysis would imply. The Glottertaler Riesling Auslese 1998 (42 g.s., 8.5 g.a. 12.9 alc.) was a complete contrast – delicious with plenty of botrytis, dried-apricot, and fresh William's pear flavours.

Weingut Schloss Neuweier

Mauerbergstrasse 21, D-76534 Baden-Baden (Baden-Baden)
tel 49 (0)7223 96670, fax 49 (0)7266 0864
email kontakt@weingut-schloss-neuweier.de
internet www.weingut-schloss-neuweier.de
estate 10.5 ha, 85% Riesling
best vineyards Neuweier Schlossberg GG and Mauerberg GG
average annual production 65,000 bottles
Member VDP

The Mauerberg has weathered granite and some heavy loam soil, and its wine resembles the powerful Rieslings of Würzburg (all the wines at this estate are bottled in the Franken *Bocksbeutel*).

The Schlossberg has weathered granite and porphyry, and its wines are classically elegant. The Kabinetts are delicious but the Spätlese have more character and can match more powerful dishes. As they do not have much botrytis here, Auslese musts are generally blended into in their top Spätlese. Neuweier Mauerberg Riesling Spätlese Trocken Goldenes Loch 2001 had a scent of orange blossom and a light sweetness on the palate. The Neuweier Schlossberg Alte Reben (old vines) 2001 was more extrovert and serious with greater length and structure.

Württemberg

Johann Friedrich, Duke of Württemberg, invited 9,600 guests to his wedding in 1609, each of whom, on average, drank forty-three litres of wine over three days. Nowadays the average consumption is about forty litres per head per annum in Württemberg. It has been said that in the late sixteenth century, Württemberg was largest wine-growing region in Germany, with about 40,000 hectares, but I believe that this was based on monastic records and included Franken, and probably Austria as well. Anyway, in 1988 there were 9,791 hectares. By 2003, this had increased to 11,336 hectares, of which Riesling was twenty-one per cent.

The Württemberg region stretches from just southwest of Würzburg to Stuttgart, with little pockets as far south as the Bodensee (Lake Constance). However, seventy-five per cent of the vineyards lie between Heilbronn and Stuttgart, around the valley of the Neckar and its tributaries. The climate is Continental, with relatively high rainfall, hot summers, and sudden autumns, causing difficult vintages to be more frequent than in other regions. Winters are cold; this is the only region in Germany where the temperature can drop to -9°C (16°F) for several nights in succession. This makes Eiswein less of a gamble, and volumes can be larger. Producers might make several different wines with different levels of concentration and possibly picked in different sites.

The soils in the region are mixed, with *Keuper* (marl and gypsum) being the most frequent. The majority of the vines are on the south faces of large, rolling hills, and are quite exposed to the weather.

Cooperatives produce seventy-five per cent of the wines, and approximately the same proportion is drunk in the region. The car and technology industries help incomes, but the *Württembourgeoisie* has not, as yet, really discovered fine wine. Wine producers have traditionally not worried about quality, but now wines from other regions of Germany and from the rest of the world are creeping in. These days they do worry.

Riesling here has sufficient fruit and alcohol to balance its acidity, and is best fermented to dryness. Because winter starts so early here there are few Auslesen made, but those that are can be superb.

The VDP classification is *Grosses Gewächs* ("Great Growth"), of which there are thirty-four. And only dry Riesling qualifies. Vineyards are marked GG under "best vineyards".

Burg Schaubeck,
the thirteenth century
castle of Michael
Graf Adelmann in
it's "English garden"

Weingut Graf Adelmann

Burg Schaubeck, D-71711 Kleinbottwar
tel 49 (0)7148 6665, fax 49 (0)7148 8036
email info@graf-adelmann.com
internet www.graf-adelmann.com
estate 18 ha, 28% Riesling
best vineyards Kleinbottwarer Süssmund GG
und Obererberg GG
average annual production 120,000 bottles

Burg Schaubeck was built in the thirteenth century.
In 1978, the estate passed to Michael Graf Adelmann,
and he has made numerous improvements in the
vineyards and the cellars. The *Weingut* is famous for
its Lembergers, but its Rieslings are just as fine. The
main vineyards are on one steep, southwest-facing
slope, on a series of rolling, windy hills that range
from 210 to 340 metres (689 to 1,115 feet) altitude,
halfway between Heilbronn and Stuttgart. The soil
is red marl.

The fine wines are labelled "Brüssele" and the
exceptional ones "Brüssele Spitze". The wines we
tasted were all Kleinbottwarer Süssmund Riesling
Brüssele Spitze: 2000 Spätlese Trocken (7 g.s.,
7 g.a., 13 alc.) was a grand wine, still in its infancy,
with concentration and terroir and a lovely flavour
of ripe apricots. 1993 Spätlese Trocken was slightly
sweeter (10 g.s.) and was cultured and pretty, with
the lingering taste of mature Riesling. The count
described it as *pummelig* ("plump and cuddly").

The 1983 Spätlese Trocken showed wonderful
maturity – a joyful wine, it was very late-picked and
relatively dry. 1993 Auslese (20 g.s.) was *feinherb*,
richer and more full-bodied, with ripeness, depth,
and a touch of mirabelle plums. 1989 Auslese was like
Miss Haversham in *Great Expectations*: fading and
old but still beautiful. 2000 Auslese Edelsüss ("noble
sweet"), from the last picking of a catastrophic year,
when rain and hail ruined the normal vintage, was
an infant wine, but it filled the mouth with elegance
and botrytis richness.

Weingut Ernst Dautel

Lauerweg 55, D-74357 Bönnigheim
tel 49 (0)7143 870326, fax 49 (0)7143 870327
email info@weingut-dautel.de
internet www.weingut-dautel.de
estate 10.5 ha, 23% Riesling
best vineyards Besigheimer Wurmberg GG,
Bönnigheimer Sonnenberg GG
average annual production 65,000 bottles

The Dautel family has been growing wine near
Besigheim since 1510. Ernst Dautel qualified
at the Geisenheim Wine Institute and immediately
decided that the family should leave the local
cooperative, and in 1984 he built his new *Weingut*.
He no longer uses Kabinett or Spätlese as quality
descriptions but instead has star ratings, four stars
being the best. Besigheimer Wurmberg Riesling ***
Trocken 2001 (3.5 g.s., 7.4 g.a., 13 alc.) was from
a steep terraced limestone vineyard. Despite having
so little residual sugar, it was very smooth, with lots
of fruit and a faint taste of barley sugar. The 1998 ***
had a similar character but had developed more
complexity in its flavours, and the 1990 Spätlese
was subtle and complete, a splendid wine.

Bönnigheimer Sonnenberg is on a gentle hill
with *Keuper* soil. Sonnenberg Riesling Trocken **
2001, from old vines, had an enticing, soft style, as did
the 1993 Spätlese that was delicious, old, and dry.

Weingut Karl Haidle

Hindenburgstrasse 21, D-71394 Kernen-Stettin im Remstal
tel 49 (0)7151 949110, fax 49 (0)7151 46313
email info@weingut-karl-haidle.de
internet www.weingut-karl-haidle.de
estate 17.6 ha, 48% Riesling
best vineyards Stettener Pulvermächer GG,
Häder, and Mönchberg
average annual production 135,000 bottles

Behind Karl Haidle's house is the steep
Pulvermächer, the finest vineyard of the area,
planted in 1494 by the local church, sixteen years

before the Haidle family were first recorded as wine-growers. Karl Haidle, the tough and wiry owner, started to sell his wines in bottle in 1949, when life was terribly hard in Germany.

Stettener Pulvermächer Spätlese Trocken 2001 was perfection, delicate at first and almost with a Mosel fruit intensity. Grosses Gewächs 2001 (8 g.s., 7.6 g.a., 13 alc.) had an exotic grapefruit flavour and a lovely aftertaste, thanks partly to its higher residual sugar and alcohol. The Auslese 1998 (20 g.s., 8.2 g.a., 13 alc.) was rich and mouth-filling, with white-peach flavour and a dry finish. Auslese 2000 (59 g.s., 8 g.a., 12.5 alc.) was a fabulous, rich, botryitized Riesling.

Weingut des Grafen Neipperg

Im Schloss, D-74190 Schwaigern
tel 49 (0)7138 941400, fax 49 (0)7138 4007
email neipperg@t-online.de
estate 29 ha, 20% Riesling
best vineyards Schwaigerner Ruthe GG,
Neipperger Schlossberg GG
average annual production 180,000 bottles

The family has been making wine from the same vineyards for 750 years, perhaps longer. The present incumbent is Karl Eugen Erbgraf zu Neipperg, whose brother Stephan owns famous châteaux in Bordeaux's St-Emilion.

Neipperger Schlossberg runs along a plateau behind the old *Schloss*. 2001 Kabinett Trocken was a fragrant, light Riesling, delicious but undemanding. Schwaigener Ruthe is on a steep stony slope on the opposite side of a valley, and the Spätlese Trocken 2000 was much more expressive, despite the rain during the vintage, with an unobtrusive touch of apricot on the nose and in the flavour.

Spätlese Trocken 1998 was a great Riesling – ripe and full-bodied with fine balancing acidity; it will continue to improve. Botrytis followed the rain in 2000, and the Auslese Edelsüss had a very modern style, with some mineral touches, good acidity, and a lingering aftertaste.

Weingut Wöhrwag

Grunbacher Strasse 5, D-70327 Untertürkheim
tel 49 (0)7113 31662, fax 79 (0)7113 32431
email info@woehrwag.de
internet www.woehrwag.de
estate 20 ha, 40% Riesling
best vineyards Untertürkheimer Herzogenberg GG
and Mönchberg GG
average annual production 150,000 bottles

Hans-Peter Wöhrwag is called "Württemberg's Mr Riesling". His Rieslings are described as *Rheinisch* ("like those of the Rhine") as a compliment, because they have great mineral purity. In the vineyards he has drastically reduced yields – he picks late and has also slowed fermentations from four days to four weeks at 14 to 16°C (57 to 61°F).

Untertürkheimer is a suburb of Stuttgart which is dominated by the steep vineyards. Untertürkheimer Herzogberg ("the duke's vineyard") is the estate's monopoly vineyard. Kabinett Trocken Goldkapsel had refreshing spritz, with rare mineral elegance. Spätlese Trocken was deep and long: spicy, with lots of fruit which, combined with higher alcohol (13 degrees), gave it a sense of sweetness on the finish.

The Grosses Gewächs Riesling was from old vines and it was even riper and more concentrated and powerful. It needed time to begin to show its great character. The noble-sweet rarities were a revelation: Auslese was from the same old vines as the previous wine, but with twenty per cent botrytis, giving it great charm, nobility, and longevity. Auslese Goldkapsel with 100 per cent botrytis had double the fruit and richness, with flavours of white peach and fresh apricot, and great acidity.

His fantastic Eiswein are from 1 ha of dedicated netted vines. The one I tasted (he makes several each year), was made with perfectly ripe grapes without any botrytis. It was brilliant-green in colour, with a crystal, mineral concentration and ripe acidity – an unforgettable Riesling.

Franken

The Franken vineyards were vast in area in the sixteenth century, but they really never recovered from the Thirty Years' War, when thirty to fifty per cent of the population of Franken died. In 2003, there were 6,250 hectares of vineyard in all, with just 243 hectares of Riesling: only 4.1 per cent of the total. This low figure is because Riesling requires the best, warmest sites to ripen properly, and needs far more work in the vineyard, but gives lower yields. It is the most prestigious grape of the region, though hugely outplanted by the finest Silvaner in the world.

The Continental climate of Franken means that springs are late summers are hot, autumns early and frosty, and winters cold. Vintages are also more variable than in other regions of Germany, and as recently as 1985 warm weather in February caused the sap in the vines to rise; whereupon a sharp cold spell, with temperatures dropping to -30°C (-22°F), killed millions of vines. It is a climate suitable for making Eiswein, but it is not conducive to botrytis; botrytized Riesling Auslesen are rare.

Karl-Martin Schmitt of Weingut Schmitt's Kinder (*see* page 86) explains that, in the climate of the five Randersacker vineyards on the hills overlooking the Main, Silvaner is best in the top third of the slopes, Riesling in the middle, and Müller-Thurgau at the bottom. Müller-Thurgau ripens much earlier than Riesling and is planted closer to the river where Riesling would never be planted.

The best sites, those suitable for Riesling, are generally owned by the top estates; in any case, the cooperatives, seven of which dominate wine production in Franken, with fifty per cent of the total, are too lazy to bother with Riesling. Instead they produce passable Silvaner, dull Müller-Thurgau and horrible Bacchus; they sell many of their wines at *Dumpingpreisen* ("dumping prices") to supermarkets in Germany.

Most of the Franken vineyards are close to the river Main. The heart of the region is the beautiful city of Würzburg, where the three largest and oldest *Weingut* cellars are found – Juliusspital, Bürgerspital, and Staatlicher Hofkeller. Three serpentine bends in the Main River in the shape of a huge "W" embrace the villages, near which four of the most famous vineyards are to be found: Escherndorfer Lump, with its *Muschelkalk* (limestone soil); Iphöfer Julius-Echter-Berg, with *Keuper* soil (mica, marl, and sandstone); Würzburger Stein, with *Muschelkalk*; and Bürgstadter Centgrafenberg, with red sandstone beneath layers of loam and clay.

The market square and
town hall of Iphofen,
the prettiest wine village
in Franken

In my opinion, Franken Rieslings (QbAs, Kabinetts, and Spätlesen) must be dry and are for drinking with food, either in the year following the vintage or two or three years later; they do not improve after that. It is my view that Franken Rieslings are best when *trocken* – except those that have botrytis – because the fruit and alcohol in the wine naturally balance the acidity. Franken wines have been bottled in a special flagon (called a *Bocksbeutel* – made in the shape of a goat's scrotum) for at least four centuries. The disadvantage of *Bocksbeutels* is that they are difficult to store except in their original case.

The VDP classification is *Grosses Gewächs* and at the time of writing there were fourteen classified vineyards; only dry wines made with Riesling, Silvaner, Spätburgunder, and Weissburgunder qualify. Vineyards that qualify are marked GG under "best vineyards".

The village of Eschendorf in Franken, with the charmingly named Lump vineyard rising from the main street

Weingut Bürgerspital zum Heiligen Geist

Theatrestrasse 19, D-97070 Würzburg
tel 49 (0)9313 503441, fax 49 (0)9313 503444
email zeitler@buergerspital.de
Internet www.buergerspital.de
estate 120 ha, 26% Riesling
best vineyards Würzburger Stein GG, Absleite, and Innere
Leiste GG, Randersacker Pfülben GG
average annual production 900,000 bottles

This charitable trust "for the sick and poor of Würzburg and travelling pilgrims" was founded in 1319; the sick and poor are still nursed and fortified with wine in the hospital. Today, it owns 120 ha, and has the highest proportion of Riesling of any well-known estate in Franken. But the quality of the Bürgerspital wines dropped sharply from 1989. Helmut Plunien was appointed cellarmaster 1999 and joint director in 2000.

Improvements were in progress when I visited the *Weingut* early in 2001. Back in the 1960s, the cellars had been redeveloped on much too large a scale; they were fermenting 700,000 litres at a time then, in stainless steel with cultured yeasts, which meant that the wines lacked character. The clock had to be turned back – smaller oak barrels had to be installed so that fermentation could be done with indigenous rather than cultured yeasts, and the old clumsy machines, including the large centrifuges, had to be replaced with clean, efficient, modern equipment.

Helmut drastically reduced yields in the vineyards, and selection at the harvest is much stricter. To demonstrate the effect of the changes, Randersacker Teufelsberg Riesling QbA.The 1997 (such a fine vintage) had no nose and no character, whereas the 1999 was very concentrated with a touch of honey on the finish. Würzburger Stein Riesling Spätlese Trocken 1998 was coarse and unpleasant, but the 1999 was very spicy and had much fruit and

life. Thus a significant improvement was achieved in 1999. 2000 was a particularly difficult year because of rain during the vintage and grey rot, but in 2001 and 2002 the wines were again on song.

Fürstlich Castell'sches Domänenamt

Schlossplatz 5, D-97335 Castell
tel 49 (0)9325 60160, fax 49 (0)9325 60188
email weingut@castell.de
internet www.castell.de
estate 65 ha, 6% Riesling
best vineyards Casteller Schlossberg GG, Hohnart,
Kugelspiel, and Trautberg
average annual production 400,000 bottles

The Castell family has lived at Castell since the eleventh century, and in 1659 it was the first to plant the Silvaner grape in Germany. Castell is a large hill with the ruins of the original castle at the top, and the best vineyard, the Schlossberg, on the steep south-facing slope.

The village consists of the Castell Bank – one of the few private banks still in existence – a large baroque church built by the Castells, their magnificent "new" mansion built in 1691, the winery itself, and a few houses. The domaine vineyards are fully organic, officially recognized by Naturland, and the cellars are thoroughly modern.

In addition to the domaine wines, the Castells help a unique sort of local wine cooperative, with eighty members owning some 50 ha of vines. The domain vineyards are organic and the estate advises the co-op members on viticulture. The co-op grapes are vinified in the estate winery, but of course kept separate from the estate wines. The domaine then helps the co-op members to market their wines.

In 1996, Ferdinand Graf zu Castell-Castell took over the wine operation with great enthusiasm and prompted a renaissance in quality, 2000 being was the estate's most successful vintage for decades. Schloss Castell Riesling Kabinett Trocken was refreshingly dry with an elegant peachy bouquet

Ferdinand Graf zu Castell-Castell – the twenty-sixth generation of the family – runs the Fürstlich Castell'sches Domänenamt

and flavour; Casteller Hohnart Kabinett Trocken showed great purity and the typical, slightly earthy, character of the local gypsum/*Keuper* soil. Casteller Schlossberg Riesling Spätlese Trocken (8.4 g.s., 7.8 g.a., 13 alc.) had great finesse and concentration with a hint of lychees on the finish.

Weingut Rudolf Fürst

Hohenlindenweg 46, D-63927 Bürgstadt
tel 49 (0)9371 8642, fax 49 (0)9371 69230
email info@weingut-rudolf-fuerst.de
internet www.weingut-rudolf-fuerst.de
estate 15.6 ha, 18% Riesling
best vineyards Bürgstädter Centgrafenberg GG, Volkacher Karthäuser GG
average annual production 95,000 bottles

I met Paul Fürst in 1991; I had been so impressed with his Bürgstadter Centgrafenberg Spätburgunder Trocken 1989 that I wanted some to show at tastings alongside 1990 burgundies. His Rieslings are not as famous, but they are equally fine.

Centgrafenberg is very steep and faces due south, giving wonderful exposure to the sun, and has warm, red-sandstone soil. Paul's house and modern winery are adjacent to the vineyard, so the hand-picked grapes can be brought directly to the press in small containers and the whole bunches gently pressed, thus avoiding unpleasant flavours from the pips and maximizing the character of the terroir in the eventual wine. Using indigenous yeast ensures that the fermentation is carefully monitored rather than rigidly controlled, so that some wines continue quietly to bubble for months on the light lees.

Bürgstädter Centgrafenberg Riesling Kabinett Trocken 2000 had a perfectly fresh, crystalline, lemony character with plenty of complexity balanced by fine acidity and restrained alcohol (11 alc.). The Spätlese Trocken 2000 was more serious; it had great purity and a wonderfully precise Riesling style, with real expression of fruit, again balanced by good acidity. Spätlese 1999 (70 g.s., 8.5 g.a., 10 alc.), that had remained on light lees in a 2,400-litre *Doppelstück* until bottling in September 2000, was a superb wine, with ripe, honeydew-melon on the palate and potential for ageing – a unique and memorable work of love and art.

Staatlicher Hofkeller Würzberg

Residenzplatz 3, D-97070 Würzburg
tel 49 (0)9313 050923, fax 49 (0)9313 050966
email s.henkelmann@hofkeller.de
internet www.hofkeller.de
estate 150 ha, 22% Riesling
best vineyards Würzburger Stein and Innere Leiste, Randerackerer Pfülben
average annual production 850,000 bottles

The Hofkeller is now owned by the Bavarian state and, like other large estates in Germany, it has been going through a difficult period. However, steps were taken to restore Hofkeller's reputation by root and branch changes in all the systems, from the management of the vineyards, to the picking of the grapes and the modernization of the vast cellars.

Among the Rieslings that I tasted, both the 2002 Riesling Spätlese Trocken from Würzburger Innere Leiste and from Würzburger Stein were fresh and dry, with elegance and fine structure, and were showing a marked improvement on the wines from previous vintages.

Weingut Juliusspital

Klinikstrasse 1, D-97070 Würzburg
tel 49 (0)9313 931400, fax 49 (0)9313 931414
email info@juliusspital.de
internet www.juliusspital.de
estate 127 ha, 18% Riesling
best vineyards Würzburger Stein GG and Innere Leiste GG, Iphöfer Julius-Echter Berg GG, Randersackerer Pfülben GG, Rödelseer Küchenmeister GG, Volkacher Karthäuser GG
average annual production 1,000,000 bottles

Julius Echter von Mespelbrunn, prince bishop of Würzburg, founded the hospital in 1576 for, "every kind of sick and poor who require care or treatment, and travelling pilgrims and village people". The estate has many great vineyards, farms and forests donated over the centuries to help fund it, and it is still an active general hospital.

Trocken Rieslings from Iphofen, where the soil is *Keuper* (mica, marl, and sandstone) have a certain baroque boldness. Iphofer Julius-Echter Berg Kabinett Trocken 1998 (0.7 g.s., 7.2 g.a., 12 alc.) had virtually no residual sugar, considerable authority and an enduring aftertaste with hints of pink grapefruit.

Trocken Rieslings from Würzburg, where the soil is *Muschelkalk* have a gothic elegance, and are more mineral and sharper, but without any bitterness. Würzburger Stein Spätlese Trocken 2000 was rich, with great length and extract – the perfect food wine. Auslese 1999 Long Gold Kapsel (109 g.s., 8.5 g.a., 10.5 alc.) was unique: it had achieved fantastic purity and complexity, the result of selective picking of perfectly ripe grapes with no botrytis. A superb wine but unfortunately, only 400 half-bottles were made. Because the winter is early in Franken, a Riesling TBA is a great rarity, and the director, Horst Kolesch, thinks that the Stein Trockenbeerenauslese 1990 might be the greatest one made in Franken in the twentieth century. It was a symphony of fruit (dried apricots and raisins) and a touch of orange marmalade in harmony with the huge residual sugar and acidity.

Weingut Horst Sauer

Bocksbeutelstrasse 14, D-97332 Escherndorf
tel 49 (0)9381 4364, fax 49 (0)9381 6843
email info@weingut-horst-sauer.de
internet www.weingut-horst-sauer.de
estate 10.2 ha, 12% Riesling
best vineyards Escherndorfer Lump GG
average annual production 78,000 bottles

Escherndorfer Lump has the reputation of being one of the six best vineyards in Franken, but until the last decade few of the growers there were making wines that lived up to this. Horst Sauer left the local cooperative in 1977 and is now recognized as one of the finest Riesling growers in Germany. He has the wiry physique and weathered face of a medieval wine-grower and is an absolute perfectionist in the vineyard and in the cellar. His only problem is that he has only 12 per cent Riesling in his vineyards, and 58 per cent "new", early ripening grapes, that he is trying to replace with Riesling and Silvaner.

Horst's vineyards are immaculate and the grapes are brought straight down from the vines and, unless botrytized, gently whole-bunch pressed at not more than 1.8 bars of pressure for three hours or so, which prevents the more astringent flavours, getting into the wine. After a slow fermentation, the Rieslings are left on light lees for three to six months before bottling.

Horst's Rieslings are strictly modern, with crystal purity and mineral freshness. Lump Spätlese Trocken 2000 (105 Oechsle and 13.5 alc.) was robust and satisfying, in contrast with Spätlese Trocken 1999; this was like a rose which has completely opened, the aromas released and the acidity already soft. Auslese 2000 had the flavour of white peaches, ripe but not overripe, luscious but with fresh acidity to balance. Trockenbeerenauslese 2000 promised to be eternal. It was made with completely botrytized grapes, and had incredible concentration and acidity.

Weingut Schmitt's Kinder

Am Sonnestuhl, D-97236 Randersacker
tel 49 (0)9317 059197, fax 49 (0)9317 059198
email weingut@schmitts-kinder.de
internet www.schmitts-kinder.de
estate 14.5 ha, 12% Riesling
best vineyards Randersackerer Pfülben GG, Sonnenstuhl GG, Marsberg, Teufelskeller
average annual production 110,000 bottles

In 1974, Karl inherited the fine eighteenth century Schmitt Weingut in the centre of Randersacker, but it was no place for a modern winery. So, ten years later he built a house and state-of-the-art cellar at the foot of the Sonnenstuhl vineyard. Karl is a scientist as well as a wine-grower, and has his own weather station in the vineyards.

The cellar contains magnificent oak barrels for fermenting (at 18°C/64°F); some wines are matured in these, while others go into stainless steel. Any movement of the must or wine is by gravity rather than by pumping.

We tasted the difficult 2000 vintage. Franken growers have a voluntary rule that *trocken* wines should not exceed 4 g.s. instead of the legal limit of 9 g.s. Karl is not mad about very dry Rieslings unless they are perfectly balanced, which his are. Randersackerer Pfülben Spätlese "Trias" Trocken 2000 (7.5 g.s., 8.4 g.a., 13.5 alc.) was a great wine with the concentration of an Auslese. Pfülben Auslese 2000 came from a 1-ha plot of old vines which had maximum botrytis, giving 115 Oechsle, great richness, complexity, and length.

Weingut Schloss Sommerhausen

Ochsenfurter Strasse 17–19, D-97286 Sommerhausen
tel 49 (0)9333 260, fax 49 (0)9333 188
email weingut@sommerhausen.com
internet www.sommerhausen.com
estate 28 ha, 20% Riesling
best vineyards Sommerhausen Steinbeck and Reifenstein, Randersacker Sonnenstuhl.
average annual production 170,000 bottles

Sommerhausen has the famous *Muschelkalk* and clay soil of central Franken. Martin Steinmann is the eleventh generation of his family to be a wine-grower in Sommerhausen and now runs the estate. His finest vineyard, Sommerhauser Steinbach, is on a hill overlooking the river Main.

The 1999 Riesling Spätlese Trocken was open, with a flowery bouquet and fine concentration on the palate; the 2000 Spätlese was a giant of a wine with 102 Oechsle, and after cold maceration at 4°C (39°F) for eighteen hours and a long fermentation it had reached 13.5 alc. There were still 7 g.s. – *trocken* by all standards except those of Franken. Made with perfectly healthy grapes (without botrytis), it had an affinity with certain Clare Valley Rieslings (*see* page 135).

By contrast, the Sommerhäuser Reifenstein vineyard is close to the river and the mists creep up at night, until the morning sun burns them off. Botrytis flourishes here. The Spätlese 2000 is a *grande dame*, made from grapes with some botrytis but mainly super-ripe. It stopped fermenting in its stainless-steel vat of its own volition, leaving a wine with great concentration and 35 g.s.

The Auslese 2000 had botrytis in abundance, so much so that Martin had to blend in a little of the Spätlese; it still had 80 g.s. This wine promised to develop over the long term into a sumptuous Riesling.

The *Weingut* is also famous for its single-vineyard vintage Sekts, a full-bodied Auxerrois, and a beautifully balanced Riesling.

Weingut Hans Wirsching

Ludwigsstrasse 16, D-97346 Iphofen
tel 49 (0)9323 87330, fax 49 (0)9323 873390
email info@wirsching.de
internet www.wirsching.de
estate 72 ha, 20% Riesling
best vineyards Iphöfer Julius-Echter Berg GG,
Kalb, and Kronsberg
average annual production 510,000 bottles

The Wirsching family has been growing wine in Iphofen since 1630; it is now one of the largest privately owned estates in Germany. Dr. Heinrich Wirsching has directed the difficult changes from "ancient to modern" with great skill. His vineyards were reorganized in a major *Flurbereinigung*, and he took the chance to increase

his holdings in the top sites by buying up small parcels from growers who wanted to give up. Then he modernized his cellars.

It is terribly dry in the vineyards in the summer at Iphofen, on the great slopes of Kronsberg and Julius-Echter Berg, and it is imperative to plant cover crops between the vines to retain the water from September to May. In May, the crops are ploughed in along with cow and horse dung to create humus.

Julius-Echter Berg is the best part on the middle and upper slope of the mile-long Kronsberg hill. It faces due south, and is protected from the north and east by the Stiegerwald forest that crowns the hill. The soil is weathered sandstone over gypsum-*keuper*.

Julius-Echter Berg Riesling Kabinett Trocken 2000 had a fine ripeness that balanced the natural acidity. Spätlese Trocken 1999 was dry, with the structure to develop. The plot of vines for the Auslese 1999 had been intended for Eiswein, but the vineyard manager wanted to lay manure and the smell would have spoiled the wine, so the grapes were picked on November 22. The wine was very concentrated, with only 11 alc. The Beerenauslese 1993 had a deep-yellow colour – pure Riesling – subtle, powerful for a BA, with flavours of dried fruit and Seville orange marmalade. Peerless.

Biodynamic ploughing in the *grand cru* Kitterlé, Alsace

France

Alsace

The early history of wine in Alsace is almost the same as that of Germany in general and the Pfalz and Baden in particular. The Romans developed the vineyards, but when the Alemanni tribe crossed the Rhine in the fourth century, they slowly destroyed the existing culture. The Merovingian king Clovis forced them back in 496 and encouraged Christianity, with the result that, a century later, there were about forty abbeys in Alsace. Each abbey had its vineyards, and of course kept faithful records of everything. By the eighth century the Rhine was navigable for relatively large cargo boats from Colmar and Strasbourg on their way to the North Sea, and wines were being exported as far as England, Denmark, and Sweden.

Charlemagne continued to encourage the Church to plant vines throughout the empire but, after the death of his son, Louis I, the empire was divided. Battles between warlords continued until 870, when Alsace came under German rule. This lasted for the next seven centuries. The original ledgers of official tolls show over eleven million litres of wine was sent outside Alsace by boat on the Rhine via Colmar in 1393. Strasbourg and Colmar combined sent over sixty million litres in 1481. At that time, Alsace and Bordeaux were the two most successful wine regions in the world.

The first likely written reference to Riesling is in Alsace, a plan showing *zu dem Russelinge* dated 1348 (*see* page 16). In 1477, Rissling (there were various spellings) was documented in Alsace. This probably refers to the grape, but it is not certain that it does because of a possible confusion with another variety called Räuschling – a brownish-skinned grape that today is known as *Knipperlé* (in Alsace).

In 890, Sainte Richarde, the wife of Charles the Fat, gave the vineyards of Weinbach in Kientzheim (now Domaine Weinbach) to the monks of Etival Abbey in the Vosges Mountains, and in 1619 they gave them to the Capuchin friars, who in 1730 listed 700 *Riesselin* vines in their inventory among about 15,000 vines of other grape varieties, including 7,700 *Petit Richelin*, 3,000 red *Genti* ("noble"), 3,000 Muscat and 500 *Toquer* (Tokay-Pinot Gris) and *Chasselin* (Chasselas). This shows how little Riesling was planted. The monks also specialized in breeding snails; at their annual banquet for the local notables, the main dish was Escargots au Riesling.

Riesling was the aristocrat of grapes at this time and it was mainly planted in the best sites, in *clos* that were owned by the church and the nobility. The wine was rarely sold outside Alsace. Planting in the vineyards was probably *en foule* ("layered"), which fits in with the research of Jean-Marcel Deiss – showing that

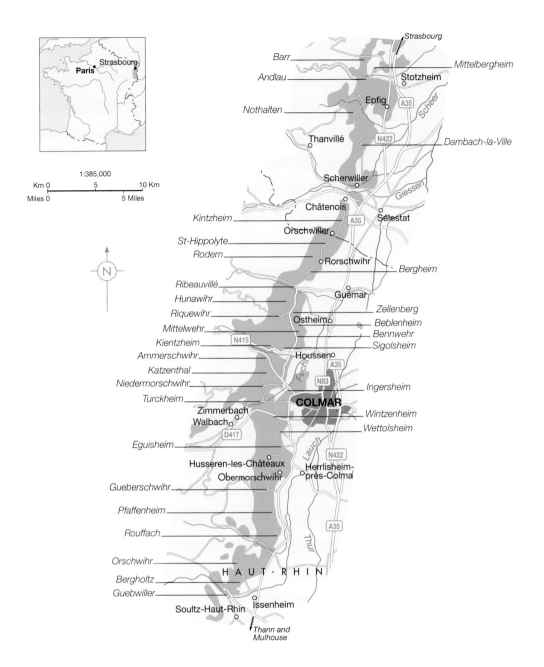

most vineyards were planted with a mixture of varieties, that, when vinified, gave wines that tasted of the terroir rather than the grape variety. Wines made with a blend of wine from any of the four "noble" grapes (Riesling, Gewurztraminer, Pinot Gris, and Muscat) can be labeled Edelzwicker (noble blend).

The 1648 Treaty of Westphalia, that ended the Thirty Years' War, handed Alsace to France. In 1662, 1682, and 1687, Louis XIV of France offered free land in Alsace to settlers, who came mostly from Germany, Switzerland, and of course France. But the wine villages had suffered horribly during the Thirty Years' War: Bergheim had a population of 2,600 in 1610, and only twenty in 1650. There wasn't enough labour to work the vineyards on the slopes, and so vines were planted on the Rhine Valley floor, where quantity could be produced, but not quality. Only from about 1750 was Riesling widely planted in the villages. Ordinary wine for consumption in Alsace continued to be the main focus until the German annexation, which lasted from 1870 to 1918, when a considerable proportion of the region's wines was bought by large export businesses in the Rhine and Mosel for blending with their thinner wines.

Phylloxera arrived in the late 1860s. Grafting was made illegal in Germany, so the only solution was the planting of various German and American hybrids. However, in 1880 J. Dirler, *Gourmet et Propriéteur de Vignes*, proudly offered Rieslings from Guebwiller of 1865 and 1834 (at four *francs* per bottle) and from Ribeauvillé of 1876 and 1870 vintages (at 2.25 *francs*). Michael Broadbent MW (in *Vintage Wine*, Little, Brown, 2002) gave five stars (his maximum) to a Hugel Riesling 1900 tasted in 1989: "…good old Riesling nose, lovely, scented but not oxidized; fairly dry but losing its punch and acidity". The average production between 1901 and 1908 was a pathetic six hectolitres per hectare, and it was only in the 1930s that the noble grape varieties were generally produced and labelled as such. In 1939, Alsace was annexed again by Germany; the men were forced to join the German army and the vineyards were left untended. In 1944, the Americans bombarded and obliterated a number of wine villages where the Germans had dug in. Statistics were not reliable until 1969, when Riesling was only 12.7 per cent of the vineyard area, while Sylvaner was 27.3 per cent and Gewurztraminer 20.6 per cent. By 1982, Riesling was 19.6 per cent, Sylvaner 20.7 per cent and Gewurztraminer 20.4 per cent. Today, Riesling is the most widely planted grape variety with twenty-three per cent, followed by Pinot Blanc/Auxerrois/Chardonnay combined and Gewurztraminer. This is in spite of the fact that Riesling only expresses its real quality and character in the steep vineyards, and Pinot Blanc, with its cousin Auxerrois, are successful on the flat land, which is easier to cultivate and where the grapes can be picked by machine. Pinot Blanc and Auxerrois reach ripeness earlier, give much higher yields, are excellent for making sparkling Crémant d'Alsace, and sell at considerably lower prices.

The history of Alsace wines is German, overlaid with 300 years of French influence. The roots are German but the psychology is French. People speak French in public, but a difficult German dialect in private – or to confuse. French appellation laws forbid planting Riesling outside Alsace, which is ridiculous.

Poles waiting to be planted at the ends of rows of vines in the vineyards of the Kientzler Estate in Ribeauvillé

The enchanting *route du vin* ("wine route") runs some 240 kilometres (150 miles) as the crow flies along the slopes of the Vosges Mountains through medieval villages from Marlenheim near Strasbourg in the north to Thann near Mulhouse in the south. Haut-Rhin and Bas-Rhin are no more than administrative regions, though the climate in the north is a little cooler and the wines tend to be lighter and drier. Between Ribeauvillé and Colmar the wines seem to develop greater elegance and balance. South of Colmar, temperatures are slightly higher in summer and the wines become progressively more voluptuous.

Climate and altitude are important for the vines. Cold winters keep the bugs away. Alsace is said, too, to be the sunniest region of France – though during our honeymoon it rained every single day for a fortnight in June. Normally, though, hot and dry summers with cool nights ensure a long ripening season. It should also be noted that the higher the altitude – up to about 450 metres (1,476 feet) – the longer the growing season, and the picking of Riesling can continue into December.

Late-harvest wines

In the 1960s and 1970s, Hugel showed the world the glories of late-harvest Alsace wines, but it was not until 1984 that Vendanges Tardives and Sélections de Grains Nobles (or SGN) were legally defined. Vendanges Tardives Rieslings are possible in two styles. The first is from the most obvious botrytis vintages – 1995, 1989, 1988, 1983, 1976, and 1971. The wines are quite deep-gold in colour with the powerful raisin and honey flavours of shrivelled botrytized grapes, and tends to be from vineyards based on limestone.

The second style is more reticent and is made with very late-harvested *passerillé* – shrivelled, but not botrytized – grapes in, for example, 2001, 1997, 1990, and 1975. These wines are lighter in colour and less sweet on the palate, though still richly concentrated with high acidity. These tend to come from granite-based vineyards. The legal minimum potential alcohol at picking for Riesling Vendanges Tardives is 13.1 degrees. Sélection de Grains Nobles Rieslings are very rare and can only be made with a high proportion of botrytized grapes. The minimum potential alcohol for Riesling SGN is 15.2 degrees.

Rye planted as a cover
crop between the rows
of vines of Domaine
Josmeyer in Winzenheim

Biodynamic viticulture

Alsace was where biodynamics began in France in 1924. Spiegel Grand Cru became the first official biodynamic vineyard in France in 1969, initiated by Eugène Meyer of Bergholz who owned just over one hectare. The reason he decided to follow biodynamic priciples was that he suffered from optic nerve paralysis caused by chemical vine treatments.

The first principle in biodynamics is to replace chemical fertilizers and this is done by spraying tiny quantities of three preparations on the soil to dynamise it, these include a cow-dung compost, silica (ground quartz), and a kind of tea from achillea, camomile, nettles, oak bark, dandelion, valerian, and others. What amazes me is how tiny the quantities used are, and although they all take time to make, they cost virtually nothing. This helps to create a balanced environment in which chemical insecticides, fungicides, and herbicides are no longer needed. The effects of the rhythms of the sun, the moon, and the planets on plant life are also used to enable growers to plan their vineyard activities. Hoeing is important, bringing vitality to the vine when done in the morning and retaining water in the soil in the afternoon.

When biodynamics was first explained to me in 1990 I was sceptical. But, organic viticulture does not go far enough in building up the resistance of the vines, particularly in a cool climate. Biodynamics has had sensational results: the wines express their terroir so clearly in their aromas, flavours, and above all their natural balance. In 2003, the number of fully registered estates in Alsace was over thirty and many more are in the process of converting (which takes a minimum of three years).

Grand cru

In 1932, a judicial tribunal was set up to decide about the right of a grower to use the name of vineyard as an official appellation on the label. The vineyard in question was Kaefferkopf in Ammerschwihr, which for centuries had been one of the best-known vineyard names in Alsace. However, a less appropriate test-case could hardly have been found. The right was eventually agreed for a limited number of grape varieties, but the growers would not agree to the stipulation and so no permission was granted. In 1990, Kaefferkopf was recognized as one of the fifty-one *grands crus,* but ratification was not given in 1992 because the growers demanded that the whole original area be included. One of the stipulations of *grand cru* is that the vineyard geology must be uniform; in this case one part was granite-based and the other limestone, producing very different wines. It was not until 2004 that this problem was potentially solved – exactly how is still to be revealed at the time of writing.

The *vignerons* in each village have known for centuries which sites produce the best wines, but all villages are not equal, nor are all parts of one vineyard. Indeed, in the past, if you wanted to be a successful *vigneron*, the simple answer was to marry the girl who stands to inherit the best plots, even if she was your first cousin. In the 1970s, before Alsace Grands Crus were given the appellation, some wanted to use this knowledge to ensure that *grands crus* would be limited to the best parts of the best vineyards. Johnny Hugel, who presided over the committee responsible for the proposals, worked hard to ensure that the classification would be élitist, like that of Burgundy. This, however, was not politically correct in the late twentieth century. Hugel resigned from the committee. He and the Trimbach family fought against the eventual form of the *grand cru* system, by which vineyards were classified in their entirety, and, to date, they refuse to participate.

It was not until 1984 that the appellation *grand cru* became law. In 2001, the regulations were reinforced, but there continue to be disappointing wines made. The opponents of the *grand cru* system say that fifty-one classified vineyards is too many, that they are too large, and that the quality of the wines produced is uneven (although it might be remembered that *grand cru* burgundy is incredibly uneven). Also, they claim that half the grapes are handled by the cooperatives who sell the wines to supermarkets for half the price of the smaller, high quality producers. Nevertheless, *grand cru* is a huge success and qualities all round are far higher. A new official local initiative was launched for the growers in each village to introduce their own regulations to improve the quality of their wines. Such local rules can be much stricter than the general ones, and it will be very interesting to see what effect this will have. Higher density planting, maximum yields, minimum natural alcohol levels, and chaptalization are the main issues that local growers want to address.

Grand cru Riesling, characteristically, is full of vigour and primary fruit flavours, with balancing acidity when young. Some then close up for two or three years before secondary aromas and flavours develop. Having reached full maturity, the wines can last for decades. *Lieux-dits* are single vineyards with a long history and are potential *premiers crus*. They were in the process of obtaining some official status in 2004. *Grand cru* vineyards represent twelve per cent of the area and only three to four per cent of the total production of Alsace appellation wines, or around 350,000 dozen bottles.

The *grand cru* yield is lower than elsewhere in Alsace, but there may also be instances where the quality of the wine is not good enough for the *grand cru* classification, and the grower decides not to apply for it. The classification of the wine as *grand cru* is not automatic, even though the vineyard is *grand cru*. Only Riesling, Gewurztraminer, Tokay Pinot-Gris, and Muscat qualify for the *grand cru* classification, and the maximum yield is fifty-five hectolitres per hectare, that can be increased in any given vintage by up to twenty per cent. Each wine-grower must declare before March 1 each year which grape varieties and vineyards are destined for the production of *grands crus*. There are also strict regulations concerning density of plantation, distance between rows, height of vegetation, pruning, distance between supporting wires, and number of buds per vine; there is also a minimum of eleven degrees of potential alcohol for Riesling.

Professor Claude Sittler of the Louis Pasteur University in Strasbourg has defined thirteen distinct terroirs in the vineyards of Alsace; most of these are mixtures of several geological origins but two are more specific, and Riesling is most expressive and distinctive in them. First, granite and gneiss is found on certain upper slopes from the north at Andlau to Châtenois and from Kaysersberg to Wintzenheim – the wines from these high-mineral soils combine depth and power with aristocratic steeliness and the potential to develop over time. The grapes for Vendanges Tardives tend to be *passerillés* (Sélection de Grains Nobles has to be made with botrytized grapes to achieve the legal minimum sugar level).

Second, limestone soil tends to appear at intervals slightly lower on the slopes from Châtenois to Bergholz. The limestone helps to make soil that is rich in organic matter and high in acidity and the wines are broader and richer in style, with the acidity to develop in time. Depending on the site, the grapes for Vendanges Tardives tend to get greater botrytis and Sélections de Grains Nobles are possible in more vintages.

The lovely pink sandstone of the Vosges is dotted at intervals along most areas, and contributes to extra complexity in Riesling wines. Other soils are based on the deposits from the Vosges spread out from ends of the many valleys and deposits of the basin of the Rhine itself. Add to some of the above loess, clay, and lime in places, and it is easy to see that Riesling can have hundreds of different expressions. No vineyards in the world have such geological diversity.

Of the fifty-one *grands crus*, it is my view that great Rieslings are currently produced in half of them, though of the rest, all but five with heavy clay soil have a proportion of Riesling. Most of the vineyards are between 230 and 330 metres (750 to 1,080 feet) altitude, though Sommerberg is over 400 metres (1,310 feet), and Rangen is up to 470 metres (1,540 feet). They would all be steep enough

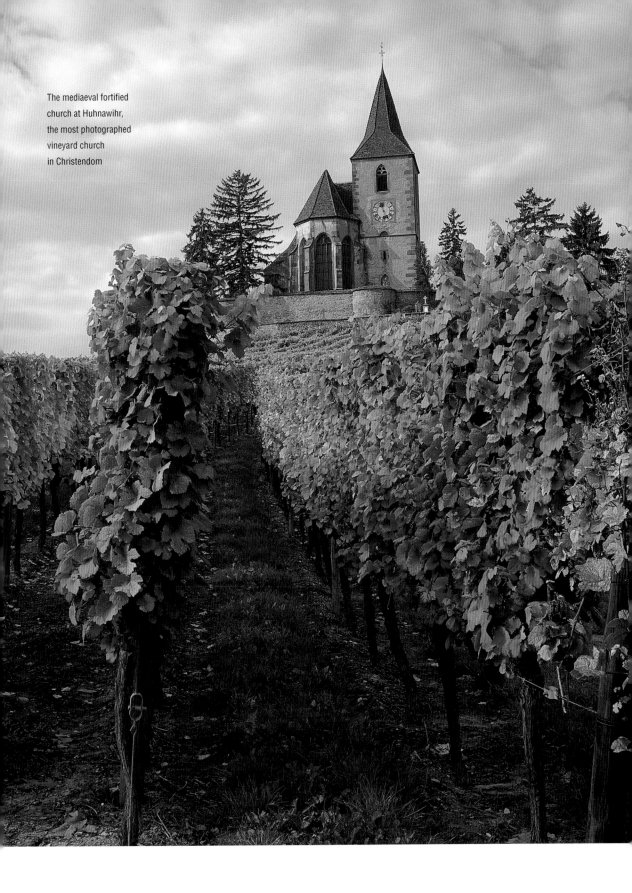

The mediaeval fortified church at Huhnawihr, the most photographed vineyard church in Christendom

to make good ski runs, were it not for the vines. The areas of the individual *grand cru* vineyards are from the tiny Kanzlerberg, 3.23 hectares, to huge Hengst, 75.78 hectares, and the intention was that the whole area of each should be homogeneous in its soil types – but, of course, this is not possible with such geological diversity. What is certain is that all the noble Rieslings come from sites on the middle and upper slopes facing south or southeast, benefiting from long exposure to the sun, though the Vosges Mountains on the west mean an early sunset.

Despite the strict *grand cru* regulations, there are wide variations in style, quality, and potential longevity of different Rieslings from one *grand cru*. This is because the cooperatives, the wholesalers, and the family estates have different objectives. Domaines using biodynamic methods of viticulture are best able to produce Rieslings that express the true terroir character of a *grand cru*.

The soil structures are incredibly diversified, especially along the fault lines at Andlau, between Ribeauvillé and Riquewihr, and at Turckheim, Guebwiller and Thann. The vineyards in brackets are *lieux-dits,* the named vineyards around the villages that were in the process being legally classified as this book went to press, and where fine Rieslings are also produced. The wines from the best producers benefit from ageing for at least three to five years and some for ten or twenty years from the vintage.

Independent growers who bottle and sell their own wines are responsible for some twenty-seven per cent of Alsace wine. A new generation of open-minded young wine-growers are energizing their family domaines. Léonard and Olivier Humbrecht MW of Domaine Zind-Humbrecht set the pace but there are many others, over thirty of whom have also introduced biodynamic methods in their vineyards and their cellars.

In 2001, some forty-five per cent of Alsace wine was produced by cooperatives, notably Wolfberger and those of Turckheim and Pfaffenheim. Alsace cooperatives are far superior to, and their wines more consistent than, those of other regions in France and elsewhere in Europe. Some medium-sized négociants make superb wines with their own grapes and fine typical wines with grapes bought from other growers. Traditional family négociants, led by the quality-conscious *Grandes Maisons d'Alsace* such as Kuentz-Bas, Hugel, and Trimbach, spearhead exports. In total, négociants produce about eighteen per cent of Alsace wines.

At the time of writing it is expected to be six month before the details of Kaefferkopf are released (*see* chart, opposite).

The finest grands crus for Riesling

Village	Grand cru	Soil	Exposure	Style of Riesling
Bergbieten	Altenberg de Bergbieten	*Keuper*, gypsum, sandstone	South & east	Fresh and floral
Andlau	Kastelberg	Schist, granite	South	Discreet elegance, virility
Andlau	Wiebelsberg	Sandstone, quartz, iron	South	Elegance, power
Andlau & Eishofen	Moenchberg	Glacial scree, conglomerate	Southeast	Floral, delicate, with balanced fruit and acidity
Nothalten	Muenchberg	Sandstone, conglomerates, tufa, volcanic ash	South	Low yields, good concentration
Bergheim	Altenberg de Bergheim	Limestones, marls	South	Power, complexity
Bergheim	Kanzlerberg	*Keuper* & *Muschelkalk*	South	Fruit aromas, richness
Ribeauvillé	Giesberg	Sandstone, *Muschelkalk*, marls	South	Elegant, powerful
Ribeauvillé	Kirchberg de Ribeauvillé	Sandstone, *Muschelkalk*, marls	South	Finesse, strong aromas
Ribeauvillé	Osterberg	Sandstone, *Muschelkalk*, marls with magnesium	South & east	Power, elegance
Hunawihr	Rosacker	Sandstone, *Keuper*, *Muschelkalk*, marls with magnesium	East	Aromatic, minerally
Riquewihr	Schoenenbourg	*Keuper*, sandstone, *Muschelkalk*, marls	South	Powerful, rich aromas, ideal for VT and SGN
Mittelwihr & Béblenheim	Mandelberg	Limestone-marl, conglomerates	South	Fruit, finesse
Sigolsheim	Mambourg	Limestone with magnesium, marl conglomerates	South	Powerful bouquet, elegance
Kientzheim & Sigolsheim	Furstentum	Limestone-marl, conglomerate	Southeast	Powerful aromas, fine balance
Kientzheim	Schlossberg	Granite and Devonian shale	South	Richly floral, delicate, distinguished
Katzenthal & Ammerschwihr	Wineck-Schlossberg	Two micas granite	Southeast	Floral, elegant, with fruit
Ammerschwihr	Kaefferkopf	Not available	Not available	Not available
Niedermorschwihr & Katzenthal	Sommerberg	Two micas granite	South	Perfect Riesling character
Turckheim	Brand	Two micas granite, *Muschelkalk*	South & southeast	Subtle complexity, great fruit, regal balance
Wintzenheim	Hengst	Conglomerates, marls, limestone, sandstone	Southeast	Soft and refined when mature
Eguisheim	Eichberg	Conglomerates, marls, limestone, sandstone	Southeast	Opulent, full, with fruit and finesse
Roufach & Westhalten	Vorbourg	Conglomerates, marls, limestone, sandstone	Southeast	Powerful, with apricot, peach aromas
Bergholz & Guebwiller	Spiegel	Sandstone, conglomerates, marls	Southeast	Racy, long
Guebwiller	Kessler	*Muschelkalk*, sandstone	Southeast	Floral, supple, complex
Guebwiller	Kitterlé	Sandstone, quartzite conglomerate, volcanic sandstones	South & east	Subtle, opulent, rich
Guebwiller	Saering	Sandstone, conglomerates, marls	East	Floral, dry, with fine fruit
Thann & Vieux-Thann	Rangen	Carboniferous volcanic rock, ashes	South	Richness with elegance, acidity

Domaine Bernhard-Riebel

20 rue de Lorraine, 67730 Chatenois, Bas-Rhin
tel 03 88 82 04 21, fax 03 88 82 59 65
email bernhard-riebel@wanadoo.fr
estate 17 ha, 30% Riesling
best vineyards Lieux-dits Rittersberg, Weingarten

This domaine is a Riesling specialist. There are no *grands crus* in Scherwiller, which claims to be *La Capitale du Riesling*. There are two different types of granite on the steep vineyards. Scherwiller has the Lieu-dit Rittersberg, with pale mica-granite, below the ruins of Ortenbourg and Ramstein castles; Chatenois has the Lieu-dit Weingarten, with red felspar granite, below the vast restored castle of Haut Konigsberg that dominates the whole region. Unfortunately, over a long period of time, the local *vignerons* had lost interest in these two vineyards because they are so steep.

The vineyards are fully converted to biodynamic practices and this shows in the quality of the wines. Tasted in 2001, Weingarten 1999 had the classic precision and cut-glass mineral character of a granite-based Riesling and deserved to be kept for a few years. The 1998, because it was picked very late, was concentrated and ripe. The 1997 was smooth and deep with a hint of Pfalz pungency and a positive granite terroir character. Rittersberg 1998 was delicate, minerally, with fine acidity, elegant, and dry, yet so complete; it was from 50-year-old vines. The 1997 was a classic Riesling, more mature and slightly deeper in flavour; 1996 had crystal-clear, ripe Riesling flavour, with high but not sharp acidity and just 2 g.s. – wonderful dry Riesling.

In complete contrast, we ended the tasting with Riesling Vendanges Tardives 1997 from an unnamed vineyard with very old vines, a lovely, subtle, and reserved wine that opened up in the

Jean-Christophe Bott, passionate wine-grower and *biodynamiste* of Domaine Bott-Geyl in Béblenheim

glass to reveal its depth and persistent flavours. On the basis of this tasting, the two *lieux-dits* should be *grands crus*.

SCEA Paul Blanck et fils

32 Grand'rue, 68420 Kientzheim
tel 03 89 78 23 56, fax 03 89 47 16 45
email blanck-alsace@rmcnet.fr
internet www.Blanck-Alsace.com
estate 38 ha
best vineyards Furstentum GC, Schlossberg GC, Mambourg GC, Lieux-dits Rosenbourg, Paterberg

Founded in 1922 by Paul Blanck, the third generation now runs the company. The genial extrovert Philippe looks after external affairs, and his cousin Frédéric is oenologist. They create a multitude of different wines.

My notes are based on two separate tastings – the 1998s in 2000 and the 1999s in 2001. Lieu-dit Rosenbourg 1998 had fine mineral flavours with depth and length, deserving to be kept for a few years, while Lieu-dit Paterberg 1998 was more elegant, with fine fruit and good acidity.

Blanck owns 6 ha of Furstentum GC, where the soil is mainly brown calcareous sandstone. 1998 was quite broad in structure and most attractive, while 1999 was rich and concentrated – almost sensual.

Schlossberg GC is one of the top-dozen Riesling vineyards in Alsace, and the soil is one of the most complicated in structure. The crystalline granite and sandstone scree on the steep-terraced slope forces the roots of the vines to explore deep into the soil to find water and nutriment. It is particularly noticeable that old vines add even more to the complexity and remarkable staying power of Riesling here.

Domaine Bott-Geyl

1 rue du petit Château, 68980 Béblenheim
tel 03 89 47 90 04, fax 03 89 47 97 33
email bottgeyl@libertysurf.fr
estate 13 ha, 20% Riesling
best vineyards Mandelberg GC, Schoenenbourg GC, Sonnenglanz GC, Furstentum GC, Lieux-dits Grafenreben, Burgreben

After completing his wine studies in 1990 at the age of twenty, Jean-Christophe Bott returned to the family domaine to work; he also began to spend his winters working in wineries in Australia and South Africa. In 1993, his father Edouard, mayor of Béblenheim, saw that his son had developed very different ideas from his own, and with more than enough to do as mayor he handed over the domaine to Jean-Christophe. In 1995, he was chosen as *Vigneron de l'Année* in *Gault Millau*, and since then his wines have won the acclaim of many major wine writers. The domaine is biodynamic.

His seventy parcels of vines extend to 13 ha from Ribeauvillé to Kientzheim. Grafenreben, with clay and limestone soil, gives a rich and positive, muscular style, which takes three or four years to express itself. 2002 Riesling (2 g.s., 8 g.a., 14 alc.) was a powerful, rich wine, while the Vendanges Tardives 2002 had perfect balance with little botrytis and lots of ripe fruit. Mandelberg GC has optimum exposure to the sun and the soil is relatively stony with marl and limestone. Riesling shows its full colours in this terroir: supple, sturdy, and yet suave, like an orchestra playing with cohesion. Schoenenbourg GC has a terroir of gypsum and marl (*Keuper*) covered with Vosgien shale and thin layers of seashell limestone (*Muschelkalk*). It is a relatively heavy soil with good water retention and a sub-soil with rich mineral elements on a steep, south-southeast facing slope. 1998 was soft, full, round, and complete – a memorable wine.

Domaine Albert Boxler

78 rue des Trois Epis, 68230 Niedermorschwihr
tel 03 89 27 11 32, fax 03 89 27 70 14
estate 12 ha
best vineyards Sommerberg GC, Brand GC, Lieu-dit Eckberg

Jean-Marc Boxler and his son Jean run this fine domaine, whose reputation is built on the superb quality of the Rieslings from their two *grands crus*.

They use indigenous yeasts to retain the essence of their terroirs. Half their wines are fermented and matured in *foudres* and half in stainless steel. Bottling is done the following September, giving the wines a long period on the light lees to develop complexity and structure.

Eckberg Riesling 2000 (10 g.s., 13.5 alc.) had a beautiful delicate flavour and roundness on the palate with a touch of sweetness on the finish. 1995 was a fantastic wine, with deep flavours backed up by strong botrytis on the finish, but a special Cuvée Vieilles Vignes of the same vintage was even richer. In complete contrast, Brand GC 2000 (5 g.s., 13.5 alc.) had a brilliant, primary fruit nose and a restrained, modern, clean, precise character, needing a few years to achieve the wonderful, ripe maturity of the 1998.

Sommerberg GC is a long, steep, south-facing granite scree slope. Vieilles Vignes 2000 was very distinguished, spicy, and concentrated with a great future; Vendanges Tardives 1989 was a superlative finish to the tasting and had great botrytis, honey sweetness, and power, all in perfect harmony.

Domaine Marcel Deiss

15 Route du Vin, 68750 Bergheim
tel 03 89 73 63 37, fax 03 89 73 32 67
estate 27 ha
best vineyards Altenberg de Bergheim GC, Schoenenbourg GC, Mambourg GC, Lieux-dits Engelgarten, Grasberg, Burg

To Jean-Michel Deiss, the terroir is more important than the grape variety, and he claims to have proved this when he asked a group of friends to taste separately Sylvaner, Pinot Blanc, Pinot Gris, and Riesling grapes grown in Schoenenbourg GC. They agreed that they had the same flavour. In other words, the terroir subsumed the varietal character. Jean-Michel stresses that, before 1918, the best grape varieties were often grown and picked together to make the blends known as *Edelzwicker* ("noble

mixture") or *Gentil* ("noble"). For him, a vine needs other varieties planted with it, so he would for example, plant a group of Muscat vines in a vineyard that is predominantly Riesling. A delightful example is his Gentil Burg with Riesling exoticized by Gewurztraminer. His triumph was to have this tradition accepted for *grand cru*. He described this as, "a milestone in my life as a wine-grower; it marks a break with the dominance of variety over terroir, which the Alsace region has suffered for the past 100 years."

Deiss's 27 ha are made up of 120 parcels on many different terroirs. All the following wines are 100 per cent Riesling. Grasberg 1997 was a delectable, rich, subtle wine from seven parcels of vines planted in 1954. Altenberg de Bergheim GC 1997 was still young and closed but characteristically rich, in perfect balance, and complete – wonderful wine.

Schoenenbourg GC 1997 had much more complexity of flavours but with the same richness; it was so perfectly balanced that it was ready to drink and would last for twenty years. Sélection de Grains Nobles Schoenenbourg GC 1989, tasted in 1993, was one of the most exotic Rieslings that I have ever tasted. Its finesse and harmonic sweetness was paramount, with the botrytis in the background – exquisite wine.

Jean-Michel looks like a bohemian artist and he is as modest as he is flamboyant. He is a rebel and a traditionalist. He looks at vines as humans and humans as collectors of experience. He wants to shock and to please. He is more French than the French. A biodynamist and a practical farmer.

Domaine Dirler-Cadé

13 rue d'Issenheim, 68500 Bergholtz
tel 03 89 76 91 00, fax 03 89 76 85 97
email jpdirler@terre-net.fr
estate 17.3 ha, 21.5% Riesling
best vineyards Saering GC, Spiegel GC, Kessler GC, Kitterlé GC

Jean Dirler took over the responsibility for the domaine from his father Jean-Pierre when they agreed to go biodynamic in 1998. Half their domaine is in the four contiguous *grands crus* on the edge of the Guebwiller geological fracture zone, and there are marked differences in the soil, though clay and weathered sandstone seem to be common factors.

Spiegel GC 1999 had great fruit enhanced by natural richness (20 g.s.), whereas Kessler GC 1999 was a very serious, long-term Riesling with plenty of acidity to hold it together for years. Saering GC 1996 had the typical, slightly pungent nose of the Rieslings of this vintage, and was rich, but bone-dry (1 g.s.).

I also tasted several exceptional Vendanges Tardives Rieslings, which had mineral concentration and obviously needed several years longer to acquire a perfect balance of richness and acidity.

Hugel et Fils

3 rue de la 1ère Armée Francaise, 68340 Riquewihr
tel 03 89 47 92 15, fax 03 89 49 00 10
email hugel1639@wanadoo.fr
internet www.hugel.com
estate 30 ha, 36% Riesling
best vineyards Schoenenbourg GC, Sporen GC

Today, Hugel is run by five eleventh and twelfth generation Hugels from their pretty seventeenth century "corner shop" in Riquewihr, with its rabbit warren of cellars beneath. Their motto is, "The best treatment is no treatment", and they practise non-interventionist viticulture and winemaking. The musts are fermented in stainless steel and 1,000 to 8,000-litre oak casks. Most wines finish fermenting naturally after a few weeks and are bottled early to preserve their fruit, but those with strong botrytis continue fermenting for months. The company's 30-ha estate around Riquewihr is backed up by about 350 growers (contracted by handshake, not in writing) who own approximately 130 ha.

Riesling Jubilée (previously Réserve Personelle) is its signature wine and the grapes are from its own vines in Schoenenbourg GC, which rises steeply from the village of Riquewihr, facing south. This is a true terroir wine. I have tasted a number of vintages and it always has the richness given to it by old vines and perfectly ripe grapes, plus finesse.

Tasted in 2001, Vendange Tardive 1990 had a brilliant green-gold colour, great concentration, and complexity of mineral flavours on the palate, with a fine, refreshing acidity on the finish; while the 1989 had tremendous botrytis richness and density but without the minerality and acid balance. The 1976 Vendange Tardive, tasted in 1987, had the typical deep colour and nose of botrytis and was spicy and long, with the creamy effect of slow fermentation in oak.

Sélections de Grains Nobles Rieslings are very rare. In 2001, the 1995 was in its infancy but already showed its enormous concentration and breeding and a flavour of barley-sugar – a golden treasure.

Josmeyer

76 rue Clemenceau, 68920 Wintzenheim
tel 03 89 27 91 90, fax 03 89 27 91 99
email contact@josmeyer.com
internet www.josmeyer.com
estate 25 ha
best vineyards Brand GC, Hengst GC

All wines under the Josmeyer label are made entirely with grapes from the domaine vineyards, but the company also buys grapes from other growers under contract; these are sold under the Jean Meyer label. Jean Meyer himself is a deeply passionate *viticulteur*. Jean's son-in law, Christophe Ehrhart, is in charge of the vineyards, which are now run biodynamically.

Another of Jean's passions is matching wine and food, and he invited us to "Un Lundi au Soleil" (a tasting for sommeliers) followed by a tasting of original tartines and Riesling. Examples of three matches included: Tartine Alsacienne de Presskopf with Riesling Kottabe 2001 – a charming wine for drinking in its first summer, which had the natural acidity to reduce the effect of the slight sweetness of the calf dish. Tartare de Féra en Tartine with Riesling Les Pierrets 2000 – the exotic, almost volcanic character of the wine reminded me of a fine Riesling Spätlese from Forst and brought out the subtle flavour of the freshwater fish. Tartine de Mousse de Saumon et Ciboulette with Riesling Brand GC 2000 – the wine had power and acidity from its granite terroir which brought out the subtle flavours of the salmon.

Handsome oak *foudres* are used for fermentation and maturation, and winemaking is non-interventionist . Hengst GC is on limestone and clay soil and the Sélection de Grains Nobles 2002 (104 g.s., 8.7 g.a., 11.2 alc.) was still in on its lees in cask, so I can only write that it had explosive concentration and intricate complexity.

Domaine Kientzler

50 route de Bergheim, 68150 Ribeauvillé
tel 03 89 73 67 10, fax 03 89 73 35 81
estate 10 ha, 25% Riesling
best vineyards Geisberg GC, Osterberg GC, Kirchberg GC

Behind Ribeauvillé the great south-facing slope is divided into a patchwork of square parcels of terraced vines. Kirchberg is closest to the mountain, Geisberg is in the middle and Osterberg faces more towards the valley; each vineyard has different soils derived from the Ribeauvillé faults. André Kientzler has eleven parcels in the parish.

Geisberg has limestone, coloured sandy marls with gypsum and stones. This is his most important

The huge "Sainte Catherine" barrel, christened in 1715 in the cellars of Hugel in Riquwihr

vineyard for Riesling and the basis of his formidable reputation. His work in the vineyards and in the cellars is very precise, but he is not yet biodynamic.

The 2000 Geisberg GC was very complex yet elegant and delicate, promising a long, slow development in bottle. The 1998 was bigger and stronger, and at 3 years old it was promising to develop its secondary aromas in another couple of years. The 1989 Vendange Tardive had splendid botrytis and was just beginning to become drier as if it were saying "enjoy me now". SGN 2001 had wonderful structure with a perfect harmony of richness, complexity, and acidity to last for another decade or two. The 2000 was a baby, overwhelming at first, but slowly revealing extraordinary concentration.

Domaine Marc Kreydenweiss

12 rue Deharbe, 67140 Andlau, Bas-Rhin
tel 03 88 08 95 83, fax 03 88 08 41 16
email marc.kreydenweiss@wanadoo.fr
estate 12 ha, 50% Riesling
best vineyards Kastelberg GC, Wiebelsberg GC, Moenchberg GC

"We do not inherit the land of our ancestors; we lend it to our children." Marc has this Indian proverb as his motto and it has led him to biodynamism. He and his wife Emmanuelle started the domaine with the magic vintage of 1971, and Riesling Kastelberg GC 1971 is still the high point of family celebrations. In 1983, another great vintage, Marc, having decided to go for quality, drastically reduced his yields (to 40 hl/ha) and started to look for the expression of terroir in his wines: he has five completely different soil types in his vines.

In 1989, he began the three-year process of becoming fully biodynamic. Unusually in Alsace, since 1995, he has allowed all his wines to go through the malolactic fermentation; he finds that the effect of biodynamic culture is to give even more acidity to the grapes.

Riesling Wiebelsberg GC comes from warm, weathered, sandstone soil. The 2000 had a bouquet of flowers and was very rounded and powerful, while the 1998 was even more powerful with fine acidity and a touch of botrytis. Vendange Tardive 1997 had a unique dry richness with great length, but without botrytis. The star of the tasting was Kastelberg GC, from a steep site which was planted by the Romans. Vendange Tardive 1999 had great freshness and fine acidity and richness (30 g.s.), structure and length. The grapes were picked late in November and the development was so slow that it could not be bottled until December 2000.

As a footnote, the 2-ha Clos du Val d'Eléon, on a steep shale soil, is planted with 70 per cent Riesling and 30 per cent Pinot Gris, which are picked and fermented together.

Kuentz-Bas

14 route du Vin, 68420 Husseran-les-Châteaux
tel 03 89 49 30 24, fax 03 89 49 23 39
email kuentz-bas@calixo.net
internet www.kuentz-bas.fr
estate 11 ha
best vineyards Pfersigberg GC, Eichberg GC

The company's own vineyards provide about forty per cent of its grapes; the rest are bought under contract from local growers. The first level is Riesling Tradition, from bought-in grapes fermented in stainless steel for bottling in March following the vintage. It is quite full and ripe with fine acidity. The second level is Réserve Personelle, from domaine grapes fermented in oak barrels. Pfersigberg GC ("peach hill") is the domaine's best vineyard for Riesling. 1998 was dry, full-bodied, and aromatic; in contrast, the 1997 had a touch of botrytis with extra fruit and complexity. Cuvée Caroline Vendange Tardive 1997, picked on December 15, had great distinction, and opulent

concentration of fruit and acidity and expression of its limestone-marl soil. To celebrate their bicentenary, they made a Special Cuvée 1995, with a lovely mature, creamy taste.

François Lehmann

12 avenue Jacques Prieirs, 68340 Riquewihr
tel 03 89 47 95 16, fax 03 89 47 87 93
estate 3.5 ha, 22.5% Riesling
best vineyard Schoenenbourg GC

We tasted 2000 to 1997, 1987, and 1982 vintages of François' Riquewihr Riesling. Each of the younger vintages showed a family resemblance of softness, with structure and finesse, with power. The two oldest wines were still full of character and showed what a genius can do with a village appellation in dreadful vintages. The vintage and the terroir were even more precise in Schoenenbourg GC: 2000 still in its infancy, 1999 beginning to show its style, 1998 in full blossom, and 1996 with rose-petal scents and the slightly "green" nose of this vintage and high natural acidity. It was picked on the same day as the Vendange Tardive from a different parcel of the vineyard.

As François uses indigenous yeast for all fermentations, the results are not always as expected. Schoenenbourg GC Vendange Tardive 1998 had strong botrytis and the must stopped fermenting at just 10 alc. and 90 g.s.; rather than provoking a further fermentation he decided to let nature alone. It was a unique Alsace Riesling with a slightly Germanic note and infinite length. 1996 Vendange Tardive had the same "green" nose as the 1998s above but with extra layers of dried-fruit flavours, which gave it the concentration and harmony to last for decades. The botrytized grapes were eliminated, to give a remarkable dry wine that François insisted should be decanted to allow it to breathe before drinking. 1994 had concentrated mineral extract and fine acidity in balance, with (for him) a hint of bracken and box hedge. François is a genius.

Domaine Albert Mann

13 rue du Château, 68320 Wettolsheim
tel 03 89 80 62 00, fax 03 89 80 34 23
email info@mann-albert.com
estate 20 ha, 23% Riesling
best vineyards Schlossberg GC, Furstentum GC,
Hengst GC, Pfersigberg GC, Steingrubler GC

Maurice and Jacky Barthelmé Mann share all the
responsibilities in this superb domaine, and run
it on strict lines to achieve absolute purity of flavours,
reflecting the terroir of each wine. They take infinite
care of the soil and the vines – that are mainly
biodynamic. Some great parcels, including
Schlossberg GC, which is on light, precious scree
that could be washed away by erosion, benefit from
gentle ploughing by horse and are being cultivated
biodynamically. Whole-bunch pressing and
fermentation with indigenous yeast in both stainless
steel and large oak barrels help to retain maximum
terroir character. The maturation is completed with
long contact with the light lees.

Since starting in 1989, they have doubled the area
of vines, and now have ninty parcels, including five
grands crus with completely different terroirs. Of
these, Schlossberg GC, with its manganese, granite,
and sandstone scree is, in my opinion, one of the three
best vineyards for Riesling in Alsace. The 1999 was
so "modern", with wild flowers on the nose, and pure
vitality and an intricate interplay of minerals on the
palate. 1998 had a bouquet of roses with concentrated
fruit and the high acidity of the vintage to guarantee
a long life. 1997 had a nose that sang of Riesling and
concentrated, juicy, ripe fruit. Furstentum, with its
limestone and sandstone soil, gives a broader style
and 1998 was magnificent, with a touch of honey from
the botrytis of the vintage, but dry. Rosenberg (next
to Steingrubler GC) is on limestone soil, and Vendange
Tardive 1997 showed how a late-picked Riesling from
a lieu-dit could compare with a grand cru; it had real
sophistication and fine acidity.

Meyer-Fonné

24 Grand-Rue, 68230 Katzental
tel 03 89 27 16 50, fax 03 89 27 34 17
email felix.meyer-fonne@libertysurf.fr
estate 10 ha, 33% Riesling
best vineyards Wineck-Schlossberg GC, Kaefferkopf GC,
Lieu-dit Poeffler

Felix Meyer and his father François run this small,
progressive domaine. Félix was schooled by
Léonard Humbrecht, of Domaine Zind-Humbrecht
(see page 115), and put his philosophy into practice.
The fifteen parcels of vines are fully biodynamic
and the terroir character of each Riesling
is emphasized by modern reductive winemaking
using temperature-controlled fermentation with
indigenous yeasts in stainless-steel vats. They
never filter the wines.

Riesling Lieu-dit Pfoeller is on a Muschelkalk
soil; the 1999 had a broad spectrum of mineral
flavours, demanding at least three years to reach
its full potential. Kaefferkopf 1997 had a fine,
restrained Riesling nose and was a lovely
full-bodied, rich wine.

Wineck-Schlossberg GC 1999, from the steep
slope around the castle on heavily weathered granit
á deux micas, known as Turckheim black-and-white
granite, was very closed and had all the right
qualities of this, the perfect terroir for classic, pure,
racy, slow-to-develop, long-to-live Rieslings. 1998
was much more open, softer, and mature because
it had a touch of botrytis, characteristic of some
wines of that fine vintage.

Frédéric Mochel

56 rue Principale, 67310 Traenheim, Bas-Rhin
tel 03 88 50 38 67, fax 03 88 50 56 19
estate 8 ha, 50% Riesling
best vineyard Altenberg de Bergbieten GC

Frédéric Mochel is a master of Riesling and owns
a good proportion of Altenberg de Bergbieten

Grand Cru, which is so far north as to be on the doorstep of Strasbourg. The vineyard faces southeast and the heavy, clay-marl, *Keuper* soil, with gypsum and sandstone, retains water in summer. Tasted in 2001, both the 1999 and the 1998 had a delicate, fragrant bouquet, quite severe and dry with a hint of grapefruit in the flavour.

Mochel has a parcel of Riesling vines planted about 100 years ago in Altenberg, the wines of which he sells under the label Cuvée Henriette. The 1998 had lovely fruit; the 1997 had great purity of flavour, with power and length; and the 1996 still retained the delicate nose of wild flowers and was positively dry in style. Cuvée Guilhaume Riesling 1997 was from a completely different vineyard, a wonderful dry wine with great concentration and distinction, which sells at nearly double the price of the *grand cru* wine.

This domaine is well worth a detour, especially if you want a really top-quality, dry Riesling.

René Muré, Clos St-Landelin

route du vin, 68250 Rouffach
tel 03 89 78 58 00, fax 03 89 78 58 01
email rene@mure.com
internet www.mure.com
estate 21 ha, 33% Riesling
best vineyards Vorbourg GC (Clos St-Landelin)

Michel Muré was a *vigneron* in Rouffach in 1620. Today, René Muré, his daughter Véronique and son Thomas run the business. Vorbourg is one of the largest *grands crus* in Alsace, and Clos St-Landelin consists of 15 ha in the heart of the total 72 ha. It is very steep and dry-stone terraced. It is one of the hottest vineyards in Alsace and also attracts botrytis, to the benefit of late-picked grapes. It is the Rolls Royce of the business.

On separate occasions I have tasted many Clos St-Landelin Rieslings. 2001 had a rich but not heavy quality, with fine acidity, thanks to the limestone, and a memorable aftertaste of ripe apricots. 1998 had pure fruit, brilliant acidity with a touch of botrytis, and perfect balance, and 1997 was a classic Riesling that needed at least five years from the vintage to mature. The Vendange Tardive 1989 from that wonderful botrytis year was immensely rich and concentrated.

Domaine Ostertag

87 rue Finkwiller, 67680 Epfig, Bas Rhin
tel 03 88 85 51 34, fax 03 88 85 58 95
estate 12.5 ha, 33% Riesling
best vineyards Muenchberg GC, Lieux-dits Epfiger Fronholz, Nothaltener Heissenberg

André has worked and studied with Dominique Lafon in Burgundy, one of the leading proponents of non-interventionist methods in the cellars and biodynamic culture in the vineyard. André follows both these principles and is always experimenting with his wines. Epfiger Fronholz is on a mound of granite overlaid with white sand from weathered quartz. André's 1999 was a classic dry Riesling (6 g.s.) with lovely aromas and flavours with a mineral background and a touch of botrytis. Nothaltener Heissenberg is on weathered granite, *grès de rose* (pink Vosges sandstone), and limestone that gives a hot, light soil for early ripening. André told me that the 1999 was fermented in barriques and aged with the lees for six months, which gave the wine oxygen and structure; then six months in stainless steel to allow it to harmonize. For me, the barriques (only four per cent of which were new) had given it a sense of low acidity and sweetness, without actual sugar, and he suggested that this transformed a wine with relatively little character to one with a very distinct character. He is not dogmatic about his methods but wishes to show what can be done. The 1995 however was in complete contrast and bore a resemblance to a lovely creamy, earthy Pfalz, with some botrytis and a bright-gold colour.

Jean Dirler who runs the family estate with his father
Jean-Pierre in their biodynamic vineyard in Guebwiller

Muenchberg GC, in Nothalten, was planted by Cistercian monks in the twelfth century – the same period as Steinberg in the Rheingau and Clos Vougeot in Burgundy were planted, also by Cistercians. The vineyard is an amphitheatre facing due south and is 95 per cent Riesling, that loves the warm stony soil with its mixture of volcanic tufa, pink shale, and Permian conglomerates, that help the grapes to ripen perfectly. 1998 was like a Mosel in its finesse, but with much more power and alcohol. 1999 had wonderful concentration of mineral flavours and fruit with total ripeness from late harvesting, obviously a wine for maturing for a few years in bottle. Vendange Tardive 1995 had depth and botrytis sweetness, balanced with powerful mineral character and acidity.

Domaine Rolly-Gassmann

1 rue de l'Eglise, 68590 Rorschwihr, Bas-Rhin
tel 03 89 73 63 28, fax 03 89 73 33 06
estate 17 ha
best vineyards Lieux-dits Pflaenzerreben, Kappelweg, Silberberg

La Simplicité, c'est la seule recette ("Simplicity is the only recipe"). This is the Rolly-Gassmann philosophy: to let nature work in its own rhythm, without intervening too much.

Pierre Gassmann is responsible for the wines and vineyards of this family domaine. Its vineyards are not yet biodynamic, but he uses organic compost, and no chemical fertilizers, herbicides or insecticides. His wines have slightly more residual sugar than those of some other growers, but if people are not told this, they love them. Gassmann is passionate about his terroir, which is as confused as that of nearby Bergheim and Ribeauvillé. He has vines in at least ten *lieux-dits*: Silberberg is on *Muschelkalk* that gives depth and richness, and weathered gneiss that gives a lovely freshness and mineral quality evident in the 1998 Riesling. Pflaenzerreben is on a different limestone, and the 1994 had a softer, ripe style, with balancing acidity. Kapellweg is also on *Muschelkalk*, and the straight 1994 was fresh and subtle without any signs of ageing, while the Vendange Tardive 1994 had much greater depth and volume, with 13.5 alc. and relatively high residual sugar; yet it was in balance, and still young at heart. Pflaenzerreben Vendange Tardive 1997 had a bouquet of wild flowers, great freshness, complexity, richness, and sugar.

Domaines Schlumberger

100 rue Théodore-Deck, 68500 Guebwiller
tel 03 89 74 27 00, fax 03 89 74 85 75
email dvschlum@aol.com
estate 140 ha, 28% Riesling
best vineyards Kitterlé GC, Saering GC,
Kessler GC, Spiegel GC

Alain Beydon-Schlumberger is the seventh generation of the family to run this domaine. It is the largest in Alsace, with 2,500 parcels of vines spread over 140 ha. That means 850 kilometres (503 miles) of vines, which requires a team of twenty-five vineyard workers; the 50 kilometres (30 miles) of drystone walls supporting the terraces need another five workers; 100 pickers are needed for the harvest.

Half the vines are in the four contiguous *grands crus* on the edge of the Guebwiller geological fracture zone where there are marked differences in the soil, though clay and weathered sandstone are common factors. Cellar techniques are modern but the musts are fermented in large oak *foudres* in the traditional way. The house's trademark style is rich and voluptuous, partly because of the soils and partly because the climate here is fractionally hotter in summer than in vineyards further north. Riesling is the most important grape.

Saering GC lies on the lower slopes where there is a weathered limestone and sandstone soil. The 1999 (tasted, like all these wines, in 2003) had developed a bouquet of freshly cut flowers; the palate was dry, with flavours that were wonderfully expressive of the terroir.

Kitterlé GC is higher up the slope and partly south-facing, with sandstone and some volcanic elements. The 1995 was gold in colour, showing the botrytis character of this vintage in Alsace and was rich, powerful, and dry, but lacking the poise of the 1997, which was pale yellow-green in colour with a young, vibrant Riesling nose, no botrytis, and fine fruit – delicious to drink over many years, and a real treasure.

Schlumberger produces splendid Vendanges Tardives in propitious years and made Riesling Sélection Grains Nobles in 1945, 1971, and 1999, the last being "Cuvée Ernest" (90 g.s., 6.6 g.a., 12.4 alc.) – a wine of superlatives.

F. E. Trimbach

15 route de Bergheim, 68150 Ribeauvillé
tel 03 89 73 60 30, fax 03 89 73 69 04
email contact@maison-trimbach.fr
estate 30 ha, 40% Riesling
best vineyards Clos Ste-Hune (Rosacker GC),
Geisberg GC, and Osterberg GC

The first recorded Trimbach was Jean in Riquewihr

in 1626. In the 1840s, Jean-Fréderic Trimbach became mayor of Hunawihr and the family moved there, within a stone's throw of the jewel in the family crown, Clos Ste-Hune. This minute 1.3-ha Riesling vineyard is in the *grand cru* Rosacker on a geological fracture zone with various different layers of limestone, sandstone, pebbles, and rich clay. Eventually, the Trimbachs moved to Ribeauvillé towards the end of the ninteenth century.

After nearly two centuries and some recent geological surveys, the Trimbach family still have little idea why Riesling on this tiny plot is so special. The winemaking is strictly orthodox – slow pressing, quick transfer of the must into large oak *foudres* or stainless steel for fermentation with cultured yeast. The Rieslings are then kept as reductive as possible to reduce oxidation. "The Trimbach style", as applied to Riesling, is "Presbyterian": slim, tight-lipped, and somewhat austere when the wines are young. Part of this style comes from the limestone soils around Ribeauvillé, which produce the antithesis of the extrovert, full-bodied, open style of Alsace Rieslings from south of Colmar.

Straight Trimbach Riesling is made with grapes bought "on a handshake" from growers who have been supplying grapes for decades; it had fine fruit and consistency. Riesling Réserve is from vineyards in the commune of Ribeauvillé and was much richer in character. Clos Ste-Hune 1996 was too young when I tasted it in 2001, but I could perceive the positive Riesling nose, the dry style, the relatively high level of alcohol, and the strong, austere, but not hard, acidity.

Jean says that Clos Ste-Hune generally needs five to eight years to reach maturity. Vendange Tardive 1989 was a glorious golden-green, indicating youth, with the flavour of heather honey but not as sweet, still tasting young, with great length of flavour.

Riesling Cuvée Frédéric-Emile comes partly from Geisberg but mostly from Osterberg, in the patchwork of parcels on the hill behind the estate's cellars in Ribeauvillé. The soil structure is different from that of Clos Ste-Hune but is just as mixed; the wines are richer and more relaxed in style because there is more limestone in the soil. The 1997 was already showing its quality and depth of character, but would reward patience.

Trimbach Vendanges Tardives are usually made with very late-harvested *passerillé* grapes with little or no botrytis because the vineyards are too windy for the mould to flourish – it likes still conditions to do its work. The 1983 Vendange Tardive Cuvée Frédéric-Emile had blossomed into a magnificent wine and had acquired the gentle, creamy flavour of great, mature Riesling.

Domaine Weinbach
Colette Faller et Filles

Clos des Capucins, 68240 Kaysersberg
tel **03 89 47 13 21**, fax **03 89 47 38 18**
email **contact@weinbach.com**
internet **www.domaineweinbach.com**
estate **27 ha, 40% Riesling**
best vineyards **Schlossberg GC, Furstentum GC, Mambourg GC, Lieu-dit Altenbourg**

In 890, Sainte Richarde, the wife of Charles the Fat, gave the vineyards of Weinbach to the monks of Etival Abbey. Just over a millennium later Théodore Faller bought the domaine and in 1998 the family celebrated its centenary. The estate is now run by Colette Faller and her daughters, Cathérine and Laurence. It has 7 ha of Riesling in Schlossberg, which was the first vineyard to be classified as *grand cru* in 1975.

The steep granite, sandstone, and shale slope has weathered to form a crystalline scree, and terraces had to be built to prevent erosion, as well as to make it possible to tend the vines. The culture of the

vines in this unique terroir is simple and natural, with animal compost and no chemical fertilizers, no insecticides, no anti-fungal products. Yields are firmly controlled.

In the cellar, simple, clean techniques are used to allow each wine to develop its own character naturally. The must is channelled into oak *foudres*, where the wines remain until bottling. To retain the terroir characteristics in the wine, indigenous yeast is used to ferment the must.

The family produces a fabulous collection of different Rieslings. Riesling Réserve is a high-quality domaine wine, well-balanced, with fine fruit. Cuvée Théo is an alluring, natural wine from the best vines in the 5.5-ha pebbly, sandy Clos des Capucins that surrounds the house. The classic Schlossberg GC has great elegance that it derives from the granite soil on the upper slope of the vineyard. Cuvée Cathérine Grand Cru Schlossberg is named after Colette's elder daughter and is picked around November 25: St Catherine's Day.

I tasted three Cuvée Cathérine 1999s. The first was from old vines on the lower slope of the Schlossberg where the soil is deeper and richer: it exploded in the mouth with juicy, mineral complexity and it will be worth waiting another three years at least for it to mature. The second was picked later from vines halfway up the slope and was so fine and rich with mellow, ripe acidity that it was guaranteed a long, long future.

The third was Cuvée Cathérine L'Inédit ("unpublished") from the oldest vines, planted in the 1940s, and only made in vintages when the weather allows perfect grapes to be picked at such a late date. Picked in the last week in November with 110 Oechsle, this was an unforgettable wine with all the qualities: richness but not sweetness, finesse, the perfect balance of ripe acidity, sugar

Olivier Humbrecht MW of Zind-Humbrecht in one of the estate's biodynamic vineyards in Turckheim

(22 g.s.), and alcohol. Sadly, only 125 cases were made. They also produce Vendanges Tardives in most years and, more rarely, Sélections de Grains Nobles.

Zind-Humbrecht

34 rue Maréchal-Joffre, 68000 Wintzenheim
tel 03 89 27 02 05, fax 03 89 27 22 58
estate 40 ha, 30% Riesling
best vineyards Rangen GC, Goldert GC, Brand GC including Clos St-Urbain, Hengst GC, Lieux-dits Clos Windbuhl, Herrenweg, Clos Hauserer, Heimbourg Clos Jebsal, Rotenberg

In 1959, Léonard Humbrecht married Geneviève Zind, bringing together two families with some of the finest vineyards in Alsace. He added to the domaine by buying vineyards once famous for the quality of their wines but which had been allowed to decline. He built an ultra-modern winery with ranks of superb oak *foudres* so that every wine could be monitored at every stage in its development – vital when using indigenous yeasts with their extended and unpredictable fermentations.

The scene was set for his son Olivier to come onto the stage. After his studies and after time spent travelling and working in other wine countries, he became the first Frenchman to become a master of wine, and the first to do so in a foreign language. He was fascinated with the pioneering work of Jean-Pierre Frick and Marc Kreydenweiss in biodynamic methods in Alsace, and he and his father decided that this was the way forward.

Already concentrated and terroir-driven, their wines became even more so, to such an extent that wines which have little residual sugar can nevertheless taste sweet.

Brand Riesling GC 1999 was so concentrated and rich without being sweet that it took time to open in the glass and reveal its complexity and authority. The hot, parched, granitic soil planted with old vines yielded a meagre 22 hl/ha of must with a massive 107 Oechsle.

Clos St-Urbain Riesling 1998 is within the Rangen GC. The power and majesty of this wine is difficult to describe, but it is the ultimate expression of its vertiginous terroir of volcanic lava rocks and ashes. In 1998, the grapes were so ripe and so perfect that the whole crop was picked in complete bunches in one day; it registered 135 Oechsle (Sélection de Grains Nobles was not the objective). Only 150 cases were made.

In the 1970s, Léonard had bought 5.5 ha, including Clos St-Urbain, of the ancient 18.8-ha Rangen GC vineyard at Thann. He restored the steep terraces, replanted the vines and was rewarded with fabulous wines. In 1999, I tasted the 1987 Rangen Grand Cru; it was an awful vintage and yet this extraordinary Riesling, pungent with green acidity, sang out that it needed a further five years fully to mature, though it was already delicious.

Clos Hauserer Riesling 1999 from marl and limestone soil just below Hengst GC was beautifully balanced and almost refreshing, though it topped 100 Oechsle. Clos Windsbuhl Riesling 1999 took ages in the glass to develop into a delicious, subtle, complex wine with great length, perhaps because it took twelve months to ferment.

Heimbourg, which is the second-steepest vineyard between Brand and Turckheim, was abandoned from World War I until Zind-Humbrecht bought it in 1991. It is on limestone and marl, and the Riesling 1999 was picked a little earlier – not too ripe and with no botrytis – to make a nicely balanced wine with fine acidity.

Austria

Austria

Grapes have been grown in what is now Austria for a long time. Cultivated grape pips (wild grape pips are a slightly different shape) dating from around the seventh century BC have been found in a necropolis north of the Neusiedler See, from the Hallstatt culture of the first iron age.

A little stream and a tiny vineyard near Weissenkirchen in Wachau named Ritzling prompted a claim that Riesling originated in Austria, but there is no documentation to back up this idea; indeed, the recent discovery of the old Weisser Heunisch vine in Germany, and the proof that Weisser Heunisch is the parent of Riesling, would seem to point to German ancestry. It is known that the bishops of Salzburg planted Riesling in the seventeenth century in the Sausaler Valley (no wine is grown there now), but the first authoritative book about wine-growing in the Austrian Empire was a three volume-work written by Franz Schams, a Hungarian, and published between 1832 and 1835. At that time, wines from the Viennese hills and those from the Klosterneuberg monastery were the best-known in the capital. There was a little Riesling and Grüner Muscateller (later to develop into Grüner Veltliner), but the main grape was Grobe, which, Schams wrote, was even more widespread in earlier times. In the Wachau, the wine-growers were unshakable in their faith in Grobe, dismissing all other grapes as "foreigners". This grape has virtually disappeared, though there might still be the odd plot in the Wachau. Schams also found whole vineyards of Riesling in Gumpoldskirchen, particularly in the experimental estates of Graf Haugwitz and Graf Harrach. In the Pulkau Valley in the Weinviertel region, he found that Riesling, "one of the old grape varieties", was being replaced by Grüner Muscateller – the precursor of Grüner Veltliner (Austria's own grape). Today, Grüner covers one-third of the vineyard area compared with Riesling's three per cent. But, it is Riesling that has pushed forward the reputation of Austria's wines.

Austria was re-founded as an independent nation in 1955, following a ten-year occupation of most of the wine regions by the Russian army after the end of World War II. At this time, Professor Lenz Moser revolutionized Austrian viticulture, introducing *Hochkultur*, or vines trained on high trellises. The yield more than doubled under this system: wonderful for the cooperatives but not wonderful for quality. In 1985, traces of diethylene glycol, an illegal chemical sweetener, were discovered in Austrian white wines. Although glycol never did anyone any harm, it almost destroyed the industry and it took a new generation of wine-growers and enormous work to establish a new reputation at a much higher quality level.

Dry Rieslings and Grüner Veltliners from the Wachau, Kamptal, and Kremstal were rediscovered, and there was a surge in interest in red wines for the home market. The general regulations for white wines in Austria used to be similar to those of Germany, but in the late 1980s the growers of Riesling and Grüner Veltiner

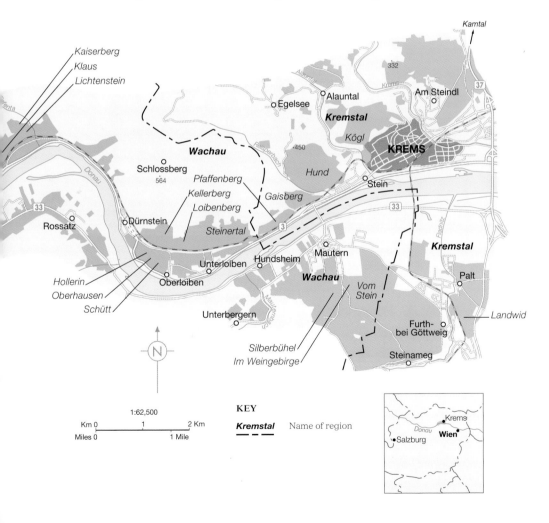

KEY

Kremstal   Name of region

- - -

The main salon of the
baroque Kellerschlössel,
now the headquarters
of the Freie Weingärtner
Wachau

in particular decided that this was irrelevant because all their wines were dry, except botrytized Auslesen, BAs, TBAs, and Eiswein. Perhaps five per cent of growers still use the German system of Kabinett and Spätlese. Ausbruch used in the Burgenland, is between BA and TBA, and the Wachau has its own regulations.

The village name is followed by the vineyard name on Austrian labels, but usually the village name is omitted; sometimes *Ried*, which just means "specific vineyard", replaces the village name. All the great Rieslings in Austria are from the Wachau, Kamptal, and Kremstal. Fine Rieslings are also to be found in the Traisertal, the valley just east of the Kremstal, and, more haphazardly, in the vineyards of Vienna. Riesling Eiswein is occasionally produced. Making TBA is possible, but easier with other grapes as in Neusiedlersee.

The wine regions

The Wachau produces the finest wines in Austria. It consists of just 1,500 hectares of vines stretched along twenty-one kilometres (thirteen miles) of steep, south-facing curves in the great Danube ravine. There is no more perfect illustration of the meaning of terroir than the Wachau. Days are warm and nights cold – important for Riesling, because it prolongs the ripening period, enhancing aromas and flavours, acidity, and finesse. The grapes ripen slowly; there is just enough rain to give some stress to the vines and to make irrigation unnecessary, except in certain sites in the hottest summers.

The vineyards are generally at 250 to 600 metres (820 to 1,960 feet) up the slopes. The stone terracing increases the heat during the day, and in autumn, misty mornings can create the perfect environment for botrytis, as well as protecting the vines from November frosts. The depth of the valley gives protection against the extremes of the Continental climate, and the finest vineyards are generally on the south-facing steep terraced slopes from Spitz to Unterloiben.

The geological structure gives a unique character to the wines from each site. The basic soil consists of weathered granite and gneiss, which has a similar structure of granular, crystalline rock containing quartz, feldspar, and mica. Added to these are ancient sediments formed into crystalline slate, and more recent sandy sediments brought down by erosion, particularly in sites closer to the river.

The climate of Spitz is fractionally cooler than that further downstream, but the real difference occurs at Mautern, where the wines are softer, and come from less steep vineyards open to the morning and afternoon sun – a slightly warmer climate and deeper, more fertile soil mean more rounded wines. Riesling and Grüner Veltliner are the two great vines. Riesling represents a mere eight per cent of the vineyards, because it is so pernickety about where it is planted; it does best in the middle terraces and sometimes higher up the slopes. Grüner Veltliner "grows like a weed" (Tony Bodenstein) but can never quite achieve the distinction of Riesling. It is happy near the river, but performs best in the middle terraces.

The Wachau has its own quality classification for dry wines. Steinfeder is the lightest and driest (min. 73 Oechsle, max. 10.7 alc.); Federspiel (min. 83 Oechsle, max. 11.9 alc.) has more character and depth; Smaragd (min. 90 Oechsle, min. 12 alc.) is powerful, rich, but still dry, with the potential to develop for decades. The rules were formulated by Vinea Wachau Nobilis Districtus, an association with about 170 members representing eighty-five per cent of the vineyard area.

After Wachau, the next important region for Riesling is Kamptal. All the finest vineyards (and the cellars) are within a radius of about five kilometres (three miles) of Langenlois, the main town, and cover 4,200 hectares of vines. The hills are lower than in the Wachau and the valley is more open to the hot Pannonian climate; nights are cold, however, allowing for slow ripening of the grapes.

As in Wachau, ninety per cent of the wines are white. Riesling is particularly successful in vineyards where the conditions and the weathered granite and slate soils resemble those of Wachau. Other vineyards have sandy valley-floor sediment and loam-loess soils that are less suited to Riesling. The greatest vineyard of the region and for Riesling is Heiligenstein ("Holy Rock") which rises to over 300 metres (980 feet), an obtrusion of granite overlaid with some volcanic rock and sandstone as well as wind-blown sand and loess.

A small hollow separates the Heigenstein hill from that of Gaisberg, another top vineyard, on loess and brown soil containing iron over granite. The vineyard in the hollow is called the *Grub* ("pit"), and traces have been found of a campsite used by Neolithic hunters in the ice age around 15,000 years ago. Scattered bones of mammoths and reindeer surround it, and the oldest bone flute ever discovered was unearthed here, all below a layer of loess blown by wind from the melted glaciers.

Lamm vineyard lies below the *Grub*. These four vineyards face southwest over Langenlois and are not as steep as the main vineyards of the Wachau, so the soil is deeper and there is only a little terracing.

The twists of the Danube ravine and the steep granite slopes end at Kremstal, but the southeast wind brings heat from the Pannonian plain, giving Krems a similar climate to that of the Kamptal. The vineyards cover some 2,500 hectares.

Wachau

Freie Weingärtner Wachau

Dürnstein 107, A-3601 Dürnstein
tel 43 (0)2711 371, fax 43 (0)2711 37113
email office@fww.at
internet www.fww.at
estate 600 ha, 18% Riesling
best vineyards Loibenberg, Kellerberg, Achleiten,
Singerriedel, Tausendeimerberg

From 1663 to 1938 much of the land and vineyards
of Wachau belonged to the von Sternhemberg family.
In 1938, Prinz Ernst von Sternhemberg offered his
tenants the freeholds of their plots of vines for token
sums. They accepted and founded Freie Weingärtner
("free wine-growers"), but it was not until the 1950s
that they began to realize the benefits. Today, its
members cultivate forty per cent of all the vineyards
of Wachau. A total of 4.5 million Euros was invested
between 1997 and 2000 in a compact,
ultra-modern winery, where the grapes and the
wines are handled very gently. The majority of the
wines are matured in oak in the original cellars.

Its finest vineyard for Riesling is perhaps
Achleiten, and I tasted a series of Smaragds: 2001 was
beautifully precise and rich; 1999 was smooth, subtle,
and long with fine mineral tones; 1995 had weight
and complexity, with a touch of botrytis typical of the
vintage; and 1993 was gentle, elegant, and mature.

Weingut Franz Hirtzberger

Kremser Strasse 8, A-3620 Spitz an der Donau
tel 43 (0)2713 2209, fax 43 (0)2713 2405
email weingut@hirtzberger.com
estate 16.5 ha, 40% Riesling
best vineyards Singerriedl, Rotes Tor, Hohenrain,
Honivogel, Setzberg

Franz Hirtzberger's father, also called Franz, was
determined to make great wines despite the difficult
times after the end of World War II. Franz junior and

his wife Irmgard took over the estate in 1983, and
have taken the quality of the wines right to the top.

Some growers think that Federspiel is
unimportant, but Franz believes in selecting ripe
grapes early for Federspiel, so he not only makes
fine examples but increases the natural sugar level
of the remaining grapes for the later-picked Smaragd.
His Riesling Federspiel from the terraces is fresh
and delicious, with plenty of ripe fruit and around
12 alc. He is so intent on selective picking that
he puts the picking dates on the labels of his
Smaragd wines. Hohenrain 2000 picked on October
13 and November 7, had great power and the flavour
of wild herbs.

Setzberg is a cool site near a little ravine with
gneiss in the soil, which gives a long, slow ripening
period to the grapes, and graceful power to the
wines; the Smaragd of both 2001 and 2002 were
superb long-term Rieslings.

Franz considers Singerriedl ("singing cricket")
to be his finest vineyard, giving the best combination
of structure, weight, and fruit. The 2001 proved this
perfectly and 2002 was perhaps even finer, with great
potential. 1998 had very deep colour from botrytis,
a powerful nose, and great depth balanced with fine
acidity (9 g.s., 8.3 g.a, 14 alc.).

Weingut Emmerich Knoll

Unterloiben 10, A-3601 Dürnstein
tel 43 (0)2732 79355, fax 43 (0)2732 793555
email emmerich@knoll.at
estate 13.5 ha, 45% Riesling
best vineyards Pfaffenberg, Loibenberg, Kellerberg, Schütt

Emmerich Knoll's family are first recorded in
Unterloiben around 1728, but it is in the last thirty
years that they have hit the headlines. He is a quiet,
seemingly restrained man until the vintage, when he
develops an extra 100 horsepower. He is one of the
forerunners of great modern Austrian winemaking,
though he is traditional in his methods. He is non-

interventionist and allows his finer wines to ferment naturally in large barrels so that each wine has its own character; he then hopes that they will be kept until they are fully mature. He dislikes people who drink his wines too young.

Pfaffenberg is just inside Kremstal so the Wachau classification does not apply. Riesling Kabinett 2001 had spritz, freshness, and structure, reflecting its long, slow fermentation. Riesling Reserve 2001 had plenty of botrytis but was still a lovely dry wine with mineral and lime tones. From within Wachau, Kellerberg Smaragd 2002 was supremely elegant and perfectly balanced (5 g.s., 7 g.a., 13 alc.). Vinotekfüllung Smaragd, the best cask of Riesling of 2002, was sensationally elegant and yet rich, with low sugar, high, ripe acidity and high extract, thanks to extremely late picking and precise selection of the grapes from the best part of the vineyard planted with old vines. A great wine for drinking from 2010.

Weingut Nikolaihof Wachau

Nikolaigasse 3, A-3512 Mautern
tel 43 (0)2732 82901, fax 43 (0)2732 76440
email wein@nikolaihof.at
internet www.nikolaihof.at
estate 20 ha, 45% Riesling
best vineyards Vom Stein, Im Weingebirge,
Steiner Hund (Kremstal)

The original cellar here was built by the Romans, and in spite of being just a stone's throw from the Danube and 4-metres (13-feet) below river level, it never floods.

Nikolaus and Christine Saahs run the estate biodynamically. One of the effects of biodynamism is the wines have less primary fruit and deeper vinosity. There is an old saying in Austria: *"Jeden Fass kocht sein eigener Wein"* ("every barrel cooks its own wine") and fermentation here is with indigenous yeasts in large oak barrels, with minimal intervention.

Vom Stein is on stony granite soil; Riesling Federspiel 2001 had lime, mineral freshness, was slim and dry but, curiously, did not taste as dry

as the analysis (1.9 g.s., 11.5 alc.). In complete contrast the Smaragd 2002 had the concentration and complexity to be in its prime in 2012.

Steiner Hund in Kremstal on the other side of the Danube is also on granite. The Reserve 2001 had clear mineral tones with intensity balanced by ripe acidity. The Riesling Premium Auslese 2000 was profound, with concentration and perfect balance.

Weingut F.X. Pichler

A-3601 Oberloiben
tel 43 (0)2732 85375, fax 43(0)2732 85375
estate 10 ha, 40% Riesling
best vineyards Kellerberg, Seinertal,
Loibner Berg, Oberhausen

Franz Xavier Pichler is nicknamed *Effix* to differentiate him from his father, Franz. He is meticulous and works by tradition and intuition. Perhaps a word for this is experience. Franz Xavier has the ambition to make perfect wines. No Steinfeder "Why bother?" he asks. It's a waste of good grapes, he believes, and it's better to reduce the yield to make even finer Smaragd.

His Smaragd Rieslings are like a diamond tiara. Von den Terrassen represents the smaller diamonds – the 2000 was absolutely correct. Oberhäuser 2000 from the lower slope represents the diamonds that outline the centre – a delicious wine for early drinking. Then the larger diamonds, the single-vineyard Rieslings: Loibnerberg, Kellerberg, Steinertal. Loibnerberg has a granite-based terroir that gives intense concentration and distinction. Kellerberg is his finest and most consistent vineyard, giving fresh and rich mineral tones when young and great complexity when mature. Steinertal seems to have certain special qualities in each vintage: a flower-scented nose, freshness in perfect balance, followed by a lingering farewell. In certain vintages, Franz Xavier makes a tiny quantity of Riesling that he labels "M" for Meisterwein ("Master Wine") or "U" for *Unendlich* ("Eternal"). To date, "M" has been made in 1992, 1994; "U" in 1998, 2000.

Franz Xavier Pichler, known as "FX", the pope of Wachau wines

Weingut Prager

Weissenkirchen 48, A-3610 Weissenkirchen
tel 43 (0)2715 2248, fax 43 (0)2715 2532
email prager@weissenkirchen.at
internet www.weingutprager.at
estate 14 ha, 65% Riesling
best vineyards Achleiten, Hollerin, Steinriegl,
Klaus, Kaiserberg

Toni Bodenstein is married to Ilse Prager and they run this estate immaculately. All the vines are from massal selection: yields are drastically reduced by pruning and green harvesting; insect populations are controlled by pheromones; indigenous yeasts are used for all the fermentations in stainless steel or large oak casks. Of the great 2001 Smaragd Rieslings: Hollerin was supremely delicate, filigree, Mozartian. Klaus had hints of gun-flint on the nose; it was closed at first, but opened up. Achleiten was a rich, complete wine, to age. From almost 1 ha of Riesling at 460 metres (1,300 feet), Wachstum Bodenstein was a truly great Riesling, with a medley of autumnal fruit on the nose and great complexity that deserved some years in bottle. Klaus 1997, tasted in 2000, was very young, with green acidity to guarantee long life, and a nose of freshly mown grass, with scintillating flavours as exquisite as a many faceted diamond.

Workers' shed below the steep vineyards of Oberloiben in Wachau

Kamptal

Weingut Willi Bründlmayer

Zwettlerstrasse 23, A-3550 Langenlois
tel 43 (0)2734 21720, fax 43 (0)2734 3748
email weingutbruendlmayer.at
internet www.bruendlmayer.at
estate: 60 ha, 25% Riesling
best vineyards Heiligenstein, Steinmassl

This is the most important *Weingut* in Kamptal and one of the largest wine estates in Austria. Willi has always used organic methods. He has some vineyards trained to a unique lyre system for better leaf and fruit exposure. He finds it gives better quality, provided that yields are controlled This system has no connection with the Lenz Moser system.

The Rieslings are fermented in stainless steel at 15–20°C (59–68°F) using indigenous yeast and then transferred to large oak barrels without clarification,

The yield of these unique, old vines is a tiny 23 hl/ha. When a vine dies its replacement is always a cutting from vines in the same plot.

Schloss Gobelsburg

Schlossstrasse 16, A-3550 Langenlois
tel 43 (0)2734 2422, fax 43 (0)2734 2422
email schloss@gobelsburg.at
internet www.gobelsburg.at
estate 35 ha, 25% Riesling
best vineyards Heiligenstein, Gaisberg

The original castle at Gobelsburg was built in 1074 and replaced by a baroque mansion in the eighteenth century. In 1740, the owner ran out of money, became a monk, and gave all his possessions (and debts) to the Cistercian Zwettl Abbey, which had already acquired vineyards around Heiligenstein and Gobelsburg by 1174. The monks made wine until in 1995 the abbot sold a sixty-year lease to Michael Moosbacher and his wife Eva. In no time, work in the vineyards had started, the cellars were cleared out, and new 2,500-litre oak barrels were installed. Alte Reben is from 60-year-old vines in the Gaisberg vineyard, which has sandy soil, volcanic rocks, and limestone. The 2000 had an apricot flavour (a character I find in wines from this vineyard) and was emphatic and rich. The vines in this plot have darker, thicker stems and very aromatic grapes due to continuous massal selection over centuries. Heiligenstein 2000, from granite and volcanic soil, had greater structure; deep fruit in harmony with its mineral character. Heiligenstein Riesling 1971 was pure-gold, with absolute purity: theosophical, gentle, and mineral.

Weingut Joseph Hirsch

Hauptstrasse 76, A-3493 Kammern Langenlois
tel 43 (0)2735 2460, fax 43 (0)2735 36089
email info@weingut-hirsch.at
internet www.weingut-hirsch.at
estate 20 ha
best vineyards Heiligenstein, Gaisberg, Lamm

where yeasts from the previous year are added to continue the fermentation over a long period. We tasted the 2000 vintage, starting with Steinmassl, a vineyard with granite soil: it was flowery and elegant, with fine acidity, easy to drink. The greatest vineyard of the Kamptal, Heiligenstein, is where Willi has most Riesling. The Heiligenstein Lyra ("lyre system") was richer by far than the standard version, with great extract and the potential to develop.

Joseph Hirsch and his son Johannes are a dynamic duo. Riesling is best in the upper parts of their vineyards because the granite and volcanic rock is closer to the surface; the microclimate is also better.

A neighbour's twenty-five goats provide manure for the vines. There are four selective pickings during the vintage and whole bunches are pressed at low pressure, followed by a long fermentation in stainless steel or large oak barrels with indigenous yeasts. It is the first Riesling estate in Austria to use 100 per cent Stelvin screwcaps; they have been a great success.

Heiligenstein 2000 was ready to drink and had a perfume of wild roses with a flavour of light honey on the palate – but with power and precision. 1998 was powerful, clear in taste, with a fine, dry finish and less botrytis.

Gaisberg comes from old vines, and the 2002 had a fine Riesling nose, plenty of fruit and depth from the brown earth and mineral terroir in this vineyard.

Weingut Jurtschitsch Sonnhof

Rudolfstrasse 39, A-3550 Langenlois
tel 43 (0)2734 2116, fax 43 (0)2734 211611
email office@jurtschitsch.com
internet www.jurtschitsch.com
estate 55 ha
best vineyard Zöbinger Heiligenstein

The Sonnhof farmhouse was built in 1541. The courtyard leads to the modern vinification centre, which is built into the vineyard slope and is on four floors. The view looks over the town of Langenlois.

Josef Jurtschitsch bought the Weingut in 1868, and today it is run by three brothers: Paul the winemaker; Karl, sales and marketing; and Edwin, vineyard manager. In 1972, the vineyards were all converted to an ecological farming system.

There are a galaxy of different Rieslings made here and the following stood out: Alte Reben 2000 had plenty of fruit backed by good concentration and low acidity. Zöbinger Heiligenstein 2000 was

delicious, sober, and aromatic, more suited for ageing. The sweeter Heiligenstein Auslese 2000 suggested it would become an elegant and subtle Riesling, with precise acidity and finesse.

Weingut Fred Loimer

Haindorfer Vögerlweg, A-3550 Langenlois
tel 43 (0)2734 2239, fax 43 (0)2734 22394
email weingut@loimer.at
internet www.loimer.at
estate 25 ha, 25% Riesling
best vineyard Seeberg, Steinmassl

Alas, I did not manage to visit Fred Loimer, a dynamic young grower. In 1999, he bought the former Haindorf Castle cellar, and Andreas Burghardt designed a futuristic, minimalist "black box" over the baroque cellar. I have been impressed with his Rieslings from Steinmassl (fermented in oak barrels) and Seeberg (fermented in stainless steel), both on sandy loam soils over granite and gneiss.

Kremstal

Weingut Martin Nigl

Priel 8, A-3541 Senftenberg
tel 43 (0)2719 2609, fax 43 (0)2719 26094
email weingut.nigl@wvnet.at
internet www.weingutnigl.at
estate 25 ha
best vineyards Piri, Hochäcker

Martin Nigl took over this estate from his father in 1987, resigned from the Krems cooperative, and started to make his own wines. His success with Riesling and Grüner Veltliner has been remarkable. His late-picked Rieslings from the Piri and Hochäcker vineyards are labelled "Privat" and have the quality of a fine Wachau Smaragd. I have not been able to visit the estate, nor have I tasted enough wines to make judgements, but those I have tasted have been fine, including a young, but scintillating Piri Privat 2002.

Weingut Undhof Salomon

Understrasse 10, A-3504 Krems-Stein
tel 43 (0)2732 83226, fax 43 (0)2732 8322678
email salomon@undhof.at
internet www.undhof.at
estate 20 ha, 50% Riesling
best vineyards Pfaffenberg, Kögl

The estate has belonged to the Salomon family
since 1792, Undhof having been the farm of the
Und monastery before its dissolution. In the 1920s,
this was one of the first estates in Austria to produce
and bottle dry Rieslings. I was particularly impressed
with its 2002 vintage Rieslings. Kögl is north of
Krems, and Pfaffenberg is contiguous with Wachau;
both are steep and terraced, and both have similar
gneiss and schist soil. Both were immaculately dry
and refreshing, and the Kögl Reserve picked two
or three weeks later was the equivalent of a Wachau
Smaragd, with great concentration, to be kept for
a few years.

Weingut Dr. Unger

Kirchengasse 14, A-3511 Furth bei Göttweig
tel 43 (0)2732 85895, fax 43 (0)2732 6601
email weingut@drunger.at
internet www.drunger.at
estate 40 ha
best vineyard Silberbügel

After Dr. Unger's death, his young daughter
Petra, who is more like a ballerina than a winemaker,
took over. All her wines are expressive and beautifully
crafted, especially her Eiswein. Her Rieslings are rich,
concentrated, and smooth, especially those from
the Silberbügel vineyard, which has rich loess over
a granite sub-soil.

The Classic Riesling has a maximum of 12.5 alc.,
and the 2001 had spritz and fine acidity. The Reserve
2001 was as clear and refreshing as a mountain
stream; in contrast with the 2000 that had 90 Oechsle
and 14 alc., with ten per cent botrytis – yet was very
dry. The 1998 showed great maturity and breadth;

and the Trockenbeerenauslese 2000 (170 Oechsle
and 10.2 alc.) had unbelievable concentration and
breeding, with overtones of dried apricots and honey.

Vienna

Weingut Mayer am Pfarrplatz

Pfarrplatz 2, A-1190 Wien
tel 43 (0)1370 3361, fax 43 (0)1370 4714
email mayer@pfarrplatz.at
internet www.mayer.pfarrplatz.at
estate 27 ha, 50% Riesling
best vineyard Nussberger Preussen

This is the most famous *Heurige* ("wine-grower's
inn") in Austria; Beethoven wrote part of his
Ninth Symphony here in 1817. It looks quite
small, but it can absorb 500 people inside and
600 outside. Underneath the house is a cellar
to hold the year's production, nearly half of which
is drunk on the premises. Franz Mayer's Australian
son-in-law, Wagga and Roseworthy Colleges,
manages the estate.

The Nussberg slope is on chalky limestone soil
and retains water throughout the summer; the best
Rieslings have great charm and integrity. Meyer's
Vienna Classic Riesling 2001 is a fine example of this.

Weingut Stift Klosterneuburg

Rathausplatz 24, A-3400 Klosterneuburg
tel 43 (0)2243 411
email weingut@stift-klosterneuburg.at
internet www.stift-klosterneuburg.at
estate 100 ha, 20% Riesling
best vineyard Franzenhauser

The monastery was founded by Margrave Leopold,
Austria's national saint, in 1114. Franzhauser
is a steep vineyard overlooking Vienna and
Klosterneuburg has Austria's first and most
important wine school.

Australia

Australia

In Sydney, on January 24, 1791, two bunches of grapes were picked – the first in the country. Between 1820 and 1840, vineyards were planted in most of the temperate regions of Australia. In South Australia, the arrival in the Barossa Valley in the 1840s of the first German Lutheran *émigrés* gave an impetus to the planting of Riesling. Indeed, it was the most widely planted premium white grape in Australia until 1992, when it was overtaken by Chardonnay.

The very popularity of Riesling in Australia caused feeble imitations to be labelled Riesling. It was only in 2001 that it was forbidden to label other grapes as "Riesling" on cask (or bag-in-the-box) wines. Hardy's, in particular, one of the giants of Australian wine, fought to the bitter end against this change in the law. There was one case of mislabelling that could almost be forgiven. The climate in New South Wales's Hunter Valley is too hot for Riesling, and the names of both Semillon and Chardonnay meant absolutely nothing in the Australia of the 1950s. So from 1960, Lindemans' winemaker, Karl Stockhausen, used the names "Hunter River Chablis" for early picked Semillon, and "Hunter River Riesling" for later-picked Semillon, with some Verdelho, Traminer, Trebbiano, and Chardonnay added for good measure. After about ten years this wonderful "Riesling" lost its original green, herbaceous acidity and developed incredible complexity.

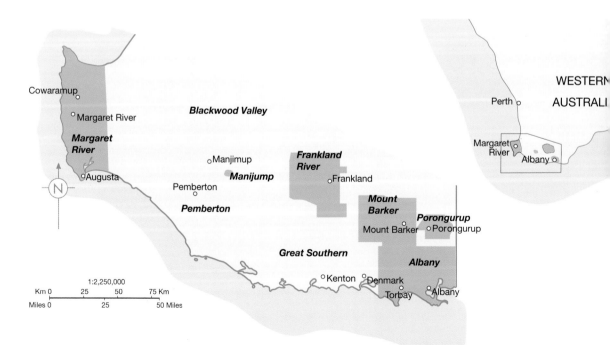

There used to be a simple way to spot an Australian Riesling in a blind tasting – it smelled phenolic, of paraffin. Three reasons have been suggested. Firstly, the ripening period is short compared with that in cooler climates. Secondly, thick skins might give phenolic tastes – the skins of Coonawarra Riesling can be seven times as thick as those of Mosel Riesling. Thirdly, Riesling grapes are averse to being picked by machine, as is quite common in the flatter New World vineyards – the eventual wines can lose their identity. Careful management of the vineyards, harvest techniques, and cellar practices, plus the use of stelvin screwcaps have solved these problems; and in theory, the latter will double the life of the Rieslings.

Australian Rieslings in general are one-dimensional compared with those of Europe, and this is part of their appeal. Tasmanian Riesling is particularly light and flowery; Great Southern has mineral hints and lime fruit; Eden Valley is steely and puritan; Clare Valley has lime fruit, purity, elegance, length, and power. Victorian Rieslings are too diverse to fit into any of these categories.

The manner in which Australia's finest dry Rieslings mature in bottle is quite different from that of their European counterparts. They are actually intended for drinking young, but as the primary fruit character disappears a certain complexity replaces it. I do not see this as being an improvement in the flavour of the wine, but rather as a subtle and academic change in its character that makes it fascinating in a vertical tasting. Whereas the young wines demand to be enjoyed with food, old ones taste better on their own. European dry Rieslings develop and improve

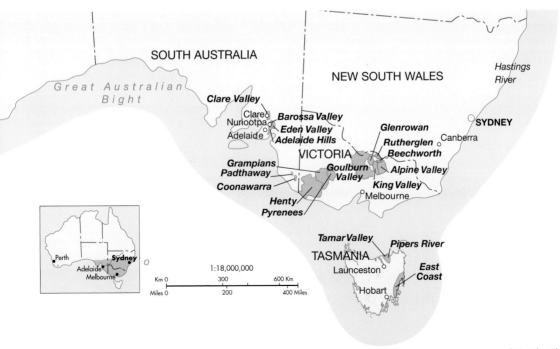

The elegant flower
of the agave adding
drama to Henschke's
vineyards in the
Eden Valley

with time more radically and last longer. Australian Rieslings of the early seventies have lasted well; some were bottled under screwcaps.

South Australia

Nearly half the grapes of Australia are pressed in South Australia, and mostly in the vast wineries in the Barossa Valley. This includes grapes that are trucked-in from other states, especially from the great mass-production regions, Murray River in Victoria and Riverina in New South Wales. Over half the grapes in South Australia itself come from the Riverland, also on the Murray. These wines are the basis for brands labelled "produce of South Australia" or "South-East Australia".

The Barossa Valley, at 230 metres (750 feet) altitude, is one of the hottest wine regions in Australia, and the contiguous Eden Valley is positively cool at 550 metres (1,800 feet). The vineyards of Barossa Valley are stretched out over about thirty-two kilometres by ten kilometres (twenty miles by six miles) at the widest point, interspersed with regiments of stainless-steel tanks every few hundred yards along the main road. Almost all the vineyards are on the flat valley floor, and the hills that separate Barossa from Eden Valley lie soft and naked in the summer sun. The soil is really too rich for Riesling, and the grapes must be watched carefully and picked early to prevent them from losing acidity. Tartaric acid can, of course, be added in Australia. The wines must be blended with those of Eden Valley or Clare Valley to have a balance of elegance and acidity.

Eden Valley is hardly a valley at all. Instead, it is a series of hills and plateaux from about 400 to 550 metres (1,300 to 1,800 feet) altitude. The vineyards are spread out and isolated from each other, partly because localized spring and autumn frosts dictate where vines may be planted. In other places there is not enough water or the aspect does not allow Riesling to ripen. The soil is poor and stony in places, with quartz and schist; this suits Riesling, which is the most widely planted grape in the region. The cool climate gives freshness to the wines and the ripening period is much longer than in the Barossa, and acidity levels higher.

In my opinion, the finest New World Rieslings are from the Clare Valley. Clare Valley always makes me think of Lord of the Rings: Clare is the Shires where the Hobbits live and the rest of Australia is Middle Earth. Clare is a region of narrow lanes with hedges and bushy-topped trees, and people who all know each other. The valley – or rather "valleys" because there are several – have huge variations of soil. In one vineyard, such as Florita in Watervale, you can find Riesling cheek-by-jowl with Shiraz on different soils. Watervale has predominately limestone soil, which is good for Riesling. Polish Hill River has poor soil with shales packed with minerals and is even better. There are also big differences in microclimate. It was not until the 1950s that it was realized that the climate was so suited to Riesling.

Coonawarra and Padthaway are dominated by the big companies and a certain amount of Riesling is produced in both regions. Their dry Rieslings tend to be rather heavy and dull, but there some great botrytized wines, especially from Padthaway.

Victoria

Superb wines are produced all over Victoria, mainly by relatively small wineries, whose wines are not easy to find outside Australia. One result is that none of the major companies can control wine production and each winery or estate has developed its own vineyards and its own market. Fine Riesling vineyards are scattered from the mountains in the far northeast to the sea in the far southwest.

Western Australia

The ancient rocky hills of the Porongurups, the gentle rolling slopes around the small town of Mount Barker, and the broad stoney hills near Frankland River are all sub-regions of the Great Southern region and homes to some of the most inspiring Rieslings in Australia. Winters are cold and rainy, and summers are hot, reaching 32°C (89°F), with cool nights of 6°C (43°F) – perfect for dry Riesling, and an occasional fine botrytized style when the winter rains come sooner than expected. Leeuwin Estate is the only winery to own an internationally recognized Riesling vineyard in the Margaret River region. The other wineries in this region, and also further north towards Perth, consider the climate to be too hot and source their Riesling from Great Southern. Most grapes are picked at night when cool, but they tend to lose freshness when they are transported over long distances and the eventual wines can be dull. Nevertheless, Western Australia produces a mere four per cent of Australia's wines, but ninteen per cent of its premium quality wines!

Tasmania

Andrew Pirie, doctor of viticultual research, founded Pipers Brook Vineyards in 1974. He was convinced that Riesling and Pinot Noir would make fine, subtle wines in Tasmania – quite different from those of mainland Australia. They are certainly some of the most delicate in Australia. The climate is cool, the ripening period is long, the soils are volcanic, and climate changes are improving the ripening of the grapes. Currently, major investments are being made in the existing wineries.

South Australia

Annie's Lane

Annie's Lane, Watervale, SA 5452 (Clare Valley)
tel 61 (08) 8562 1955, fax 61 (08) 8562 4127
email cellardoor@annieslane.com.au
internet www.annieslane.com.au

Annie's Lane is part of the giant Beringer Blass Wine Estates group. Annie's Lane runs along the brow of the hill, at about 400 metres (1,300 feet) altitude, that divides cosy Watervale from the exposed valley to the east. I have not visited it but I have always enjoyed Annie's Lane Riesling. Recently it has launched a premium Coppertrail Riesling.

Grosset

King Steet, Auburn, SA 5451 (Clare Valley)
tel 61 (08) 8849 2175, fax 61 (08) 8849 2292
email info@grosset.com.au
internet www.grosset.com.au

Jeffrey Grosset's Polish Hill is agreed to be the finest Riesling of Australia, and his Watervale Riesling is also greatly sought-after. His partner is Stephanie Toole of Mount Horrocks. Their wines are quite different, although he is her consultant winemaker.

The Molloy vineyard has been the major source for Polish Hill. The soil is shale, rich in minerals but very cold and poor in nutriments. And, with reduced yields, he can only make about 2,500 cases a year from 7 ha of vines. Watervale soil is red clay over limestone and, given the right conditions, a small quantity of sweet wine can also be made with very late-picked and/or botrytis-affected Riesling grapes.

Jeffrey's commitment is enormous. He has the most advanced canopy-management techniques, and he uses minimal irrigation, and virtually no chemicals in pest and disease control. Picking is by hand. The whole bunches are gently pressed at 10°C (50°F) and kept cool for two days until the fermentation starts, all in stainless steel. After time on the light lees, the wine is bottled with Stelvin screwcaps.

As president of the wine-growers of Clare, Jeffrey proposed that Stelvin screwcaps be used on all their Rieslings; sixteen estates agreed. Riesling producers in many other countries have followed suit.

In 2003, I tasted a series of Polish Hill Rieslings. The 2002 was still reductive on the nose but had fine mineral elegance – perfectly structured, with fine, balanced acidity; perhaps his best vintage ever? 2001 was beginning to move into the intermediate stage between primary fruit and mature aromas. 2000 had precise fresh lime on the nose, fine acidity, and was absolutely straight; lovely. 1999 had hints of banana on the nose, with sweet fruit and a dry finish: a brilliant wine. 1998 had a flowery bouquet, the acidity becoming softer and the flavour rounder but the finish was still positively dry; a complete wine at its peak. 1997's fruit was dominant and the acidity seemed slightly lower, making the wine a little less intense. 1996 was mineral and rich with a clean, dry finish. 1995 was more golden in colour, with flavours of lime fruit and minerals and a polished finish. 1994 was a lovely older wine with a touch of botrytis. 1992 was a gentle, feminine old Riesling, full of flavours.

Henschke

Henschke Road, Keyneton, SA 5353 (Eden Valley)
tel 61 (08) 8564 8223, fax 61 (08) 8564 8294
email info@henschke.com.au
internet www.henschke.com.au

In 1862, Joseph Henschke from Germany planted some vines in North Rhine, as Keyneton was then called. Stephen is the fifth generation and he took over the business in 1979, after having studied at the Geisenheim Wine Institute. His wife Prue is a viticulturist. They have about 100 ha of vines, of which 26 are their famous Shiraz and 19 are Riesling.

Tilly's Vineyard Riesling 2002 was delightfully refreshing. Julius Eden Valley 2000 was from three separate vineyards and had an exciting green-apple flavour on the front of the palate, with fresh, brisk acidity and fine balance (7.2 g.a., 12.5 alc.).

Lenswood Green's Hill 2000, from the cooler Adelaide Hills vineyard, with loam and shale soil, was more Australian in style with more body, fruit, and acidity (8.1 g.a., 12.8 alc.). Eden Valley 1990 Museum Release was a shade of yellow, showing its maturity, with a gentle, perfumed, flowery bouquet; bone-dry and with classic Riesling flavours. Eden Valley Noble Rot Riesling 1998 was picked in late May and had botrytis flavours of honey and dried apricots.

Jim Barry Wines

Main North Road, Clare, SA 5453 (Clare Valley)
tel 61 (08) 8842 2261, fax 61 (08) 8842 4380
email jbwines@jimbarry.com
internet www.jimbarry.com

This is a family enterprise founded in 1959. In 1964, Jim bought 31 ha of land, 3.5 of which were the original Armagh vineyard of old Shiraz vines. He was also fortunate to be able to buy the main part of the Florita vineyard in Watervale from Lindemans. Florita Riesling 2000 was fresh, with a strong terroir character and needed time to develop. 1996 was herbal on the nose, with fine balance of fruit and acidity. 1995 had quite a deep colour, showing good maturity. 1994 had great depth, acidity in balance, and a sense of sweetness, without being sweet. 1993 was luscious and yet dry. 1984 was a great old wine, with flavours of dried apricots.

Knappstein Wines

2 Pioneer Avenue, Clare, SA 5453 (Clare Valley)
tel 61 (08) 8842 2600, fax 61 (08) 8842 3831
email cellardoor@knappsteinwines.com.au
internet www.knappsteinwines.com.au

Tim Knappstein founded this company in 1976, and after some years sold it to Brian Croser's Petaluma. Andrew Hardy runs the estate, which is quite

Geoffrey Grosset's old stone winery in Clare Valley: sold out as usual

separate from Petaluma's own vineyards in Clare. I have tasted many vintages of its dry Riesling and they are always delicious. The Knappstein Hand-Picked Riesling 2002 tasted in London had a clear lemony nose, plenty of fruit, and beautiful balance, while not being as dry as some Clare wines.

We tasted some botrytized Rieslings at the property. The 1999 was the first made since 1992 and it had a typical Clare bouquet of lime and wild flowers, backed up by delicious honey and raisin flavours. The 1989 had pronounced botrytis, but was not at all heavy – a wine to enjoy on its own or with cheese rather than with something sweet. The 1979, despite being ullaged, had wonderful flavour, richness, and acidity in balance, and was undoubtedly the finest of the old wines.

Leasingham

7 Dominic Street, Clare, SA 5453 (Clare Valley)
tel 61 (08) 8842 2555, fax 61 (08) 8842 3293
email customers@hardys.com.au
internet www.www.leasingham-wines.com.au

The Stanley Wine Company was founded in 1893 and installed in The Clare Jam Factory. By 1911, J.H. Knappstein, the largest owner in Clare Valley, had bought out his partners, and the family retained control until they sold it to Heinz (of beans fame) in 1971. The Knappsteins who worked there, including chief winemaker, Tim , were retained. Meanwhile, the label was changed to Leasingham, the name of the village that is the centre of the vineyard holdings. In 1976, Tim set up his own company just round the corner (see above).

Although this is a large company in the vast Hardy empire, it produces some fine Clare Valley wines, especially from its old vines. I have tasted a number of vintages of the Leasingham Classic Clare Bin 7 Riesling, of which the 2001 vintage was fresh and racy: dry, with a juicy, appetizing flavour.

Mitchell

Hughes Park Road, Senenhill via Clare, SA 5453
(Clare Valley)
tel 61 (08) 8843 4258, fax 61 (08) 8843 4340
email mitchell@mitchellwines.com
internet www.mitchellwines.com

Andrew Mitchell's wines are very traditional.
Most of the Riesling comes from his vineyard
on the exposed eastern side of the hills at Watervale,
where it is so cold in winter that the vineyard
workers dubbed it Alcatraz. Andrew's Watervale
Riesling was first made in 1977 and has always
been built to last. The 2000 was fresh, with a strong
personality that suggested it has great staying power.
1992 was a lovely, creamy Riesling that left a gentle,
harmonious aftertaste.

Mount Horrocks

The Old Railway Station, Curling Street, Auburn,
SA 5451 (Clare Valley)
tel 61 (08) 8849 2243, fax 61 (08) 8849 2243
email sales@mounthorrocks.com
internet www.mounthorrocks.com

Stephanie Toole is often described as "a little
dynamo." Her Rieslings are as concentrated,
but not as precise, as those of her partner Jeffrey
Grosset (see above). She believes in relating her
wine styles to food, to great effect.

Mount Horrocks Watervale Riesling is from the
Peglidis vineyard, where no irrigation is necessary
and the grapes are picked by hand. Watervale
Riesling 2000, 2001, and 2002 are grapey, vivacious,
and immediate. Stephanie also makes a wonderful
dessert wine – Cordon Cut Riesling. The canes
(branches) are partly cut and the grapes are left
hanging on the vines for up to eight weeks to
dehydrate. The 2001 was concentrated, firm, and
super-ripe, with overtones of oranges and perfect
acidity: wonderful to drink with soft and blue
cheeses and mixed autumn berries – or on its own.

Orlando Wines

Barossa Valley Way, Rowland Flat, SA 5352 (Barossa)
tel 61 (08) 8521 3111, fax 61 (08) 8521 3100
email contact_us@orlando.com.au
internet www.orlandowyndhamgroup.com

Jacob's Creek Riesling and the premium wines
St Helga and Steingarten are produced here. Jacob's
Creek is the original Riesling vineyard planted by
Johann Gramp, the founder of the business, in 1847.
Today it is the most successful brand of Riesling in
the world. A wonderful Riesling tasting was set up
in 2001 by Bernard Hickin, the white winemaker,
and I was looking forward to meeting (again) John
Vickery (see Richmond Grove, page 141).

Orlando has 100 ha in the Eden Valley, the
St Helga vineyard is at 400 to 450 metres (1,300 to
1,480 feet) altitude. We tasted eleven vintages back
to 1972 and they were a revelation. At two extremes –
the 2000, with a Stelvin screwcap, had a typical lime-
juice nose and was crisp with good acidity, needing
time; the 1972 was rich, aromatic, and spicy, with
honey on the finish.

Steingarten ("stone garden") is an isolated
2-ha vineyard on the north face of the steep hill
above Rowland Flat at 490 metres (1,600 feet) altitude,
on schist and sandy limestone. We tasted seven
vintages and two stood out: 2000 had a bouquet
of orange blossom and was wonderfully complex,
with mineral character, and 1991 was brilliant, soft
voluptuous, with fruit wrapped into its firm structure.

Petaluma Clare Estate

Spring Gully Road, Piccadilly, SA 5151
(Adelaide Hills and Clare Valley)
tel 61 (08) 8339 4122, fax 61 (08) 8339 5253
email petaluma@petaluma.com.au
internet www.petaluma.com.au

Winemaker Brian Croser has a passion for Riesling.
The love and care that is given to his Hanlin Hill
vineyard in Clare Valley allows the terroir to shine

through the primary fruit flavours and fresh acidity when the wines are young, and through their softer elegance as they grow older.

The 2002 had the characteristic Clare lime and lemon nose, with a long well-balanced flavour – a sheer delight now, it will develop over many years. Brian says that it is as fine as 1980, his greatest vintage. 1999 was a botrytis year, and the wine was quite pale in colour, with a strong lime nose and flavour tinged with botrytis honey. 1992 had a lovely gold colour, lots of lime on the nose, and was long on the palate, with a positive botrytis flavour and a soft and seductive finish. 1982 had a brilliant orange-gold colour and at first the nose gave the impression of sweetness, but it was actually dry – succulent and elegant with a lovely finish. These are just five of the twelve vintages we tasted but they show how fine Petaluma Rieslings are and how they develop with time.

Richmond Grove

Para Road, Tanunda, SA 5352 (Barossa Valley)
tel 61 (08) 8563 2184, fax 61 (08) 8563 2804
internet www.richmondgrovewines.com

Since 1955 Richmond Grove has been run by "the Master of Australian Riesling" John Vickery. Despite successive company take-overs (Richmond Grove is owned by Orlando), John's dedication to Riesling has taken the estate from ordinary to great. Richmond Grove Barossa Valley Riesling 2000 under Stelvin screwcap was full of fresh fruit – the Barossa grapes were picked very early due to a hot February.

John Vickery considers Watervale to be the village with the best terroir for Riesling in the Clare Valley. Watervale 2000 was intensely concentrated and full-bodies, with mineral and tropical flavours. The 1996, from the famous Florita vineyard, was a great Riesling, perfectly fresh and so harmonious that it could not get any better, but would keep for ages.

Skillogalee

Off Hughes Park Road, Sevenhill via Clare,
SA 5453 (Clare Valley)
tel 61 (08) 8843 4311, fax 61 (08) 8843 4343
email skilly@chariot.net.au
internet www.skillogalee.com.au

David and Diana Palmer came from England and bought this winery at the end of the 1980s. They have 8 ha of mature Riesling vines at 500 metres (1,640 feet) altitude in the little Skilly Valley. Pruning and picking are both carried out by hand.

The 2002 was pure Clare: lime on the nose, penetrating intensity and length; the 2001, a pretty bouquet of flowers with style and elegance and only 11.5 alc. 2000 had clear fruit and Riesling precision; 1996 was fresh and lively. The 1995 had sweet fruit on the palate, with a dry finish.

Tollana

Tanunda Road, Nuriootpa, SA 5355 (Barossa Valley)
tel 61 (08) 8560 9408, fax 61 (08) 8562 2494
internet www.tollana.australianwines.com.au

Tollana, part of Southcorp, has more than 200 ha in Eden Valley. The 2000 was intensely fresh, with fine fruit; 1995 was very ripe and showed the mature creaminess unique to mature, dry Riesling. 1994 was even richer and more concentrated. 1998 Coonawarra Botrytized Riesling was the finest Coonawarra Riesling I had tasted – fully mature, with barley-sugar and raisin flavours balanced by fine acidity.

Wolf Blass

Bilyara Vineyards, Sturt Highway, Nuriootpa, SA 5355 (Barossa Valley)
tel 61 (08) 8562 1955, fax 61 (08) 8562 4127
internet www.beringerblass.com.au/brands/wolfblass

Wendy Stuckey and Kirsten Glaester are the white winemakers at Wolf Blass's winery with its vast forest of stainless-steel tanks outside Nuriootpa. Beringer Blass owns 450 ha in Clare Valley, and most

The unique timber winery of Chateau Tahbilk is a national monument and still makes great wine from vines planted in 1860

of the grapes are picked by machine before dawn. Those for premium wines are picked by hand.

Yellow Label 1999 Riesling had extrovert lime and lemon flavours yet was refined at the same time. Red Label 1999, sourced from Watervale and Polish Hill River in Clare Valley, was deliciously fresh with only 11.5 alc. Gold Label, a blend of Clare Valley and Eden Valley grapes, was even lighter, with bright fruit and a faintly Germanic style.

Yalumba

Eden Valley Road, Angaston, SA 3393 (Barossa Valley)
tel 61 (08) 8561 3200, fax 61 (08) 8561 3393
email info@yalumba.com
internet www.yalumba.com

In 1849, Samuel Smith, an English brewer, settled in Angaston, on the border between the Barossa and Eden Valleys. He bought 12 ha of land on the Barossa side and ambitiously named it Yalumba ("all the land

fruit. Its acidity made it was ready to drink or capable of keeping for up to ten years. The 2000, despite difficult weather conditions, was a triumph: fresh and crisp on first taste, it developed wonderful complexity on the finish.

Pewsey Vale Contours Museum Release comes from the oldest vines and is released after four or five years in bottle. 1995 was green and gold, and after five years in bottle it was just beginning to wake-up. It had the potential to last for many years, with finesse and elegance and intensity and great length.

Colin Heggie was a typical Australian bushwacker, who owned and grazed hillside land. Hill-Smith had set his sights on Heggie's farm, and in 1971 he sold most of his Barossa vines to finance the purchase. The 48-ha vineyard was planted up to 570 metres (1,870 feet), with 10 ha of Riesling. Heggies 2000 had a particularly flowery bouquet, with a faint mineral and salt flavour on the palate.

In certain years botrytis occurs in the vineyards, but in 1999 Louisa Rose, the brilliant winemaker here, had to buy-in botrytized grapes. Her Eden Valley Late Harvest 1999 was impeccably clean on the palate, with strong raisin flavours.

Victoria

Best's Wines Estate

Western Highway, Great Western, Victoria 3377 (Grampians)
tel 61 (03) 5356 2250, fax 61 (03) 5356 2430
email info@bestswines.com
internet www.bestswines.com

In 1866, Henry Best decided that there was more money to be made from selling wine to gold-miners than from digging for gold. When the gold rush came to an end he built the original cellar at Best's Wines Estate.

Victoria Riesling is a blend of wines from the estate's Concongella and Olive Grove blocks: it is a gentle and refreshing wine that keeps beautifully for up to ten years.

around" in aboriginal). In 1989, Wyndham Hill-Smith and his sons Robert and Sam took the helm. In 1961, Hill-Smith had bought and replanted vineyards in Pewsey Vale in the Eden hills, with vines that were sited at up to 500 metres (1,640 feet). The schistose soil was ideal for Riesling, and vines were planted in contours to reduce erosion and steer frost down into the valley.

Of the total 50 ha planted here, 30 ha are Riesling. 2002 Pewsey Vale Riesling had a bouquet of wild flowers, with lime freshness and perfectly integrated

Brown Brothers

Snow Road, Milawa, Victoria 3678 (King Valley)
tel 61 (03) 5720 5500, fax 61 (03) 5720 5511
email browns@brown-brothers.com.au
internet www.brown-brothers.com.au

This remarkable family enterprise was founded in 1885,
but it took a leap forward when John Brown found
a farm on a plateau at Whitlands at 750 metres (2,460
feet) above King Valley. This and the neighbouring
farm gave him a possible 140 ha of volcanic soil in a
cool climate, where first Riesling and then other grape
varieties have produced subtle and individual wines.
Whitlands Riesling 1995 had real crispness and the
ideal balance of fruit and acidity. Family Reserve
Riesling 1994 had more power and length, with the
potential to develop in bottle. Beerenauslese 1995,
which came from the Milawa vineyard in the valley
near the winery, had terrific concentration from
botrytis, with lemon acidity and orange marmalade
fruit that lingered on the palate. Family Reserve
Noble Riesling 1985, also from the Milawa vineyard,
was soft and luscious, with great concentration
and botrytized honey flavours, but was not cloying
because, rare in Australia, it had only 9.5 alc.
This wine, first made in 1962, was the first botrytized
Australian wine to be sold commercially.

Chateau Tahbilk

Goulburn Valley Highway, Tahbilk, Victoria 3607
(Goulburn Valley)
tel 61 (03) 5794 2555, fax 61 (03) 5794 2360
email johnpurbrick@tahbilk.com.au
internet www.tahbilk.com.au

Founded in 1860, this must be one of the most
beautiful historic wineries in the New World. It looks
like a eighteenth century wooden church (see page
142). The estate has Shiraz vines, planted over 140
years ago, and its Riesling tradition is almost as long.
The 1996 Riesling was fresh and lively, dry yet rich,
and well-balanced when I visited in 1998.

Delatite

Stoneys Road, Mansfield, Victoria 3722
(Central Victoria Mountain Country Region)
tel 61 (03) 5775 2922, fax 61 (03) 5775 2911
email info@delatitewinery.com.au
internet www.delatitewinery.com.au

This is an isolated winery set against the great
backcloth of the Australian Alps. Brown Brothers
helped Robert Ritchie to establish 20 ha of vines here,
and bought his grapes. Eventually the Ritchies built
a winery, with their daughter Rosalind as winemaker
and her brother David as viticulturist. The vineyards
are on steep slopes of weathered ironstone with traces
of copper and minerals, and the cold nights at these
high altitudes make for a long ripening period – the
vintage continues to the middle of May. I love the
delicate, fresh but intense quality of the Riesling.

Mount Langi Ghiran Vineyards

Warrack Road, Buangor, Victoria 3375 (Grampians)
tel 61 (03) 5354 3207, fax 61 (03) 5354 3277
email sales@langi.com.au
internet www.langi.com.au

Mount Langi Ghiran (the home of the yellow-tailed
cockatoo) is perched on a 450-metre (1,476-feet)
cliff face. It is a cool-climate site, with loam and
red clay soil peppered with ironstone, and quartz
overlaid with granite sand – perfect for Riesling.
It was planted in 1978 on the lower part of the hill.
The vineyard has been organic since 1991.

The grapes are late-picked, fermented at 10–14°C
(50–57°F) in stainless steel for about six weeks, then
left on the lees for five months before bottling,
without filtering. The quality has been consistent
in every vintage. The 1996 had an intense nose,
green-apple acidity, flavours hinting at Alsace,
and a relatively high 13 alc. – a great wine.

Barrie Smith and Judi Cullam are the owners of The Frankland Estate
in Great Southern – and 7,000 sheep

Mitchelton

Mitchellstown via Nagambie, Victoria 3608
(Goulburn Valley)
tel 61 (03) 5794 2710, fax 61 (03) 5794 2615
email mitchelton@mitchelton.com.au
internet www.mitchelton.com.au

The tower above the winery here, with its tall, pointed Javanese temple roof, is visible from miles away. The vineyard for Blackwood Park Riesling was planted in 1978, so the vines are now old enough to give this dry wine depth of flavour and fruit, balanced with fine acidity. Classic Release is the same wine of the best vintages, released when fully mature, and develops exotic fruit flavours, with a touch of honey.

Seppelt Great Western

Moyston Road, Great Western, Victoria 3377
(Grampians)
tel 61 (03) 5361 2239, fax 61 (03) 5361 2200
internet www.seppelt.com.au

The star white wine is Drumborg Riesling, full-flavoured and distinguished. It benefits from a cool climate and cold sea breezes from the Antarctic.

Western Australia

Alkoomi

Wingebellup Road, Frankland, WA 6396 (Great Southern)
tel 61 (08) 8556 2229, fax 61 (08) 8556 2284
email alkoomi@wn.com.au
internet www.alkoomiwines.com.au

In 1971 Merv Lange and his wife Judy planted their first vines, at 360 metres (1,181 feet), reasoning that "someone will buy our grapes". The first vintage was 1976 and they have never looked back. Their Rieslings are among the finest in Western Australia and on a par with those of Clare Valley. The 2000 and 1999 were wonderfully fresh and vigorous; the 1991 and 1988 were vibrant, with great ripeness and body.

Castle Rock Estate

Porongurup Road, Porongurup, WA 6324
(Great Southern)
tel 61 (08) 9853 1035, fax 61 (08) 9853 1010
email diletti@castlerockestate.com.au
internet www.castlerockestate.com.au

In 1981, Angelo Diletti cleared the red gum trees in this cool 350-metre (1,148-feet) site near the landmark Castle Rock. The weathered granite soil and sea breezes are the two key factors in shaping the style and quality of his Rieslings. 2000 had an elegant lime and lemon character with plenty of acidity. 1994 and 1993 still had the same lovely lemon character.

Frankland Estate

Frankland Road, Frankland, WA 6396 (Great Southern)
tel 61 (08) 9855 1544, fax 61 (08) 9855 1549
email info@franklandestate.com.au
internet www.franklandestate.com.au

Barrie Smith and Judi Cullum planted their first vines in 1988 on Isolation Ridge at 270 metres (886 feet). Four separate parcels of Riesling are pick by by hand. The 2000 was very with powerful, with grapefruit on the nose and beautiful balance. The 1999 had a touch of sweetness and fine structure: an Alsace Riesling with an Australian accent.

Goundrey

Muir Highway, Mount Barker, WA 6324 (Great Southern)
tel 61 (08) 9851 1777, fax 61 (08) 9851 1997
email info@goundreywines.com.au
internet www.goundreywines.com.au

Jack Bendit, a businessman from Perth, bought this estate in 1995 and invested heavily, increasing the production by a multiple of four by 1999. It has 175 ha of fine vineyards in the valley and on a slope opposite the winery. Grapes are sourced in Great Southern and in Pemberton. The 2000 Riesling Reserve showed crisp, green-apple fruit and fine acidity.

Howard Park

Lot 377 Scotsdale Road, Denmark, WA 6333
(Great Southern) and Leston Park Estate,
Cowaramup (Margaret River)
tel 61 (08) 9848 2345, fax 61 (08) 9848 2064
email hpw@hpw.com.au
internet www.howardparkwines.com.au

A progressive company founded in 1986, making
exciting, premium-quality wines, Howard Park
sources its brilliant Riesling from Great Southern.
The 2000 had citrous freshness, vibrant flavours,
and a clear, long finish I associate with Riesling here.
The 1992 gave a tiny hint of its age on the nose and
had developed great softness of texture.

Leeuwin Estate

Stevens Road, Margaret River, WA 6285 (Margaret River)
tel 61 (08) 9757 6253, fax 61 (08) 9757 6364
email info@leeuwinestate.com.au
internet www.leeuwinestate.com.au

Founded by Denis and Tricia Horgan in 1974, Leeuwin
Estate has a wonderful modern winery, holds open-air
concerts in an amphitheatre, has a collection of
paintings, and of course, great wines; Leeuwin Estate's
Art Series Riesling are among the finest in Australia.
There is no irrigation, and to distract parrots from the
grapes, sunflowers are planted round the edges of the
vineyards and rye between alternate rows of vines.

The estate has 27 ha of Riesling planted in
sandy mineral soil and the yield is kept down to just
over two tons per acre. Any botrytized grapes are
pre-selected by hand. Sustainable viticulture and
meticulous, gentle winemaking, aim for purity
and balance. Clear, free-run juice is fermented with
cultured yeast. Art Label Riesling 2000 had a subtle,
flowery bouquet with flavours of grapefruit and lime
and a clear finish; zero sugar. 1998 was green on the
nose, but soft and mature on the palate: 1992 had a
smoky nose, with gentle, ripe fruit stretching through
to the finish – delicious.

Plantagenet

Albany Highway, Mount Barker, WA 6324
(Great Southern)
tel 61 (08) 9851 2150, fax 61 (08) 9851 1839
internet www.plantagenetwines.com

The first winery in the Mount Barker region,
Plantagent's first Riesling was planted in 1971. 1999
was pale, fresh, very dry, and pungent. The 1984 had
a lovely old nose; dry and delicious – I could have
drunk the whole bottle. Although attractive when
young, they can acquire hints of kerosene with age.

Tasmania

Piper's Brook Vineyard

Bridport Road, Piper's Brook, Tasmania 7254
(North Tasmania)
tel 61 (08) 9279 6818, fax 61 (08) 6382 7226
email enquiries@pbv.com.au
internet www.pbv.com.au

Dr. Andrew Piper founded the estate in 1974, but it
was bought by Belgian company Kreglinger in 2003.
There are great Rieslings from an original 3-ha plot,
and fine dry Rieslings in commercial quantities from
other vineyards. The sharp and precise style, with
apple and mineral flavours, gives long life.

Tamar Ridge Wines

Auburn Road, Kayena, Tasmania 7270 (North Tasmania)
tel 61 (03) 6334 6208, fax 61 (03) 6334 6050
email info@tamarridgewines.com.au
internet www.tamarridgewines.com.au

This 62-ha estate was taken over in 2003, and
Dr. Richard Smart, the soil and viticultural expert,
is planning a further 200 ha. The 2003 was delicate
with a touch of honey. 2002 had a pure nose, plenty of
body, lovely fruit, and a dry finish – head and shoulders
above other vintages – to drink or keep to 2008.

Netted vines for bird protection in Hawke's Bay

New Zealand

New Zealand

New Zealand's first vines were planted in 1819 and, until 1975, when the New Zealand Wine Institute was founded, the history is one of ignorance, false starts, mistakes, frustrations, and threats of total prohibition. Often the wrong vine varieties were planted in the wrong places for the wrong reasons. "Experts", for example, said in the 1960s that the climate in New Zealand was unsuitable for Riesling in the South Island and utterly impossible in Central Otago. But, by 2004, there were 692 hectares of Riesling in New Zealand, out of a total vineyard area of 18,112 hectares. Fine Riesling is possible in Gisborne, Hawke's Bay, Wairarapa (especially in the sub-region of Martinborough), Nelson, Marlborough, Canterbury (in the sub-region of Waipara), and Central Otago.

New Zealand is young in geological terms, and so in contrast with European vineyards, vines tend to fail on the sides of hills (except in Central Otago) because they lack nutrients and water. The best sites, except in Central Otago, are ancient riverbeds, or "benches": long, narrow, flat, stony terraces left by huge rivers as the glaciers melted at the end of the last ice age, where there are layers of stones, gravel, and sand. Often there is running water underground; this is most evident in Marlborough and also in the 800 hectares of Gimblett Gravels, the first officially defined *grand cru* in Hawke's Bay.

North Island

In Auckland and the north of the North Island, the soil can be so rich that the vines grow too much foliage and produce too many grapes; this can be partly solved by appropriate canopy management. But the climate is really too hot and the soil too heavy for Riesling north of the tiny region of Wairarapa (Martinborough) near Wellington.

South Island

The west of the island consists of mountains of the Southern Alps and glaciers. The wine regions in the north and east are flanked by soft velvet hills: green in spring, and vicuna-coloured in autumn. Marlborough consists of wide former riverbeds, Nelson is more hilly, and Canterbury (including Waipara) is sheep country, with plains and rolling hills. Central Otago is the most beautiful mountainous wine region in the world.

Central Otago is on latitude 45 and its vineyards are the most southerly in the world. Some vineyards are quite steep and on the foothills of the mountains. The soil is mainly composed of granite and schist, rich in minerals, with wind-blown loess from the glaciers, poor in nutrients and excellent for Riesling.

The wine regions have very little rainfall. In Milford Sound, over on the west coast, rainfall is nine metres (354 inches) per year; further north there is rainforest. But Cromwell, the heart of the vineyards in Central Otago, has just fifty centimetres (19.7 inches) of rain per year. Mist rising from the sea and the rivers can bring botrytis. Ultraviolet levels are very high in Central Otago, because there is a hole in the ozone layer over New Zealand and canopy management must be adapted to give protection to the grapes. Clear, dry air and altitude exacerbate the UV problem. Frost is a threat on flatter sites, where wind machines or sprinklers may be installed. The regular hot days and cool nights suit Riesling to perfection; temperatures can rise to 30°C (86°F) by day and fall to 3°C (37°F) at night. This is perhaps the most promising new region in the world for dry Riesling. In 2003, there were 700 hectares of vines, of which eight per cent was Riesling.

In the other regions, Marlborough, Nelson, Waipara, and Canterbury, mist rising from the sea and the rivers also encourages botrytis. Most of the vines are planted in stony soils. Often there is running water underground and this is most evident in Marlborough, where Riesling is also most successful.

1:7,895,000

Km 0   100   200   300 Km
Miles 0   100   200 Miles

NORTH ISLAND

Auckland
AUCKLAND
Hamilton
Waikato
Bay of Plenty
Gisborne
Gisborne
L. Taupo
Hawke's Bay
Napier
Hastings

Nelson
Nelson
Westport
Blenheim
Marlborough
Kaikoura

Wairarapa
Martinborough
WELLINGTON
Cook Strait

PACIFIC OCEAN

Waipara
Canterbury
Christchurch
Mt. Cook
3764

Mt. Aspiring
3077
L. Wanaka
Queenstown
Cromwell
Otago
Dunedin

SOUTH ISLAND

N

AUSTRALIA

NEW ZEALAND
Wellington

North Island

Dry River

Puruatanga Road, Martinborough (Martinborough)
tel 64 (06) 306 9388, fax 64 (06) 306 9275

All Dr. Neil McCullum's wines sell out within weeks of release, though he hopes that his Rieslings, which are among the finest in New Zealand, will be enjoyed at between 5 and 10 years old. The 2000 Craighall Riesling was intensely yellow-green, very dry, almost austere, concentrated, and precise, and obviously needed time. The fruit was beginning to show in the 1999 but it, too, needed time. 1996 Craighall Amaranth Riesling was developing more slowly and it had subtle grapiness and elegance, with a touch of cream on the finish. Craighall Botrytis Selection 1996 was redolent of sweet biscuits, with high acidity in balance with great concentration.

Millton Vineyard

119 Papatu Road, Manutuke (Gisborne)
tel 64 (06) 862 8680, fax 64 (06) 862 8869
email milton@bpc.co.nz
internet www.milton.co.nz

Millton Vineyard was the first estate in New Zealand to be officially certified as biodynamic. The primary fruit characteristics of its Rieslings are less pronounced, and terroir is expressed in their length and subtlety as well as how they develop over time. Picking is by hand and fermentation is in old barrels, giving the wines a particular creamy character as they mature. Indigenous yeasts are used, and the wines generally have between 18 and 30 g.s., and 10 to 11 alc. The style is more European than New World.

Riesling Opou 2002, tasted in 2003, had a lovely freshness and length of flavour, a certain softness and mystery; it will become more precise with time.

Chard Farm vines threatened by schistous rocks on a "bench" in the Kawarau Gorge, Otago

Other producers of fine Riesling

Craggy Range

253 Waimarama Road, Havelock North (Hawke's Bay)
tel 64 (06) 873 7126, fax 64 (06) 873 7141
email info@craggyrange.co.nz

Steve Smith MW is the brilliant winemaker here. His dry Rieslings are archetypal – a perfect balance of fruit and acidity with the special New Zealand tang.

Ngatarawa

305 Ngatarawa Road, Hastings (Hawke's Bay)
tel 64 (06) 879 7603, fax 64 (06) 879 6675
email ngatarawawines@clear.net.nz

Alwyn Corban, a fourth generation winemaker, has a small plot of Riesling here: his brilliant, voluptuous 1996 Noble Harvest Glazebrook Riesling, with eighty per cent botrytis, had concentrated flavours of dried fruits and lemon and a lingering taste of raisins.

Nga Waka

Kitchener Street, Martinborough (Martinborough)
tel 64 (06) 306 9832, fax 64 (06) 306 9832
email ngawaka@ngawaka.co.nz

Roger Parkinson worked in Australia and France; he makes classic, crisp, dry Rieslings, released one year after bottling, which develop beautifully. The 2000 had the finest acidity and was still closed; 1999 had lime-fruit youth, and still needed time. The later-picked 1995 was still young and delicate, with great botrytis.

Palliser Estate

Kitchener Street, Martinborough (Martinborough)
tel 64 (06) 306 9019, fax 64 (06) 306 9946
email palliser@palliser.co.nz

Founded in 1989; this it the largest estate in Martinborough, with 60 ha in production. 2000 Riesling was young when I tasted it, but had great promise. 1998 had developed wonderful complexity.

South Island

Allan Scott Wines

Jackson's Road, RD3 Blenheim (Marlborough)
tel 64 (03) 572 9054, fax 64 (03) 572 9053
email info@allanscott.com
internet www.allanscott.com

Allan attended the birth of Marlborough as a wine region, working with Montana when it planted the first vines there in 1973. 2000 had mineral character and pure Riesling taste; delicious but too young to judge. 1999 had flowers and lemon acidity with a lovely, long aftertaste and was beginning to wake up. Then the older wines: 1993 was golden with strong botrytis and lovely complexity, 1992 had lovely green acidity with less botrytis and more precision in its balance – equally fine; 1991 had ripeness and complete maturity, still with plenty of fruit. The vines are netted to protect the botrytized grapes from birds. 1991 Beerenauslese was deep-gold, with flavours of butterscotch and honey to last for decades.

Felton Road

Felton Road, Bannockburn (Central Otago)
tel 64 (03) 445 0885, fax 64 (03) 445 0881
email feltonrdwines@xtra.co.nz

For forty years in the nineteenth century, Central Otago was a gold-mining area. Bannockburn has a relic of those days: an extraordinary yellow plateau with ravines left by the water that washed the gold. Just below this, on the sun-drenched north-facing slopes, are Mount Difficulty, Felton Road, and Olssen's vineyards. Felton Road was founded in 1991 and the first wines made in 1997; Nigel Greening, a businessman from London, bought it in 2000.

The soil is schist and loess; it retains water, which is valuable because there is no irrigation. The vineyards are between 240 and 330 metres (787 to 1,082 feet) altitude. The brilliant winemaker, Blair Walter, makes three styles of Riesling: dry, medium, and a rare late-harvest. The Dry 2000 was clear and straight, uncomplicated but delicious. The 2000 Medium, always from another block, was appetizing; a wine for Asian food. 1999 Block 1 Late Harvest was late-picked with no botrytis, and fermented with indigenous yeast: concentrated, with ripe acidity and great promise.

Framingham

Conders Bend Road, Marlborough (Marlborough)
tel 64 (03) 572 8884, fax 64 (03) 572 9884
email info@framingham.com
internet www.framingham.com

Winemaker Ant Mackenzie is very proud of his eight-ha block of Riesling, planted in 1981. Yields are extremely low, which gives the wines great concentration. Straight Rieslings are not fined and the wines are allowed to stop fermenting themselves, which leaves a little residual sugar balanced with the relatively high acidity. The 2000 vintage was rich, but 1999 was dry, mature, and soft. 1997 had developed more complexity and length. 1994, his first vintage, was rounded and mature, but still retained the acidity. 1998 Reserve Late Harvest Noble Selection had been hand-picked with seventy-five per cent botrytis, and fermented with indigenous yeast to make 1,000 litres of the finest NZ botrytized Riesling I have tasted.

Fromm Winery

Godfrey Road, RD2 Blenhiem (Marlborough)
tel 64 (03) 572 9355, fax 64 (03) 572 9366
internet www.frommwineries.com

Georg Fromm is Swiss and knows about cool-climate wine production. Winemaker Hätsch Kalaberer is a wonderfully eccentric genius, and he explained that in other regions there is constant sunshine, whereas in Marlborough the sunlight is dappled by the frequent clouds. The constant airflow allows

Lois Mills, owner of Rippon Vineyard – the first and most beautiful vineyard overlooking Lake Wanaka in Central Otago

Riesling to ripen slowly and does not allow grey rot to develop, but botrytis comes later.

There is an old block of Riesling and a new block planted with the aromatic Geisenheim 198 clone. Hätsch produces a straight, dry Riesling, and a sweet Reserve in propitious years. All the wines are under the "La Strada" label. Riesling 2000, from the new block, had a fragrant nose and clean freshness, with fine, elegant, juicy fruit, balanced by ripe acidity. 2000 Reserve, from the old block, had great complexity, structure, and length, requiring time to express itself.

Giesen

Burnham School Road, Burnham, Christchurch (Canterbury)
tel 64 (03) 347 6729, fax 64 (03) 347 6450
email info@giesen.com

The three ambitious Giesen brothers, originally from the Pfalz, doubled the area of their vineyards to 190 ha in 2000, and built a new Winery in Marlborough. Their Rieslings have a slight German accent, with fine balance however dry or sweet. Canterbury Reserve Riesling 1998 was beautifully soft, rich, and elegant with residual sugar. Canterbury Botrytized Riesling 1995 had all the flavours of raisins and barley sugar of a great Auslese from the Pfalz.

Pegasus Bay

Stockgrove Road, Waipara, RD2 Amberley (Canterbury)
tel 64 (03) 314 6869, fax 64 (03) 314 6869
email info@pegasusbay.com

Lynette Hudson and Matthew Donaldson are the best winemaking husband and wife team I know. Their Rieslings are hand-picked and usually have a good amount of botrytis and some residual sugar, balanced with high acidity. The 2000 was gentle and full-flavoured; 1999 was drier, still tight, and very young;

1998, an extremely hot year, was a much deeper colour and was reaching its peak – soft and seductive; 1995 required careful handling (after a tropical storm) – a light and sensitive Riesling.

Rippon Vineyard

Mount Aspiring Road, PO Box 175,
Lake Wanaka (Central Otago)
tel 64 (03) 443 8084, fax 64 (03) 443 8034
email rippon@xtra.co.nz
internet www.rippon.co.nz

The most beautiful vineyard in the world and the first to be planted in Central Otago in 1976 by Rolfe Mills.

Since his death, his widow Lois runs it with the help of her son Nick. He studied biodynamic viticulture in France and is introducing it here. The vineyard is on a long, even slope down to Lake Wanaka, where the summer sun is reflected onto the vines increasing the heat. The estate is progressing towards full biodynamic methods in the vineyard.

The 2002 and 2001 Rieslings both had the essential freshness and lime fruit character of the region, plus an extra purity and depth of flavour that comes from older vines and non-interventionist winemaking. The 1991 had a lovely green hue and was still youthful, with a soft, gentle finish. 1998

A vertical tasting of Allan Scott's Riesling from Marlborough

saw the first Late Harvest Riesling made – fresh and light (with no botrytis), a style reminiscent of a dry Vendange Tardive from Alsace.

Seifried Estate

Redwood Road, Appleby, PO Box 7020 (Nelson)
tel 64 (03) 544 5599, fax 64 (03) 544 5522
email wines@seifried.co.nz
internet www.seifried.co.nz

In 1973, Hermann Seifried planted thirteen different grape varieties in a small block to see if any would survive. He was one of the first growers to plant Riesling in New Zealand commercially, and recently they increased their total holdings to 100 ha. Winemaker's Collection Riesling comes from a special block on poor soil protected by mountains. It is whole-bunch hand-picked and the 1999 had great concentration and was dry with fine citrus acidity. The 1998, a particularly hot vintage, was rich, integrated, and biscuity, with more than a touch of botrytis.

Seresin Estate

Bedford Road, Renwick, Marlborough (Marlborough)
tel 64 (03) 572 9408, fax 64 (03) 572 9850
email info@seresin.co.nz
internet www.seresin.co.nz

Filmmaker Michael Seresin is the owner and Brian Bicknell is the manager and winemaker of this splendid estate. The vineyards are on two adjacent river terraces, the upper of which is cool and windy; the lower is sheltered and warm and particularly good for late-ripening Riesling.

The estate is farmed organically and only grapes from its own vines are used. The grapes are all hand-picked and sorted on a conveyor belt. Fermentation is with the indigenous yeasts at 15°C (59°F). The Rieslings are not released until eleven months after bottling. The 2000 was still in its

infancy, but showed its potential; compared with the 1998, which was wonderfully clean and dry (2 g.s.), with very clear definition of ripe Riesling. Noble Riesling 1998 required four passes to select the botrytized grapes – a glorious mouthful of raisins and peaches.

Villa Maria Estate

cnr New Rewick and Paynter's Rds, PO Box 848, Blenheim (Marlborough)
tel 64 (03) 577 9530, fax 64 (03) 577 9585
email enquries@villamaria.co.nz

George Fistonich's estate is the most consistent and exciting of all New Zealand's medium and large companies. It produces two Rieslings in every vintage and I have never tasted a bad bottle. Private Bin Riesling 2000 was a typical clean, balanced, dry wine. Reserve 2000 (from two blocks by the Wairau River) had greater depth and character, with fresh lime flavours. Riesling Reserve Marlborough Noble Riesling is rare: 1998 was picked with heavy botrytis – a great wine, with glorious honey and apricot flavours.

Other producers of fine Riesling

Montana Brancott Winery

RD4 Riverlands, Blenheim (Marlborough)
tel 64 (03) 578 2099, fax 64 (03) 578 0463

Montana planted the first vineyards in Marlborough in 1973, which included a good proportion of Riesling. I was impressed with the fresh, full Corban's Estate 2000 and the lemony, rich Stoneleigh 2000.

Olssen's of Bannockburn

306 Felton Rd, Cromwell (Central Otago)
tel 64 (03) 445 1716, fax 64 (03) 445 0050

This winery made a great Cordon Cut Late Harvest Riesling 2000. Its straight Riesling 2002 was light and flowery, with great charm.

The USA

Halloween pumpkins in the Finger Lakes

The USA

Washington is the most important state for Riesling, followed by California, Oregon, and New York State. Riesling was (and still is) very popular as a light, refreshing, slightly sweet wine. The name "Johannisberg Riesling" or "White Riesling" is sometimes still used in the USA to differentiate true Riesling from so-called "Grey Riesling", an Arbois grape called Trousseau, and "Emerald Riesling", which is an American hybrid.

Washington State

Washington (and Idaho) are the only states where *Vitis vinifera* vines are not grafted onto American rootstocks to protect them from phylloxera. This is because it is thought that the sandy soil and/or the extreme cold of the winters dissuades the bug. For Riesling, the cold winters are not a threat as the rest of the year sees plenty of sun, and irrigation prevents too much stress in the vines. Most important for quality is the difference between day and night temperatures. In the summer, days can hit 30°C (86°F) and nights can fall to 5°C (41°F) which lengthens the ripening period. Botrytis does occur in certain areas, which can give more complexity to dry Rieslings or, if the grapes are picked separately, sweet late-harvest wines and genuine Ice Wines.

The Cascade Mountains act as a rain shield creating desert conditions. There are still large areas that are planted with hybrid grapes for fruit juice production, but ungrafted *vinifera* grapes thrive here because the many dams in the great Columbia River gorge provide water to irrigate all the vineyards and farms. Fertilisers are added to the water (fertigation) at some of the wineries by central computer control. Although the mountains are obvious in the distance, the vineyards are relatively flat. Today, there are around 1,000 hectares of Riesling in the state, and this is increasing. Most of the production is dominated by the two large corporations, Château Ste-Michelle and Columbia Winery, and their associate companies. Nevertheless, small wineries are springing up, quality is sharply improving, and demand is exceeding supply.

California

California is generally too hot for Riesling, except in the cooler foothills close to the Pacific or at higher altitudes. Pockets of Riesling are to be found in Anderson Valley, Monterrey, and Santa Barbara, but there are only some 900 hectares in production.

The wineries of Napa Valley have a huge prejudice against Riesling, mostly because the more profitable Chardonnay is their idol, but also because the big wineries of Washington State have grabbed the USA semi-dry Riesling market at cut prices.

Oregon

In recent years, plantings of Pinot Gris and Pinot Noir have both increased, while Riesling has dwindled to 250 hectares; it is less profitable and cannot compete with the cut-price Rieslings from Washington State. However, Riesling should do well here – there is a long ripening period, and temperatures are relatively low. The best soils for Riesling are in Willamette Valley, where there is a volcanic and iron soil called Red Jory, and a silty, alluvial soil called WillaKenzie. Riesling seems to do best on Red Jory on the upper slopes of the Yamhill Valley, which is itself in Willamette Valley. A few producers have continued to make Riesling with conviction, and independent young winemakers are following them.

New York State – Finger Lakes
(*see* map page 173)

From a distance the Finger Lakes look beautiful, but, as you get closer, you can see great creeping, unkempt cobwebs covering the slopes – these are hybrid vines and there are around 4,000 hectares.

The wines from these grapes tastes like "grape jelly with a shot of vodka". Most are used to add acidity to fruit juices and jellies. Riesling only accounts for 180 hectares, but this is set to increase exponentially. The lakes have a vital moderating influence on temperatures that make late-harvest or even botrytized Riesling possible. Most of the successful wineries are around Lakes Keuka, Cayuga, and Seneca. The climate is severe in winter and it is possible to make Ice Wines, though in the USA, mechanical picking and freezing of the grapes or juice is permitted – very different to the situation in Canada and Germany.

Washington State

Badger Mountain Vineyard

1106 S Jurupa Street, Kennewick, WA 99338
tel 1 (509) 627 4986, fax 1 (509) 627 2071

Bill Power and his son Greg founded this model winery in 1982 on a wonderful, south-facing slope. They own about 10 ha, which they farm organically; this includes 3.8 ha of Riesling. They buy grapes for two-thirds of their production. Their Riesling 2001 was dry, with great fruit intensity and character.

Château Ste-Michelle

1 Stimson Lane, Woodinvale, WA 980072
tel 1 (425) 488 1133, fax 1 (425) 415 3657
email info@ste-michele.com
internet www.ste-michelle.com

This is a huge operation: it owns about 570 ha of the 1,000 ha of Riesling in the state. Ernst Loosen from the Mosel (*see* pages 30, 71) was invited to help Château Ste-Michelle to produce a new straight Riesling, Eroica, and an intensely sweet Riesling, Single Berry Select. Ernst's contributions were his experience of terroir; he also defined minimum irrigation, reduced yields by sharp pruning, did a green harvest in August, and improved the canopy management, all to achieve ripeness, while retaining high acidity levels. Picking is at night to get complete bunches of chilled grapes in perfect condition.

Cold Creek Vineyard is 266 ha, planted in 1972, of which 70 ha are Riesling. It is an isolated, large, green patch on the barren south-facing hillside and is the main source for Eroica.

Ste-Michelle 2001 Dry Riesling was very fresh and green-apple dry; Johannisberg Riesling 2001 was richer and rounder, with more fruit, due to its extra residual sugar; Cold Creek Vineyard 2001

Tasting in full sunshine at Allan Green's Greenwood Ridge in Mendocino, while Anderson Valley is still fogbound

had layers of flavour: a terroir wine. Eroica 2001 had a minerally, flowery nose backed by a delicious white-peach flavour, with finely balanced acidity. Reserve Late Harvest Riesling 2000 had tremendous botrytis and dried apricot concentration.

Columbia Winery

14030 NE 145th Street, Woodinville, WA 98072
tel 1 (425) 488 2776, fax 1 (425) 488 3460
internet www.columbiawinery.com

Columbia Winery was founded by a group of friends in 1962 to prove that European *vinifera* vines could survive the harsh Washington winters. Since 1979, David Lake MW has been largely responsible for its success. He introduced the philosophy of single-vineyard wines and many other advances. Today, this estate is the second-largest producer in the state.

Cellarmaster's Riesling 2001 was a semi-dry wine that had stopped fermenting naturally. It had fine fruit balanced by ripe acidity. Covey Run is a separate part of the company. Dry Riesling 2001 was fresh, with delicious fruit, if not really dry.

Ste-Chapelle Winery of Caldwell in Idaho is the fourth largest winery in the three states of Oregon, Washington, and Idaho. It has an extreme continental climate, with very hot summers and winters so cold that the vines can freeze. To avoid this they are ungrafted so that they grow back from the roots. The Ste-Chapelle 2001 Dry Riesling was fresh, with finesse, and balanced, with good fruit. Skyline Vineyard Ice Wine Reserve Series 2001 (150 g.s.), produced from frozen bunches picked by hand, was scintillating.

Kiona Vineyards Winery

44612 N Sunset NE, Benton City, WA 99320
tel 1 (509) 588 6716, fax 1 (509) 588 3219
email kionawine@aol.com

Red Mountain is the latest and smallest AVA in Washington State. It consists of one hill of

150 to 460 metres (492 to 1,509 feet), facing southwest, and is thought to be the hottest place in Yakima Valley. John Williams and Jim Holmes planted 4 ha in 1975 with one-third each of Riesling, Chardonnay, and Cabernet Sauvignon.

This became the heart of Kiona Vineyards now owned by the Williams family. Dry Riesling 2000 was a big wine with lots of fruit and fine acidity, deserving to be kept for another couple of years. Late Harvest 2001 was picked after the first frosts and was a delicious, concentrated "hand-made" Riesling.

Washington Hills/Bridgman/ Apex Cellars

111 East Lincoln Avenue, Sunnyside, WA 98944
tel 1 (425) 839 9463, fax 1 (425) 839 6155
email winery@washingtonhills.com
internet www.washingtonhills.com

There are three levels of quality here – Washington Hills is the commercial brand, Bridgman the middle quality, and Apex the super-premium. Its biggest asset is Outlook Vineyard, that provides about half the grapes (it owns nearly 50 ha of vines). It is at around 400 metres (1,312 feet) altitude. The soil is ideal for Riesling, being quite shallow and stony, and over a granite sub-soil. Brian Carter is a brilliant winemaker, and his Bridgman Dry Riesling 2001 was an excellent, fresh wine aimed at the restaurant market. The sweet 2001 was late-picked, with one-third botrytis. Apex Riesling 2001, from vines planted in 1982 in Outlook vineyard, was rich, yellow-green, concentrated but dry, precise and mouth-filling – a great wine. Apex Goldbeerenauslese was tremendously complex, viscous, and with a tweak of acidity to balance.

Woodward Canyon Winery

11920 West Highway 12, Lowden, WA 99360
tel 1 (509) 525 4129, fax 1 (509) 522 0927
email info@woodwardcanyon.com
internet www.woodwardcanyon.com

This patriotic tasting room in Carlton Village sells wines from all the wineries in the Willamette Valley

Rick Small runs this winery with energy and enthusiasm. The lovely, netted vineyards are on steep slopes by the long, sinuous Woodward Canyon – where there ought to be room for a lot more Rieslings! Small's first claim to fame is his Merlot (and the 1999 was the finest that I have tasted from the USA). I feel the same about his 2001 Dry Riesling, it was bone dry, clean as a whistle, and in balance with 13.5 alc. Unlike other Washington Rieslings, it was akin to a top-quality Clare Valley Riesling: powerful but fresh, light but concentrated, with the correct acidity to carry the finish and to make it last for more than a decade. It was hand-picked from three different sites, all with old vines yielding about 25 hl/ha.

California

Bonny Doon

10 Pine Flat Road, Bonny Doon, CA 95060
tel 1 (408) 425 3625, fax 1 (408) 425 3656
email lecigare@aol.com

Randall Grahm is an iconoclast. As the climate in Santa Cruz is wrong for Riesling, he looked to Washington State and Germany to create his Pacific Rim Riesling. This is made from seventy-five per cent of a grower's wine in Washington and twenty-five per cent (the legal limit in the USA) from an import from Johannes Selbach in the Mosel Valley, to add finesse. He sells around 600,000 bottles per annum, and hopes that in the future the Washington grapes will be biodynamic.

2002 Pacific Rim Riesling was flowery, fragrant, and peachy, ideal with modern cuisine. His Estate 2002 Solidad Salinas Valley had an undemonstrative nose because the vines were so young, but a wonderful developing Pfalz-like flavour. "The Heart has its Rieslings" was from a single vineyard in the

Yakima Valley; it had flavours of William's pears, balanced with fine acidity. "Riesling is like love, sweet and tart," as Randall says.

Greenwood Ridge Estate

5501 Highway 128, Philoh, CA 95466
tel 1 (707) 895 2002, fax 1 (707) 895 2001
email everybody@greenwoodridge.com
internet www.greenwoodridge.com

"Islands in the sky" is the sobriquet of Mendocino Ridge because the vines are planted at 400 metres (1,312 feet) altitude or more, above the coastal fogs. Greenwood Ridge Riesling 2001 had a fine, ripe nose and rich flavours.

A second picking two weeks later produced a wonderful rich, sweet, botrytized Late Harvest Riesling. The straight 1990 was still young and had a glorious green-yellow colour with an exquisite flavour of ripe pears that stayed on the palate. The 1988 was gold, with a faint kerosene flavour, but with mineral and botrytis characters; old and wonderfully elegant.

Navarro Vineyards

5601 Highway 128, Philoh, CA 95466
tel 1 (707) 895 3686, fax 1 (707) 895 3647
internet www.navarrowine.com

Ted Bennett and Deborah Cahn bought this farm in 1973, because the cool climate might enable them to fulfil their passion for Alsace Riesling, Gewürztraminer, even temperamental Muscat d'Alsace and the Burgundian grapes. They encourage biodiversity and farm ecologically. They use large oak barrels (rare in the New World) for their Alsace-style wines, giving them extra complexity.

The 2001 Dry Riesling was fresh and sprightly, with plenty of fruit balanced with fine acidity. The 1998 Late Harvest was like a Vendange Tardive with less residual sugar and no botrytis, and great subtlety. 1997 Late Harvest had the highest sugar level they had ever recorded, and it took a year in barrel to finish fermenting.

Smith-Madrone

4022 Spring Mountain Road, St Helena, CA 94574
tel 1 (707) 963 2283
email info@smithmadrone.com
internet www.smithmadrone.com

The winery is camouflaged among the trees almost at the top of Spring Mountain at 500 metres (1,650 feet). This is semi-wild, Hillbilly country and we were greeted by the suitably bearded Stuart Smith, a Davis University graduate in Oenology and Viticulture. He and his brother Stuart bought the farm in 1972 and they have no irrigation, nor do they believe that it is necessary in the Napa Valley. Their original plantings were ungrafted and the Riesling block of 2.25 ha faced east to avoid the strongest sun. The red, volcanic soil is not particularly fertile and the vineyards are quite steep. The 2001 Riesling was an infant and had all the right genes – immediately fresh and delicious, but promising to become more subtle. 2000 was flowery, more delicate, and elegant. 1998 was still fresh and deserved more time to develop. 1996 was still grassy and young with perfect acidity – it took a week for a twenty-four-man team to select the grapes. This winery was a real discovery.

Trefethen

1160 Oak Knoll Avenue, Napa, CA 945558
tel 1 (707) 255 7700, fax 1 (707) 255 0793
internet www.trefethen.com

All the Riesling grapes are from Blocks 2 and 5 on the estate, the soil being alluvial loam in the cooler, southern end of Napa Valley. The 2001 had a light prickle of CO_2, and was slim but powerful, with lots of fruit – proof that fine Riesling can be produced from a vineyard on the Napa Valley floor.

Oregon

Amity Vineyards

18150 Amity Vineyards Road, SE Amity, OR 97101
(North Willamette Valley)
tel 1 (503) 835 2362, fax 1 (503) 835 6451
email amity@amityvineyards.com
internet amityvineyards.com

"Riesling is an incredible grape which, under Oregon conditions, develops lovely aromas and flavours at relatively low sugar levels," wrote Myron Redford, the owner of Amity Vineyards. Amity is in the Eola Hills, where the soil is red clay-loam above volcanic basalt rock, and is well-suited to Pinot Noir and Riesling.

First, the current vintages. Amity Oregon Dry Riesling 2001 had lovely fruit, fine acidity; 1999 was mature and delicious. Then the older vintages, mainly late-harvest but dry: 1994 – very rich but subtle with a fine dry finish; 1989 – botrytis on the nose, but dry, soft, and long; 1988 – deep-gold, botrytis colour, lovely but just beginning to show its age; 1984 (a terrible vintage) – honeyed nose, dry, but still retaining a fraction of fruit, amazing; 1982 – despite being ullaged, there was no oxidation and it was soft and seductive with natural balance; 1976 (Myron's first vintage) – still youthful, pure, light, and elegant and only 11 alc. – astonishing.

Argyle Winery

691 Hwy 99W, PO Box 280, Dundee, OR 97115
(North Willamette Valley)
tel 1 (503) 538 8520, fax 1 (503) 538 2055
email buywine@argyle.com
internet www.argyle winery.com

Richard Soles is a great Texan who went to Australia and worked for Brian Croser. Brian was interested in setting up a winery in the USA to grow Pinot Noir, Chardonnay, and Riesling. The 1999 Riesling was crisp and quite powerful, with a subtle flavour of pink grapefruit. They have planted a new, large Riesling vineyard and its first vintage will be 2005…

Belle Pente

12470 NE Rowland Road, Carlton, OR 97111
(Willamette Valley)
tel 1 (503) 852 9500, fax 1 (503) 852 6977
email wine@bellepente.com
internet www.bellepente.com

The inspiration for Jill and Brian O'Donnel comes from Alsace and Burgundy. Old vines are closely planted on a "beautiful slope", and hand-sorted grapes vinified in small lots with minimum handling guarantee wines with individual character. Their 2000 Riesling had a distinctive, dry Alsace style, with an American accent.

Elk Cove Vineyards

27751 NW Olson Road, Gaston, OR 97119
(North Willamette Valley)
tel 1 (503) 985 7760, fax 1 (503) 985 7760
email info@elkcove.com
internet www.elkcove.com

Adam Campbell runs this lovely estate organically, and puts straw between the rows to prevent erosion, retain moisture, and control weeds. Yields are restrained. The small Riesling vineyard is at 250 metres (820 feet) altitude. Willamette Riesling 2001 had a ripe, green-gold colour, and acidity and fruit were melded together. Late Harvest Riesling 2000 was beautifully concentrated and distinctive – for me, a perfect wine to drink on the verandah.

Henry Estate Winery

687 Hubbard Creek Road, Umqua, OR 97486
(Umqua Valley)
tel 1 (541) 459 5120, fax 1 (541) 459 5146
email henryest@wizards.net
internet www.henryestate.com

Scott Henry is a scientist and engineer; he developed the Scott Henry vine-trellising system, now pretty widely used in the New World and itself the inspiration for other trellising systems. He was

Fred Frank, Riesling specialist and director of
Dr. Konstantin Frank's Vinfera Wine Cellars, Lake Keuka

spurred on to do it because his clay-loam volcanic soil encouraged too much growth in his vines. By training one level of canes upwards and one downwards, with a "window" in the middle, the vigour of the vine is reduced, the leaves and the bunches of grapes receive more sunlight, and the air flows more freely, thus reducing mildew and rot.

Henry Estate Dry Riesling 2000 had exceptionally good, ripe acidity in a very friendly style. Select Harvest 2001 had a flowery nose, richness from botrytis, and great elegance. 1992 Beerenauslese had great viscosity, and apricot and peach flavours.

New York State

Dr. Konstantin Frank's Vinifera Wine Cellars

9749 Middle Road, Hammondsport, NY 14840
(Keuka Lake)
tel 1 (607) 868 4884, fax 1 (607) 868 4888
email frankwines@aol.com
internet www.drfrankwines.com

Dr. Konstantin Frank was the director of the Institute of Viticulture and Viniculture at the Polytechnic in Odessa during the 1940s. In 1951, he escaped from Russia and found himself at Cornell unable to speak English and doing menial work to earn a crust. In 1953, he met Charles Fournier, formerly of Veuve Clicquot Champagne, but then responsible for the Gold Seal brand of sparkling wines made with Finger Lakes hydrid grapes. They agreed to collaborate on a planting of *vinifera* vines, and by 1966, they had planted 30 ha by Keuka Lake. Dr. Frank had also planted his own Riesling vineyard.

Frank's grandson, Fred, now runs this, the leading winery in the Finger Lakes region. He has an encyclopaedic knowledge of viticulture and viniculture. Salmon Run Johannisberg Riesling is the estate's successful brand – made with grapes from contracted growers. This wine established the Finger Lakes' regional Riesling character – with acidity balanced by around 30 g.s. In contrast, Dry Riesling 2001 was precise, beautifully fresh, mineral, and positively dry; only to be overmatched by 2001 Dry Riesling Reserve that was complete, packed with fruit and delicate mineral flavours, and with just 3 g.s. This was the first Reserve Riesling, but a recent vertical tasting back to 1962 showed that the Franks' Rieslings are built to last.

Hosmer Winery

6999 State Route 89, Ovid, NY 14521 (Cayuga Lake)
tel 1 (607) 869 3393, fax 1 (607) 869 9409
email hoswine@fltg.net
internet www.hosmerwinery.com

Cameron and Maren Hosmer own this excellent winery and they have a brilliant winemaker, Martha Gioumousis. Dry Riesling 2001 was a delight: fresh, with a green-lime nose and a mineral elegance through to the finish. Semi-sweet Riesling 2001 had lots of fruit and 33 g.s. Late-Harvest 2000 was concentrated, with great Riesling purity and 59 g.s.

Lamoreaux Landing Wine Cellars

9224 Route 414, Lodi, NY 14860 (Cayuga Lake)
tel 1 (607) 582 6011, fax 1 (607) 582 6010
email llwc@capital.net
internet www.lamoreauxwine.com

Mark Wagner owns this beautiful winery, which is a Graeco-modern temple standing proudly on the brow of the long hill overlooking Lake Cayuga. The interior contains the essential state-of-the-art stainless-steel equipment and French oak casks for Chardonnay and classic red varietals, though a new cask cellar was in construction. He has four blocks of Riesling with three different

clones and uses organic compost rather then chemical fertilizers. The straight, dry Riesling 2001 (9 g.s., 6.5 g.a.) was fine and elegant, with aromas of exotic fruit: perfectly balanced, and long on the palate. The 2000 showed even better with the extra year in bottle. For the fermentation of the Semi-dry 2001 (25 g.s., 8.2 g.a., 13.3 alc.), he had used a different yeast, which gave it more prickle on the tongue, and the relatively high levels of acidity and alcohol balanced the sugar admirably. The 1998 Late Harvest was a great wine (107 g.s., 8 g.a.), with hints of orange peel.

Hermann J. Weimer Vineyards

3962 Route 14, PO Box 38, Dundee, NY 14837
(Seneca Lake)
tel 1 (607) 243 7971, fax 1 (607) 243 7983
email wines@weimer.com
internet www.weimer.com

In 1973, Hermann Weimer bought 60 ha of land and set up a nursery that supplied a number of *Vitis vinifera* varieties worldwide. He also set-up his own Riesling vineyard. Today, he has 18 ha of Riesling, with five different Geisenheim Riesling clones to give diversity and complexity to his wines. He was the first to produce a dry Riesling in the Finger Lakes.

2001 Dry Riesling had a lovely, precise flavour, and classic finesse. The 2000 semi-dry was totally different with twice as much residual sugar (20 g.s.) and less pronounced acidity – more like a traditional Mosel (the region he came from). Late Harvest 2001 (51 g.s., 10.2 alc.) was a brilliant Riesling, like a Nahe, with crystaline mineral character and finesse. The grapes for this wine were selected from the block of his oldest vines.

His quality is sophisticated and immaculate, and in his spare time he continues his fight against the use of hybrid vines!

Canada

Vineyards overlooking the village of Peachland on Lake Okanagan

Canada

It is difficult to believe that the explosion of quality Canadian wines made with *vinifera* grapes only really began in the 1990s. Canada had experienced the same problem as New York State in growing *Vitis vinifera* vines in that they could not survive the combination of phylloxera and the bitterly cold winter climate.

Despite the different climates and terroirs of Ontario and Okanagan, the main grapes of Bordeaux, Burgundy, and Alsace are grown with great success in both regions. Syrah from four-year-old vines in Okanagan is amazing and there are small experimental plots of other grapes in both regions. Riesling is predominantly of the German persuasion: positively dry, half-dry, late-harvest, and Ice Wine. The most serious problem is the availabiliy of suitable land – on the Niagara bench there is a move to ban further building of any sort and there is not much more of the Okanagan desert to be leased from the Indian tribes, even if they were to agree.

Canada is the largest producer of Ice Wine in the world. Regulations and standards are carefully monitored and artificial freezing is banned – unlike in the USA. The annual production is some 75,000 cases, less than five per cent of Ontario's entire wine production – and still less in Okanagan. About seventy-five per cent is made from Vidal (a hybrid) which makes good-quality Ice Wine, but Riesling with its concentrated flavour of the grape is immeasurably finer and less cloying. It takes time to learn how to grow Riesling, and then for the vines to mature so that they produce grapes that reflect the terroir from where they came and give the subtle flavours to the wines. Canada has made fantastic progress in a relitavely short time.

Ontario

The Niagara escarpment runs some forty kilometres (twenty-five miles) west from the Falls, parallel to the south coast of Lake Ontario. It has seven layers of limestone and shale-sandstone. The soils on the benches are not unlike those of the Côte d'Or. So, specific terroir is important here. Air-flow is also very important, and the escarpment prevents frost damage in the early months of the year by trapping warm air from the lake. In the summer, cool air from the lake discourages rot and mildews; in the autumn, warm air from the lake lengthens the ripening season.

A number of small-to-medium wineries and a handful of giant corporations are developing the vineyard areas. Ninety per cent of Ontario's wine business is in Niagara, the rest is in Lake Erie, North Shore, and Pelee Island in Lake Eyrie.

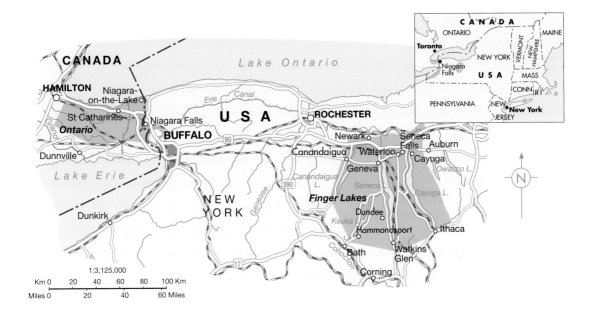

An indication of confidence comes from the partnership between Vincor International and the Jean-Claude Boisset group in Burgundy. They have created a new winery – designed by the great architect Frank Gehry – Le Clos Jordan, in the middle of the Niagara benches and it already has 200 hectares of Pinot Noir and Chardonnay planted. In the 1980s, Hermann Weis from the Mosel started a nursery in Niagara and had a big influence on the planting of *vinifera* vines in Canada and the choice of rootstocks and clones, especially for Riesling.

British Columbia (*see* map page 161)

Okanagan is *the* wine region. It is the northernmost section of the desert to the east of the chain of mountains that runs through Washington State all the way to Mexico. The annual rainfall is just fifteen to twenty-five centimetres (5.9 to 9.8 inches). The climate is very cold in winter, and in summer and autumn the days are very hot and the nights are cool – ideal for Riesling. Cold winters and dry summers mean that the vines are almost disease-free, and sprays and insecticides are not needed. Okanagan is the name of the Indian tribe that owns most of the desert land; it is also the name of the river that joins the Columbia River in Washington State. Glaciers gouged out a series of lakes, linked by the river, giving grey and green slate, schist, granite, gneiss, basalt, sand, and alluvial soil to the benches at the base of the surrounding mountains; this is where the vines are planted, at an average altitude of 400 metres (1,300 feet). Here, too, the deep lakes moderate the climate and provide almost limitless water for irrigation.

Ontario

Cave Spring Cellars

3836 Main Street, Jordan, Niagara, Ontario
tel 1 (905) 562 3581, fax 1 (905) 562 3232
email tpenna@cavespringscellars.com
internet www.cavespringscellars.com

Leonard Pennachetti founded Cave Springs Cellars in Jordan, the prettiest village in Niagara, in 1986. Today, he owns 52 ha, mainly on the best sites on Beamsville Bench. The 2000 Dry Riesling was reasonably dry and fresh: a lovely summer wine. 2000 Estate Reserve, from a low-yielding block planted in 1979 in Cave Springs vineyard, had fine fruit and was much more concentrated and serious. The 2000 Riesling "CSV" was from vines planted in 1976. It was very aromatic and rich, and had gained complexity by being left on the lees for five months before bottling.

2000 Riesling "Indian Summer" Select Late Harvest was a great Auslese-quality wine; the grapes were left on the vines and had twenty per cent botrytis – the first frosts in December gave partly frozen bunches that helped further to concentrate the juice. 1999 Ice Wine (250 g.s., 10 g.a., 10 alc.), in contrast to many Ice Wines, had about fifteen per cent botrytis.

Inniskillin Wines Inc. (Vincor)

RR#1, Niagara Parkway, Niagara-on-the-Lake, Ontario
tel 1 (905) 468 2187, fax 1 (905) 468 5355
internet www.inniskillin.com

When Donald Ziraldo and Karl Kaiser first met, Donald was running the family nursery, which specialized in vines and fruit trees, and Karl Kaiser had begun experimenting with home winemaking.

They founded Inniskillin in 1975, and since then have led the Canadian wine industry from the front. Now Inniskillin is part of Vincor International. Phillip Dowell makes all the wines except the Ice Wine,

which is still made by Karl Kaiser. 2001 Riesling was pale in colour with a refreshing, green-apple nose: herbaceous, and fruity.

2001 Late Autumn Riesling had more colour and fruit, and more of everything. 2000 Select Late Harvest Riesling had a large proportion of botrytized grapes, giving richness and concentration, to which was added "not quite Ice Wine" juice that gave even more sugar and acidity. This was from Marienne Hill vineyard on Beamsville bench, one of the best sites for Riesling: a beautiful wine.

2000 Ice Wine was green-gold in colour and was so concentrated that tears of glycerol clung to the glass; the acidity and sugar were in perfect harmony. The frost was never quite hard enough to pick the grapes in one session so they had to pick little and often on eight nights from December 27 to March 5, and then blend the different wines.

Jackson-Triggs Estate Winery (Vincor)

2145 Niagara Stone Road, Niagara-on-the-Lake, Ontario
tel 1 (905) 564 3003
email info@jacksontriggswinery.com
internet www.jacksontriggswinery.com

A magnificent, thoroughly modern winery designed for flexible use, where the winemaker, Tom Seaver, can see everything, and where the juice and the wines can be handled with the minimum manipulation and use of pumps. Dry Riesling 2001 was lime-green in colour, and the flavour had an interesting touch of tangerine. It was lower in alcohol than most dry Rieslings, which made it a delicious, dry, summer wine. Proprietors' Reserve Riesling 2001 was more concentrated and with higher residual sugar. Delaire Vineyards 2001 was a little more Alsace in style: concentrated, and minerally; Proprietors' Grand Reserve Riesling 2000 had a Germanic Rheingau character: powerful and precise, dry but not sharp. Proprietors' Grand Reserve Riesling 2001, in contrast, was more in the Mosel mould: light and delicate. The 2000 Ice Wine was picked in December and January, with wonderful concentration of sugar and acidity.

Konzelmann Estate Winery

1096 Lakeshore Road, Niagara-on-the-Lake, Ontario
tel 1 (905) 935 2866, fax 1 (905) 935 2864
internet www.konzelmann.com

Herbert Konzelmann graduated at the Weinsberg Wine School in Württemberg and moved to Canada in 1984. He now has 37 ha by the lake. He uses stainless-steel vats and traditional large, old-oak barrels that I had not seen in Canada before. The Dry Riesling 2001 is fresh and correct without being exciting, but his Reserve 2001 was much drier and with more extract and structure.

Thirty Bench

4281 Mountainview Road, Beamsville, Niagara, Ontario
tel 1 (905) 563 1698, fax 1 (905) 563 3921
internet www.thirtybench.com

Dr. Tom Muckle has 11 ha of vines on Beamsville bench, one of the best sites with a limestone terroir. Dry Riesling 1999 was very characteristic Niagara: dry but not extremely so, quite aromatic and ripe, softening after three years in bottle. The 1998 Riesling was from a year of very low yields; its mineral character balanced the rich, concentrated fruit in the wine. Semi-dry Riesling 1999 had fine style and was beautifully balanced.

Other producers of fine Riesling

Vineland Estates

3620 Moyer Road, Vineland, Ontario
tel 1 (905) 562 7088, fax 1 (905) 562 3071

Vineland Estates was established in 1988 by Hermann Weiss, owner of the impressive Weingut St Urbans-

The master of Canadian Ice Wine, Karl Kaiser, co-founder with Donald Ziraldo of Inniskillin Wines

Hof (*see* page 36) in the Mosel Valley. He also established a remarkable multi-clone vine nursery specializing in Riesling. He sold Vineland Estates to John Howard in 1992, and the latter has made it into one of the leading wineries of Niagara. The 2001 Dry Riesling was finely balanced, with lime-fruit tones, and was most appetizing, while the Semi-dry 2001 was light, fresh, and easy, with a touch of elderberry.

Daniel Lenko

5246 Regional Road 81, Beamsville, Ontario
tel 1 (905) 563 7756, fax 1 (905) 563 3317

Daniel Lenko could not show us his 2001 Riesling because it was completely ruined by the ladybird plague that hit Niagara, and so he had got rid of it. The 2000 was fragrant, fresh, and delicate, with fine acidity and a little residual sugar. The 1999 Reserve was richer, riper, and heavier, more curvaceous and sexy.

British Columbia

Domaine Combret

PO Box 1170, Oliver, B.C. VOH 1T0
tel 1 (250) 498 6966
email info@combretwine.com
internet www.combretwine.com

This winery has a different feel from others in British Columbia. I asked to taste its Riesling and a bottle of Reserve 1994 was produced. I asked if I might taste a younger vintage first and was told that all the younger vintages were still in vat on the lees, that they are normally bottled after five years, and released two or three years later.

The 1994 was bone-dry, powerful, aromatic, and aristocratic in an Alsace way, and was not showing the faintest signs of age; it was delicious.

The owner, Olivier Combret, MSc Agriculture from the University of B.C. and former President of Provence AOC, wrote a fascinating article for the

A triumphant native American on horseback in its desert landscape at the entrance to the superb new Nk'Mip winery of the Osooyos Indian Band

French magazine, *Le Progrès – Agricole et Osoyoos Viticole*, on viticulture in Okanagan. This explained why the soil here is similar to that of Schlossberg in Kaysersberg and Kientzheim in Alsace, consisting of granite, gneiss, and metamorphic rocks, plus *fluor* and magnesium. But, of course, the terroir here – in the broader sense – is very different.

Hawthorne Mountain Vineyards (Vincor)

Green Lake Road, Okanagan Falls, B.C. VOH 1RO
tel 1 (250) 497 8267, fax 1 (250) 497 8073
email info@hmvineyard.com
internet www.hmvineyard.com

This estate has the most beautiful vineyards – at high altitude, with steep rows of vines overlooking the lakes and mountains. The reception and tasting room is the original homestead, built in 1909. Fine Riesling (and perhaps the best Gewürztraminer of the region).

Inniskillin Okanagan (Vincor)

Road 11, Oliver, B.C. VOH 1TO
tel 1 (250) 498 6663, fax 1 (250) 498 4566
email InniskillinOkanagan@inniskillin.com
internet www.inniskillin.com

This winery is tiny compared with Inniskillin's main winery in Niagara. It has just 1 ha of Riesling in its original vineyard, with access to more. It produced a finely balanced and elegant Riesling in 2000.

Jackson-Triggs Okanagan

PO Box 1650, Oliver, B.C. VOH 1TO
tel 1 (604) 498 4981, fax 1 (604) 498 6505
email jacksontriggswinery.com
internet www.jacksontriggswinery.com

In 2001, one batch of Riesling was fermented to 13.3 alc., a second batch was stopped at 9. These were then blended with a tiny amount of Ice Wine. The result was 1,000 cases of Dry Riesling 2001 Proprietors' Reserve which was fresh, with the added concentration and acidity of the Ice Wine. 2000 Riesling Ice Wine –

picked January 15, 2001 – sacrificed a potential 45 tons of grapes to make 4,500 litres of superb, concentrated, voluptuous wine, with gripping acidity,

Gehringer Brothers

Road 8, RR1 Site 23, Comp 4, Oliver, B.C. VOH 1TD
tel 1 (250) 498 3537, fax 1 (250) 498 3510

The dream of the brothers was conceived in 1973. Walter graduated in viti- and viniculture at the Geisenheim Wine Institute, and Gordon at the Wine College at Weinsberg in Württemberg. In 1981, they bought the land, and in 1985 built the winery. Their vineyards are immaculate. Dry Riesling 2001 had a gently perfumed nose and was very attractive, light, and elegant. Reserve Riesling 2001 was riper and had more substance and a little more residual sugar.

Late Harvest 2001 (55 g.s., 11.5 alc.) was picked on December 20 and had the crystalline purity of a fine, modern German Riesling Auslese with great complexity. Ice Wine 2001 (232 g.s., 10 alc.) was similar to the last wine but, as the analysis implies, four times as concentrated and the closest to perfect that an Ice Wine can be – not as fine as a great German Eiswein, but a real celebration wine.

Mission Hill Family Estate

1730 Mission Hill Road, Westbank, B.C. V4T 2E4
tel 1 (250) 768 7611, fax 1 (250) 768 2267
email info@missionhillwinery.com
internet www.missionhillwinery.com

Anthony van Mandl said that when he bought this winery in 1972, it was in a filthy, run-down state, and he thought he had made the worst decision of his life. Today, it's architecture (by Tom Kundig) and its practicality rivals any winery in the world. From one direction it recalls San Gimignano in Tuscany; from the terrace you see the amphitheatre where concerts are held; behind are the vineyards and the great lake. Inside the entrance is a huge Chagall tapestry, and below is a cool, dark cellar. This is the domain of John

Simes, former chief winemaker of Montana (New Zealand's largest winery, *see* page 157), who arrived in 1992. Currently, there are 300 ha, but it is becoming more difficult to find suitable land. We tasted the dry Rieslings first. The 2001 had a floral nose and appetizing green acidity; 2000 was richer, more complex and mouth-filling, with a touch of honey; 1998 had power and high acidity but was still very fresh, needing more time (13 alc.). 1995 had elegance and lower acidity, making it fully mature and lovely to drink. 1993 had a bouquet of wild flowers, delicious in 2002. 1991 tasted much younger than the previous wine, and was in perfect balance, with fine acidity and a clean, pure finish.

Nk'mip Cellars

1400 Rancher Creek Road, Osoyoos, B.C. V0H 1V0
tel 1 (250) 495 2985, fax 1 (250) 495 2986
email winery@nkmip.ca

This is a joint venture between the local Osoyoos Indian Band (owners of the majority of land in Okanagan) and Vincor International. Opened in 2002, the winery echos Aztec shapes, angles, and curves relate to the tribe's wooden huts. The vineyards spread out like a fan below the winery near the lake and the desert rises on the hill above. The wines so far show great promise, Riesling is eagerly awaited.

Other producers of fine Riesling

Cedar Creek Estate Winery

5445 Lakeshore Road, Kelowna, B.C. V1W 4S5
tel 1 (250) 764 8866, fax 1 (250) 764 2603

The owner of this estate has invested in state-of-the-art equipment in the winery. The wines have great purity of flavour. The Dry Riesling 2001 had a fine, elegant nose and was dry with a bright, clear finish. Late Harvest 2001 was picked on January 28, 2002 (temperatures did not drop to the point at which it could be labelled as Ice Wine). The high acidity balanced the sugar and alcohol, promising a long life.

Gray Monk Winery Estates

1055 Camp Road, Okanagan Centre, B.C. V4V 2H4
tel 1 (250) 766 3168, fax 1 (250) 766 3390

Founded by the Heiss family in 1981, George Heiss Junior, the winemaker, studied wine in Germany and knows how to handle cool-climate vines. The winery lies on the 50th parallel, like Schloss Johannisberg in Germany's Rheingau. The 49th parallel is the border with the USA, and Osoyoos. Gray Monk is the northernmost vineyard of the region, and that makes a big difference to the average temperature. The Riesling did not ripen in 2001, but the 2000 (11 g.s., 7 g.a., 11 alc.) had a pronounced, flowery bouquet, and green-apple taste, with great finesse – delicious wine.

Quails' Gate Estate Winery

3303 Boucherie Road, Kelowna, B.C. V1Z 2H3
tel 1 (250) 769 4451, fax 1 (250) 769 3451

The Stewart family have made this one of the best small wineries in the region. Their 2001 Dry Riesling (7 g.s., 12.5 alc.) was beautifully made, very dry, positive, and minerally. 2001 Late-Harvest Riesling was the first they had made, but this was because they were hoping to make an Ice Wine, and picked the grapes on January 29, 2002. The temperature did not get quite cold enough, so instead they made this concentrated wine, with sweet, apricot flavours and tingling acidity. They had picked their 2000 Ice Wine (270 g.s., 9 alc.) on at -14°C (6.8°F) on December 11. It was an immaculate and multi-layered wine.

Wild Goose Vineyards

2145 Sun Valley Way, Okanagan Falls, B.C. V0H 1R0
tel 1 (250) 497 8919, fax 1 (250) 497 6853

Founded in 1990, this was the second licensed farm-gate winery in British Columbia. 2001 Riesling was brilliantly dry, with fine acidity in a light style. The 1998 Late-Harvest had had time to develop; it started sweet and finished quite dry.

The Simonsberg Mountain in Stellenbosch

South Africa
South America, and Europe

South Africa

The first Governor of the colony, Simon van der Stel, was granted a huge farm in 1685, which he named Constantia and on which the great reputation of South African wine was based. In 1992, apartheid and sanctions ceased and the wine-growers started to restore and reorganize the vineyards. At last they were free to operate independently and exports started to accelerate.

There has always been a strong German influence in South Africa. South African wine producers and ambitious young winemakers studied at the Geisenheim Wine Instutute in the Rheingau, and returned in love with Riesling. In South Africa, Riesling or "Cape Riesling" is Crouchen, an inferior vine from the south of France. Genuine Riesling is labelled either "Weisser Riesling" or "Rhine Riesling". This confusion has contributed to the drop in sales of Rhine Riesling; the South African Wine Board should be ashamed of this scandal, and should change the law so that Crouchen is accurately labelled. In 1977, the total area of Riesling was 117 hectares; in 1990, 1,600; and in 2002, 417.

The summer temperatures in South Africa are higher than those in the classic Riesling regions of Europe, but near the south coast, Constantia, Elgin, Walker Bay, and Hermanus benefit from the "Cape Doctor": a cool and powerful southeasterly wind that sweeps into False Bay and past Table Mountain to the Atlantic. Vineyards at higher altitudes are also cooler than those in the valleys. The soils are mixed, but along the south coast there is weathered granite and sandstone, and in certain other areas there is shale and granite.

Buitenverwachting

PO Box 281, Constantia 7848 (Constantia)
tel 27 (21) 794 5190, fax 27 (21) 794 1351
email buiten@pixie.co.za
internet www.buitenverwachting.com

The name of this estate is pronounced *bayten-fair-vachtung*. The estate was part of the original Constantia farm. The winery was completely restored and the vineyards re-planted in 1981. The talented winemaker, Hermann Kirschbaum, loves Riesling. The 1998 Rhine Riesling was fairly dry, light, and refreshing, with lime and lemon acidity and only 11 alc., as near as you can get to a Mosel style in South Africa.

De Wetshof Estate

PO Box 31, Robertson 6705 (Robertson)
tel 27 (2351) 615 1863, fax 27 (2351) 615 1915
email info@dewtshof.com
internet www.dewtshof.com

Danie de Wet is a man of huge stature: physically and in reputation. The whole area of Robertson

used to produce virtually nothing but fortified wines, but Danie studied at the Geisenheim Wine Institute and returned with a passion for Riesling and a great knowledge of white wines. He installed equipment for controlling fermentation temperatures and planted Riesling, Chardonnay, Sauvignon, and Muscadel. He produces six different Chardonnays and this is his most important grape variety. His reputation is based on the work he has done to improve the lives of the families who work for him, the quality of the wines of the region, and the administration of wine in general. We tasted his three

An idyllic setting for the village built for their workers by Buitenverwachting Estate in Constantia

1998 Rhine Rieslings. The straight Rhine Riesling was dry and elegant with green-lime freshness and sharp quince flavours on the palate, with the balance to develop over 5 or 6 years in bottle. Rhine Riesling "Mine d'Or" was a gorgeous wine tasting of lychees, and resembling a classic Auslese from the Pfalz. "Edeloes" (187 g.s., 10 g.a, 8.8 alc.) was a great Trockenbeerenauslese-style mouthful, amber-coloured and tremendously concentrated and refined.

Groot Constantia Estate

Private Bag X1, Constantia 7848 (Constantia)
tel 27 (21) 794 5128, fax 27 (21) 794 1999

This estate is the main part of the original farm, with its beautiful, Cape Dutch farmhouse – a national monument. The Weisser Riesling has varied over the years in the amount of botrytis it contains, but generally it has around 20 g.s. The 1998 had little botrytis, but was very ripe, subtle, and almost dry. 1999 was rich and promising in 2003.

Hartenberg Estate

PO Box 69, Koelenhof 7605 (Stellenbosch)
tel 27 (21) 865 2541, fax 27 (21) 865 2153
email info@hartenbergestate.com
internet www.hartenbergestate.com

This farm in the beautiful Devon Valley was established in 1692, but the present wine estate dates from 1978, when the Mackenzie family bought it in a run-down state. The vineyard is on decomposed granite on a clay base at 134 to 320 metres (440 to 1,050 feet), and includes some wetland where the fish eagles feed. This encourages botrytis, adding complexity to the wines.

Weisser Riesling is different in each vintage, but always has some residual sugar. It seems slightly more like a Pfalz Riesling than a New World one. The 1998 had around 20 g.s., with excellent ripeness, and around thirty per cent botrytis. It promised to reach its peak about four years after the vintage.

Jordan Winery

PO Box 12592, Die Boord 7613 (Stellenbosch)
tel 27 (21) 881 3441, fax 27 (21) 881 4326
email info@jordan-wines.com
Internet wwwjordanwines.com

Gary and Kathy Jordan are dedicated wine-growers. From the beginning, in 1982, they vowed never to buy grapes from other growers – a considerable

sacrifice while their new, virus-free vines grew. But the policy has paid off wonderfully in the quality and character of all their wines. Their Weisser Riesling is grown on unirrigated vineyards in decomposed granite soil on cool, south-facing slopes at 300 metres (984 feet) altitude. Fermented in stainless steel and tasted by me in the winery in 1999, the 1997 (7.7 g.s., 6.7 g.a., 13 alc.) was pure, fresh, dry, and powerful, with a slight resemblance to the Rieslings of Clare Valley in Australia. Later vintages have been perfectly consistent, not identical but with a similar profile, and always high-quality.

Klein Constantia

PO Box 375, Constantia 7848 (Constantia)
tel 27 (21) 794 5188, fax 27 (21) 794 2464
email info@kleinconstantia.com
internet www.kleinconstantia.com

This is the smaller part of the original Constantia estate. It produces the fabled Vin de Constance, with Muscat de Frontignan (from clones imported by Jan van Reebeeck in 1656). Its only comparison today is the great Muscat of Rutherglen in Australia.Klein Constantia makes one of the most consistent Rhine Rieslings from 20-year-old vines on weathered granite soil in the higher, cooler part of the vineyards. The 2000 (12 g.s., 5.6 g.a., 12 alc.) was wonderfully ripe, with about 20 per cent botrytis: excellent for relatively early drinking. The 1997 was somewhat drier but still with botrytis complexity and good fruit, while the 1990 (18 g.s., 9.5 alc.) was sweeter, with lower alcohol. At 9 years old, it was still in its prime.

Nederberg

Private Bag X3006, Paarl 7620 (Paarl)
tel 27 (2211) 862 3104, fax 27 (2211) 862 4887
internet www.nederberg.co.za

Gunther Broze is the legendary German winemaker who has been at Nederberg for thirty-three years. Considered the King of Riesling, he also created

James Brown, Riesling enthusiast and front man at the family owned
Hartenberg Estate in Stellenbosch

Edelkeur, the classic botrytized Chenin Blanc.
I bought a case of Nederberg Weisser Riesling Noble
Late Harvest 1983, originally sold at the famous
annual Nederberg Auction. From time to time I open
a bottle and each time I taste it it has hardly changed.
The colour is of polished Victorian mahogany, the
nose is of sultanas and ripe figs, and it has the
concentration of a TBA and the flavour and acidity
of coarse-cut Seville orange marmalade. More recent
vintages of this wine are auctioned every year.

Paul Cluver

PO Box 48, Grabouw 7160 (Elgin)
tel 27 (21) 844 0605, fax 27 (21) 844 0150
email info@cluver.co.za
Internet www.cluver.co.za

Paul Cluver is a neurosurgeon and his home is a farm
in cool-climate Elgin. The first vintage was 1997 and
the Riesling was an attractive, relatively sweet wine,
towards Mosel in style, with about fifteen per cent
botrytis. The 1998 (17.5 g.s., 14.5 alc.) was in a different
class, with a slight prickle of CO_2, concentration, and
power – more Alsace in style. In London, the 2002 was
similar to 1997. The 2001 showed deep-gold colour,
was intense and dry, with fine acidity to balance.

Thelema Mountain Vineyards

PO Box 2234, Stellenbosch 7601 (Stellenbosch)
tel 27 (21) 885 1924, fax 27 (21) 885 1924
internet www.thelema@adept.co.za

If I had to choose the best winemaker in South
Africa, I would have to say Gyles Webb. He is quiet,
modest, and very serious. Riesling is not yet a priority
in terms of price or, sadly, prestige, but he makes
unique wines each vintage and likes to see them
mature. We tasted his 1992 Riesling in 1998 and
it was understated, so stylish and harmonious!

South America

In South America, Chile is the only country so far to develop Riesling and the potential is great. Cousino Macul has a vineyard of Riesling at Santiago, with vines imported from the Rheingau in Germany in the ninteenth century. The 2003 had great character, power, and flavour. Vina Santa Monica is at Rangacua in the Rapel Valley where Emilio de Solminihac grows Riesling because "he likes it"! He makes a most attractive, light summer wine, with freshness and acidity. Further south in Curicó, Miguel Torres produces a magic Riesling Vendimia Tardia from San Francisco de Molina. I tasted the 1998 vintage which was picked long after the normal vintage on May 10: on the nose it had flowers and spices, and on the palate it had honey, with the raisin-concentration of a typical BA. The cool-climate valley of Bio-Bio another 200 kilometres (125 miles) further south is the real home of Riesling in Chile, started by German settlers in the ninteenth century. The temperature variation between day and night, which is so important for Riesling, can be as much as 17°C (63°F). Cono Sur was the first winery to export a Riesling from Bio-Bio to the UK – it was fresh, delicious, and uncomplicated.

Mendoza is the wine capital of Argentina. The fashion for Chardonnay and Sauvignon has meant that Riesling has not yet found its home there, even in the cooler sites at over 1,000 metres (3,281 feet), near Mount Tupangato, where, in theory, the climate and the stony soil should be ideal. I was informed that Riesling was being planted in the Rio Negro region 750 kilometres (470 miles) further south, where the climate is much cooler, but, as yet, I have not tasted any.

Europe (and to the east)

I have tasted genuine Rieslings from Luxembourg, Italy, Slovakia, and Slovenia, but none as yet have been worth writing home about. In all the other countries the Rieslings have been either false or bad. The extension of the EU could reveal regions and estates where good Rieslings might be produced. However, that said, Waltraud Riesling 2003 from the Miguel Torres estate in the Penedès hills in Spain was special – a juicy, nicely balanced wine, with fine acidity and 13 alc. – like a fine Alsace Riesling, and especially suited to food.

Glossary

Auslese German quality classification above Spätlese and below BA, usually sweet.

Beerenauslese German quality classification above Auslese and below TBA.

Biodynamic System of agriculture based on the teachings of Rudolf Steiner.

Botrytis Fungal disease that causes noble rot when it attacks ripe grapes. It shrivels them by reducing the water, while retaining the sugar.

Canopy Management The pruning and training of the vine to reduce vigour: also to delay ripening in hot climates and protect the grapes from sunburn.

Chaptalization Addition of sugar to the must to give a slightly greater level of alcohol: not permitted for any German wine labelled Kabinett or above.

Clones Selected clones have been developed by many research institutes.

Eiswein Grapes picked when frozen, at -8ºC (18ºF) or below, and pressed immediately to give a wine with the minimum Oeschle level of a BA.

Erste Lage German vineyard classification used in the Mosel-Saar-Ruwer.

Erstes Gewächs German vineyard classification used in the Rheingau.

Federspiel Middle of three quality categories used in Wachau.

Feinherb Slightly sweeter than *halbtrocken*.

Flurbereinigung German process of re-structuring and replanting of steep vineyards, and building roads to give improved access to the vines.

Fuder 1,000-litre, round, oak barrel used in the Mosel-Saar-Ruwer.

Grosses Gewächs German vineyard classification.

Halbtrocken German category of half-dry wines, with between 9 and 18 grams of residual sugar/litre.

Hybrid Type of vine, the result of crossing a vine of an American vine species like *Vitis labrusca* with *Vitis vinifera*, the European wine vine.

Ice Wine In Canadia this is strictly controlled and is made with grapes picked when frozen, at -8ºC (18ºF) or below, and pressed immediately. Unregulated in USA.

Kabinett German quality classification below Spätlese. No chaptalization is permitted for this or higher grades.

Keuper Soil type: clay, stones, and gypsum.

Late Harvest Late-picked wine, usually sweet.

Lees Sediment, including dead yeast cells, in the tank or barrel after fermentation.

Lieu-dit Named vineyard in Alsace below *grand cru* in quality, but with a specific character.

Loess Soil type, wind-blown, dusty sand; usually from receding glaciers. Fertile, it retains both water and heat.

Malolactic fermentation Bacterial ferm. after alcoholic ferm. Changes sharp malic acid to ripe lactic acid.

Massal selection The propagation of vines by taking cuttings from the best vines in a vineyard.

Muschelkalk Soil type, limestone with fossilized seashells.

Must Unfermented grape juice.

Négociant French wine merchant making wine from bought-in grapes, or blending bought-in wine. Many own some vineyards.

Noble rot *See* Botrytis.

Oechsle German measure of ripeness based on sugar density in the must.

Old vines There is no legal definition: a grower might mean vines of 25 years of age, or 100.

Oxidation, oxidized Grapes or wines that have been exposed to too much oxygen.

Passerillage Grapes shrivelled on the vine, usually without botrytis. Vendanges Tardives often made from such grapes.

Petrol Delicate waft of an aged Riesling, especially from a hot climate. Not a fault until it dominates the wine.

Phenolics Important flavour compounds, deriving mainly from skins and pips.

Phylloxera *Phylloxera vastatrix* is an aphid that destroyed most of the vineyards in the ninteenth century. Grafting vines onto American rootstocks gives them immunity.

Physiological ripeness Ripeness of skins and pips; better than sugar analysis for judging harvest dates.

Reductive A state in which wine has been starved of oxygen to reduce oxidation and to slow down its development. The opposite is oxidative.

Residual sugar The amount of sugar remaining in the wine after the fermentation has stopped.

Rootstock American vine immune to phylloxera onto which *vinifera* cuttings are grafted.

Schist Laminated crystalline rock.

Sekt A sparkling wine made in Germany.

Sélection de Grains Nobles Sweet Alsace wine made with selected, heavily botryized grapes.

Smaragd Top quality category in Austria's Wachau.

Spätlese German quality classification above Kabinett and below Auslese; wines may be dry or sweetish.

Spritzig German tasting term for a prickle on the tongue caused by CO_2; gives young wine extra freshness.

Steinfeder Quality classification used in Austria's Wachau, the lowest of three.

Stück 1200-litre oval oak barrel used in the Rhine.

Süssreserve Unfermented grape juice added after fermentation to increase sweetness.

Terroir French term for the combination of soil, microclimate, and exposure to the sun that makes each vineyard unique.

Trocken Dry; up to 9 g.s.

Trockenbeerenauslese German quality classification: the sweetest of all wines, made from grapes shrivelled by botrytis.

VDP Association of German Quality Wine Producers.

Vendanges Tardives Alsace category of late-picked wines, often but not always sweet.

Vitis vinifera The European species of vine.

Weingut German word for wine estate.

Vintages

These ratings (out of 10) are generalized and cannot be applied to individual wines. Riesling always produces wonderful surprises. The ageing process of European Rieslings is gentle and slow, and as they get older, especially concentrated ones, so they acquire luscious and subtle overtones. Ausleses and above from the top estates in Germany of 1976, 1971, 1959, and earlier great vintages are still fabulous, as are the great Alsace Rieslings.

The ageing process of New World Rieslings is quite different from that of Old World Rieslings. Dry wines are how most people look at New World Rieslings, and they become more refined and "intellectual" with time but do not exactly improve. It would be unfair to extend vintages back to 1983 because many of the top producers were only dreaming of making great Rieslings at that time.

Year	Germany	Alsace	Austria
2003	9 >	7 *>	8 *>
2002	8 >	9 *>	8 *>
2001	9 *>	8 *>	6 *>
2000	4 *>	8 *>	7 *>
1999	8 *>	7	9 *>
1998	8 >	8 *>	8 *>
1997	9 >	7 *>	9
1996	6 >	8 *>	6 *
1995	7 *>	8 *	8 *
1994	7 *	7 *	7 *
1993	6 *	7	7 *
1992	5 *	7	7
1991	4	5	2 #
1990	9 *>	9	8
1989	8 *	9 *	6 #
1988	7 *	8	7
1987	3 #	4 #	3 #
1986	4	6 #	5 #
1985	5	8 *	8
1984	2 #	3 #	#
1983	8 *>	8 *	9 *

Year	Aust.	NZ	Finger Lakes, Niagara	Northwest USA/Okanagan, Canada
2003	9 >	8 *>	7 *>	8 >
2002	9 >	8 *>	8	9 >
2001	8 >	9 *>	9 *>	7
2000	6 >	8 >	6	8 *>
1999	6 >	8 *>	9	8 >
1998	6 >	9 *	6	7 *
1997	8	8 *	7	7 *
1996	8 >	9 *	6	8
1995	6 >	6	9	7
1994	8 >	7	7	8
1993	6	6	8	6

> * also late-picked with botrytis
>
> > should keep and develop
>
> # probably too old

Bibliography

Andreas, Stefan, *Die Grossen Weine Deutschlands*, Verlag Ullstein, Berlin, 1962

Blom, Philipp, *The Wines of Austria*, Faber & Faber, London, 2000

Bodenstein, Toni, *Wo Urgestein den Wein formt die Wachau*, Vinea Wachau Nobilis Districtus, Spitz, 1998

Broadbent MW, Michael, *The Great Vintage Wine Book II*, Mitchell Beazley, London 1991

Brook, Stephen, *The Wines of Germany*, Mitchell Beazley, London, 2003

Campbell, Bob MW, *Cuisine New Zealand Wine Annual*, Cuisine Publications, Auckland, 2000 and 2001

Clarke, Oz, and Rand, Margaret, *Grapes & Wines*, Webster's International Publishers, London, 2001

Clarke, Oz, *New Classic Wines*, Webster's International Publishers and Mitchell Beazley, London, 1991

Cooper, Michael, *Classic Wines of New Zealand*, Hodder Moa Beckett, Auckland, 1999

Cooper, Michael, *The Wines and Vineyards of New Zealand*, Hodder and Stoughton, Auckland, 1984

Diel, Armin and Payne, Joel, *WeinGuide Deutschland*, Christian Verlag, München, 1994–2003

Duijker, Hubrecht, *The Wines of Chile*, Het Spectrum BV, Utrecht, 1999

Fleck, Udo, and Rüder, Bernd, *Weinschlösser an der Mosel, Saar, Ruwer*, Paulinus Verlag, Trier, 2000

George, Rosemary MW, *The Wines of New Zealand*, Faber & Faber, London, 1996

Hall, Lisa Shara, *Wines of the Pacific Northwest*, Mitchell Beazley, London, 2001

Halliday, James, *Australia and New Zealand Wine Companion*, Harper Collins, Sydney, 2000

Hallgarten, Fritz, *Alsace and its Wine Gardens*, André Deutsch, London, 1957

Hallgarten, Fritz and André Simon, *The Great Wines of Germany*, George Rainbird, London, 1963

Hardy, Tom, *Pictorial Atlas of Australian Wines*, Grape Vision Pty Ltd, Melbourne, 1986

Hinkle, Richard, *Alligator Dreams, The Story of Greenwood Ridge Vineyards*, Silverback Books Inc, Santa Rosa, 2000

Hoffmann, Beate, and Winterling, Gisela, *Zur Lage der Region Mittelhaardt/Pfalz*, Sommer Verlag, Grünstadt, 1998

Jameson, Ian, *German Wines*, Faber and Faber, London, 1991

Jefford, Andrew, *The Wines of Germany*, Deutsche Weininstitut, Mainz, 1994

Jefford, Andrew, *The New France*, Mitchell Beazley, London, 2002

Johnson, Hugh, *The Story of Wine*, Mitchell Beazley, London, 1989

Johnson, Hugh and Robinson, Jancis MW, *The World Atlas of Wine 5th Edition*, Mitchell Beazley, London, 2001

Knoll, Rudolph, *Plädoyer für Einen grossen Wein Riesling*, Fachverlag Dr. Fraund GMBH, Mainz, 1990

MacDonagh, Giles, *The Wine & Food of Austria*, Mitchell Beazley, London, 1992

MacDonagh, Giles, *Austria, New Wines from the Old World*, Österreichischer Agrarverlag, Klosterneuburg, 1997

Moser, Peter, *The Ultimate Austrian Wine Guide*, Falstaff Verlag, Klosterneuburg, 2002

Orffer, Professor C.J., *Wine Grape Cultivars in South Africa*, Human & Rousseau Pty Ltd, Cape Town, 1979

Piggot, Stuart, *Life beyond Liebfraumilch*, Sidgewick & Jackson Ltd, London, 1988

Piggot, Stuart, *Riesling Weine*, Ekon Verlag, Düsseldorf, 1994

Platter, John, *South African Wine Guide*, The John Platter SA Wine Guide Pty Ltd, Hermanus, 1995–2003

Robinson, Jancis MW (ed.), *The Oxford Companion to Wine*, Oxford University Press, Oxford 1994

Simon, André, *A Wine Primeur*, Michael Joseph Ltd, London, 1946

Simon, André, *The History of the Wine Trade in England VolI, II, III*, Wyman & Sons Ltd., London, 1906

Simon, André, *Wines of the World*, George Rainbird Ltd, London, 1967

Simon, André and Hallgarten, Fritz, *The Great Wines of Germany*, McGraw Hill, New York, 1963

Slessor, Kenneth OBE, *The Story of Australian Wines*, Australian Wine Board, 1964

Stevenson, Tom, *The Wines of Alsace*, Faber & Faber, London, 1993

Tovey, Charles, *Wine and Wine Countries*, Whittaker & Co, London, 1877

Vandyke Price, Pamela, *Alsace Wines*, Sotheby Publications, London, 1984

Ziraldo, Donald, *The Art of Wine at Inniskillin*, Key Porter Books Ltd, Toronto, 1995

Index

Acknowledgements

Janet and I would like to thank the countless individuals and wine producers all over the world who gave us help and encouragement with this book, and the hundred and more that are not featured. Also the national and regional wine-promotion teams in the UK and abroad who helped us with our visits. Everywhere we went, nothing was too much trouble.

Dirk Richter gave me the inspiration for this book by countless hours of talking and tasting Riesling in London, Oxford, Cambridge, and Mülheim, Mosel. Every day that we have spent together over the last thirty years I have learned something new about Riesling. In our travels, although we had only asked for a visit, we were often looked after as if we were family. In Germany, Christoph Tyrell, Christian Ebert, Stefan Ress, Rainer Lingenfelder, Dorothee Anheuser, Horst Kolesch, Armin Diel, Garry and Marlies Grosvenor, Michael Prinz zu Salm-Salm, Armin Göring and the late Christian Adams all played crucial parts in our understanding of German Riesling. Jean-Christophe Bott was our great advisor in Alsace. In Australia, Jeffrey Grosset and Stephanie Toole, Barrie Smith and Judi Cullam, the Tomlinson family at Lenton Brae, Brian Croser, Viv Thomson – all let us share the Australian way of life and their beautiful wines. Margaret Harvey set the framework for our visit to New Zealand, Bob Campbell indoctrinated us when we arrived, Lois Mills welcomed us at Lake Wanaka, and George Fistonich, Allan Scott and Kevin Judd showed us different aspects of Marlborough. Miguel Torres arranged our stay in Curicó in Chile, which set us up perfectly for our alarming crossing on a rough trackover the Andes. Myron Redford was our mentor in Oregon and invited us to an unforgettable party to celebrate the completion of the vintage. Ingo Grady arranged everything for our first days in Okanagan, including our visit to the fabulous Mission Hill Winery, and then the teams of Inniskillin and Jackson Triggs set up visits to their wineries in Okanagan and in Niagara. Our very last trip was a comprehensive visit to the Finger Lakes, perfectly organised by Susan Spence.

Hugh Johnson, Jancis Robinson, and Chris Foulkes all gave us fantastic support, especially when it was uncertain that the book would ever be published. Subsequently Hilary Lumsden and Margaret Rand had the patience and kindness to understand that I was a complete novice at writing a book. Yasia Williams and Janet worked beautifully together to choose her photographs for the book and to Colin Goody for designing the book so handsomely. Lastly, we thank our daughter Eloïse and our son Toby, who saved us from multiple mental breakdowns with our computers.